Corporate Social Responsibility and Economic Responsiveness in India

This book provides a timely contribution to the study of Corporate Social Responsibility (CSR) and state–business relations in India. The development of CSR as a new component of business–society interplays has triggered intense debates and controversies. Corporate actors, governments, and other CSR advocates describe CSR as a promising opportunity to transform companies from societal problem-makers into societal problem-solvers. Conversely, critical commentators denounce CSR either as 'window-dressing', which hides corporate greed behind shallow commitments to social justice and environmental sustainability, or as a pernicious means used by companies to sideline regulatory constraints and manage business-relevant public affairs in their own terms. Departing from these controversies, this book mobilizes an original theoretical framework to examine empirically how CSR emerges from and retroacts on growing structural tensions between profit-making and competing collective values and interests in contemporary India. It shows at a macro-sociological level and with detailed case studies (cement industry; CSR public policies) that, paradoxically, CSR enhances the autonomy of the economy by making profit-driven economic processes more responsive to non-economic concerns raised in politics, law, morality, and other spheres of modern society.

Damien Krichewsky is Post-doctoral Fellow at the Forum Internationale Wissenschaft at the University of Bonn, and Research Associate at the Centre for South Asian Studies, Paris, and the Centre de Sciences Humaines, New Delhi. Besides his work on CSR and state–business relations in contemporary India, his areas of research comprise green finance, environmental aid, as well as environmental politics in India's democracy.

Corporate Social Responsibility and Economic Responsiveness in India

Damien Krichewsky

CAMBRIDGE
UNIVERSITY PRESS

CAMBRIDGE
UNIVERSITY PRESS

University Printing House, Cambridge CB2 8BS, United Kingdom

One Liberty Plaza, 20th Floor, New York, NY 10006, USA

477 Williamstown Road, Port Melbourne, vic 3207, Australia

314 to 321, 3rd Floor, Plot No.3, Splendor Forum, Jasola District Centre, New Delhi 110025, India

79 Anson Road, #06–04/06, Singapore 079906

Cambridge University Press is part of the University of Cambridge.

It furthers the University's mission by disseminating knowledge in the pursuit of education, learning and research at the highest international levels of excellence.

www.cambridge.org
Information on this title: www.cambridge.org/9781108485364

© Damien Krichewsky 2019

First published 2019

Printed in India by Nutech Print Services, New Delhi 110020

A catalogue record for this publication is available from the British Library

ISBN 978-1-108-48536-4 HB

Contents

Tables and Maps

Abbreviations

ACC	Associated Cement Company
AITUC	All India Trade Union
ASSOCHAM	Association of Chambers of Commerce
BCF	Business & Community Foundation
BJP	Bharatiya Janata Party
BMS	Bharatiya Mazdoor Sangh
BoP	bottom of the pyramid
BSP	Bahujan Samaj Party
CCI	Cement Corporation of India
CEO	Chief Executive Officer
CII	Confederation of Indian Industries
CITU	Centre of Indian Trade Unions
CMM	Chhattisgarh Mukti Morcha
CMS	Centre for Social Markets
CPI	Communist Party of India
CPI-M	Communist Party of India – Marxist
CPI-ML	Communist Party of India – Marxist Leninist
CPSE	central public sector enterprises
CSR	corporate social responsibility
FDI	foreign direct investment
FICCI	Federation of Indian Chambers of Commerce and Industry
FII	foreign institutional investor
FIR	first information report
FTPA	Free Trade Practices Association
GCNI	Global Compact Network India
GDC	Guidelines Drafting Committee

GDP	gross domestic product
GIZ	Gesellschaft für Internationale Zusammenarbeit
GRI	Global Reporting Initiative
HMS	Hind Mazdoor Sabha
INTUC	Indian National Trade Union Congress
ITC	Indian Tobacco Company
KPI	key performance indicators
LADA	Local Area Development Authority
MCA	Ministry of Corporate Affairs
MLA	Member of the Legislative Assembly
MoEF	Ministry of Environment and Forests
MPs	members of Parliament
MNC	multinational company
NFCSR	National Foundation for Corporate Social Responsibility
NGO	non-governmental organization
NIDHEE	National Initiative for Dwellings, Health, Education and Employability
NTPC	National Thermal Power Corporation
NVGs	National Voluntary Guidelines on Social, Environmental and Economic Responsibilities of Business
OECD	Organization for Economic Co-operation and Development
PBSS	Paryavaran Bachao Sangharsh Samiti
PiC	Partners in Change
PIL	public interest litigation
SCF	Standing Committee on Finance
SDM	sub-divisional magistrate
SEBI	Securities and Exchange Board of India
SEZ	special economic zone
SST	social systems theory
TBL	triple bottom line
TERI	The Energy and Resources Institute
TSRDS	Tata Steel Rural Development Society
TWS	Tribal Welfare Society
UTUC	United Trade Union Centre
VRS	voluntary retirement scheme

Preface

Corporate Social Responsibility (CSR) is an intriguing modern phenomenon. Since the development of corporate capitalism, owners and managers have been called upon to adopt 'responsible' business practices, that is, practices which can help society overcome its problems (for example, poverty, inequalities, harsh labour conditions, corruption, environmental degradation) while also benefitting companies thanks to enhanced public trust and legitimacy. With more or less willingness, companies have answered this call by dedicating resources to show their 'responsible' commitment to social welfare and progress, beyond the normal course of business and abidance to law. Under the catchwords of 'trusteeship', 'corporate citizenship', 'stakeholder management', 'triple bottom line', 'doing well by doing good', or 'shared value', the CSR discourse tends to repeat itself – *plus ça change, plus c'est la même chose*. However, CSR has also changed substantially in terms of both form and outreach. Since the 1990s in particular, as large companies have been dragged into growing controversy regarding their harmful social and environmental impacts, CSR has expanded worldwide in business organizations and governance structures with the promise to harmonize business–society interplays.

In the face of recurring discrepancies between the objectives put forward by CSR and the actual behaviour of firms, it is clear that CSR is not as virtuous and transformational as its promoters like to claim. Nonetheless, given the institutional and cultural extent of the phenomenon, CSR is bound to have effects that formulas such as 'managerial fancy', 'window dressing', and 'green washing' fail to grasp. How has the development of CSR in companies' organizations changed the way these companies perceive and respond to problems in their social surrounding? How has CSR changed the way society perceives companies and conceives of their role within and beyond the economic sphere? Overall, is CSR about tuning capitalism to the expectations of other spheres of society, such as morality, law, or politics? Or is CSR rather intended to make morality, law, and politics more compatible with the profit-oriented processes of a globalized capitalist economy?

In India, where economic reforms starting in the 1980s have initiated a development strategy based in large part on private industrial growth, with extensive political support to large companies and a significant relaxation of regulatory constraints, the questions raised by CSR have become particularly salient. Old Indian conglomerates such as Tata and Birla, new industrial giants such as Reliance, as well as foreign multinational companies with deep pockets and state-of-the-art technology, have been the beacon of India's economic 'emergence'. But large companies have also faced intense resistance on the ground of the contentious social and environmental impact of their activities, such as land acquisition processes mired by corruption and violence, harsh working conditions, large-scale industrial pollution, and the commercialization of unsafe products. In this tensed Indian context, how has CSR affected interplays between companies' profit-oriented activities and the collective values and interests underpinning India's developmental aspirations?

Investigating these interplays between corporate capitalism, development, and CSR has taken me on a fascinating intellectual and human journey. Whether in research centres and libraries, at international conferences, in shiny corporate meeting rooms, or in the homes of local trade union leaders and activists, lost in the labyrinthine corridors of Indian ministries, or while conducting interviews in snowy Himalayan valleys and dusty villages of central India, I had the privilege to meet and exchange with inspiring people. Their interest, open-mindedness, and support have been invaluable throughout this research endeavour.

I am particularly thankful to Professor Erhard Friedberg, Professor Jean-Gustave Padioleau, Professor Denis Segrestin, Professor Christophe Jaffrelot, Professor Loraine Kennedy, Professor Stéphanie Tawa Lama-Rewal, Professor Jean-Luc Racine, Professor Leïla Choukroune, Professor Jens Beckert, Professor Rudolf Stichweh, as well as my numerous other colleagues and friends from academia for their insightful advice and the stimulating exchanges we had over the past few years. I would also like to gratefully acknowledge the institutional and financial support provided by the Centre for Sociology of Organizations (Sciences Po-CNRS, Paris), the Centre for Social Sciences and Humanities (MAE-CNRS, New Delhi), the Centre for South Asian Studies (EHESS-CNRS, Paris), the Max-Planck Institute for the Study of Society (Max-Planck Society, Cologne), the Forum International Science (University of Bonn), and the Réseau International de Recherche sur les Organisations et le Développement Durable (RIODD – International Research Network on Organizations and Sustainable Development).

The field research I conducted in Chhattisgarh benefitted immensely from the assistance of Durga Jha, whose energy, high spirits, and deep knowledge of the region have been extraordinary. I would also like to thank Viraf Mehta and Khurram Naayaab for their help and precious friendship. I am also indebted to all interviewees who shared their time, knowledge and networks for this research, including in particular the managers and workers of Lafarge India and of the other companies I studied; the politicians, bureaucrats, and experts who recounted how they crafted India's CSR public policies; the trade union leaders and social activists I met, whose dedication to social justice and democracy have often been inspiring; and the many village dwellers who introduced me into their homes and lifeworlds.

I dedicate this book to my family and friends.

Chapter 1

✠

Introduction

Corporate Social Responsibility and the challenges of business–society interplays

The recent US$66 billion merger of Bayer and Monsanto, which gave birth to a multinational biotech giant endowed with unprecedented power over food production and food security of the human kind, has raised intense controversies all over the globe. While some protagonists emphasized revenue prospects and the ability of such an entity to help feed the world's population, others described the merger as the creation of a Frankenstein-like entity, which is set to exploit peasants, destroy ecosystems, and put public health at risk for the sake of profit. Big oil companies, which supply society with energy and provide income to hundreds of thousands of people, have faced similar critics because of environmental pollution (for example, the Deepwater Horizon oil spill; climate change) and instances of collaboration with the police and military forces of autocratic regimes to repress protest (for example, Shell in Nigeria; Total in Myanmar). Leading providers of financial services, such as Morgan Stanley and Goldman Sachs, also raised controversies as some of their highly profitable activities contributed to the global economic and financial crisis that erupted in 2007–2008. The collapse of the Rana Plaza building in Bangladesh in 2013, which claimed the lives of more than a thousand workers from the garment industry, is a further case where profit-making business is entangled with competing collective values and interests.

These diverse cases epitomize structural tensions characterizing 'business–society' interplays. In fact, over the course of the past two centuries, companies have gradually developed into a core institution of modern society, and their profit-making business activities have had both positive and negative consequences for the life chances of billions of people. In the economic domain, companies have provided income to a growing number of private capital owners, as well as to waged and salaried workers who now represent 55 per cent of the 3.2 billion people employed worldwide.[1] Companies also constitute a key income source for governments, for international organizations, and for a large number of non-governmental organizations (NGOs). Besides, by developing innovative products and supplying markets with goods and services, companies have contributed to shaping modern living conditions and lifestyles, which are valued by billions of moneyed consumers and aspiring poor persons.

However, companies are also involved in issues such as rising socio-economic inequalities, discriminatory recruitment and remuneration practices, or cost-cutting programmes that lead to low wages and/or exhausting working conditions.[2] As illustrated by the 'Panama papers' scandal, many companies limit their contributions to government income by using sophisticated techniques of tax evasion and fiscal optimization. Companies' support to international organizations and NGOs also raises questions, as it often comes with strings attached.[3] As for innovation and production, cases abound where commercialized goods have been criticized for their harmful impacts on public health or the environment (for example, Monsanto's Roundup herbicide; Volkswagen's diesel cars).

Tensions between profit-making and competing collective values and interests also characterize corporate activities in politics and law. Indeed, companies are not only economic actors but also political actors and 'governing institutions' that actively participate in the production and implementation of collective rules.[4] Companies' political activities include legitimate forms of participation, such as lobbying or the funding of political parties. But companies sometimes also use illegitimate means of influence, such as the corruption of political decision-makers. Moreover, the extent of companies' political power can appear to threaten democratic principles and institutions.[5] Regarding governance functions, companies have become a source of private standards that complement and sometimes override positive law.[6] While

---

[1] See www.ilo.org/ilostat and https://data.worldbank.org/indicator/SL.TLF.TOTL.IN (accessed on 26 February 2018).

[2] On the latter, see, for instance, a recent study by Locke and Samel (2018).

[3] See, for instance, Shamir (2004), Barkan (2013), and Seitz and Martens (2017).

[4] Wilks (2013, p. 251). See also Coen, Grant, and Wilson (2010).

[5] See, for instance, Hertz (2001), Reich (2007), Crouch (2011), and Corporate Europe Observatory, The Austrian Federal Chamber of Labour, and The Austrian Trade Union Federation (2014).

[6] See, for instance, Fuchs (2007) and Bartley (2018).

such private norms can palliate shortcomings of state-based regulation, they can also weaken the legal protection of labour welfare, public health, nature conservation, and other collective values and interests that can stand in the way of business opportunities.[7]

These tensions between profit-making and competing collective values and interests are generally envisaged as problems that, as such, must be addressed. However, the formulation both of these problems and of the way they should be tackled has proved to be everything but consensual. Which profit-driven activities are socially beneficial, and which ones are socially harmful? Which moral, legal, political, or economic criteria should be used to distinguish between the two? Which trade-offs between positive and negative outcomes of profit-making are acceptable, and when do negative outcomes justify regulatory constraints? Which policies and institutional arrangements should be adopted by the state to bolster socially beneficial corporate conduct while preventing profitable but socially harmful practices? Should companies be involved as legitimate partners in the political governance of corporate conduct, for instance, through self-regulation and multi-stakeholder governance initiatives? Or does such involvement undermine democracy by transferring regulatory functions to powerful private entities that account to shareholders, not to citizens? Are collaborations with business a good way for civil society organizations to promote socially fair and environmentally sustainable production? Or are such collaborations a form of co-optation of civil society by dominant capitalist actors, whose power must be tamed with more confrontational strategies?

As part of these debates, Corporate Social Responsibility (CSR) has emerged and asserted itself across the world as a modern phenomenon that sets out to settle business–society interplays. As an offshoot of late nineteenth-century American business ethics, CSR was conceived originally as an alternative both to growing regulatory constraints and to the doctrine of 'laissez-faire'.[8] This middle-ground position, which acknowledges the societal problems generated by capitalism, while expecting core institutions of capitalism to address them, has remained the hallmark of CSR. In fact, CSR has prospered out of the core belief that by opening the eyes of business executives to the profitability of ethics and 'socially responsible' conduct, by helping them realize this vision in their company, thanks to dedicated organizational structures and management tools,

---

[7] See, for instance, Utting and Marques (2010a).

[8] See Clark (1916) and Abend (2014).

and by engaging business actors in societal problem-solving through private and public–private governance initiatives, tension-ridden business–society interactions can be transformed into harmonious and mutually beneficial ties.

Such an ambitious project put forward by CSR has triggered friendly reactions across society. Countless books and articles have been published to showcase the virtues of CSR for business and for society at large, as well as to bolster the CSR movement with new ideas and practical knowledge. Many governments and international organizations, such as the United Nations and the World Bank, have also supported CSR with programmes and projects that encourage companies to adopt socially responsible practices. Auditing and consultancy firms, including the influential 'big four' (Deloitte, Ernst & Young, KPMG, and PricewaterhouseCoopers), have further added to the CSR momentum by offering services that promise to help companies reap the benefits of CSR. Some NGOs, such as CARE or the World Wildlife Fund (WWF), have also contributed to CSR by developing partnerships with companies as part of the latter's CSR activities. Last but not least, since the mid-1990s, a growing share of the world's large companies have introduced more or less extensive CSR components in their organizational structures and activities. For instance, companies have partnered with NGOs to prevent child labour and improve working conditions along their supply chains. Companies have also adopted ethical codes of conduct to tackle issues such as employee discrimination or the corruption of public officials. Initiatives aimed at reducing the ecological footprint of production processes provide further examples of CSR activities. In short, ideas about business ethics and CSR have progressively morphed into a highly complex social phenomenon, whose reach has expanded into most aspects of business–society interplays.

CSR advocates versus CSR critics

The driving force of CSR is the claim that it can transform corporate profit-making from being a source of societal problems to becoming an efficient response to these problems. But *how is CSR changing the structural tensions in modern society between profit-making and competing collective values and interests?* Is CSR changing corporate behaviour for the common good? What if CSR was only simulating change to shield profitable business opportunities from regulatory constraints, political interventions, and the attacks of anti-corporate protest movements? Could it be that CSR does not redefine corporate profit-making to make it compatible with the common good, as CSR advocates like to claim, but that it discursively redefines the common good to make it compatible with corporate profit-making? These questions have animated decades of CSR research.[9] But research findings have not provided many sound and conclusive answers yet. On the contrary, the more CSR scholarship has progressed, the more depictions of CSR have become controversial.

Business ethics, for instance, has produced more than a century of research that conceives of CSR as a way to guide business actors towards socially desirable goals.[10] But it has also met with harsh critics. Unlike what the moral connotations of 'ethics' and 'social responsibility' suggest, according to critics, business ethics and CSR would be an instrument used by more or less cynical corporate actors to neutralize moral criticism of unbridled profit-making, in particular through the construction of an alternative morality that frames profit-making as a virtuous means to achieve the common good.[11]

Similarly, a large body of literature on 'stakeholder theory', which is concerned with interdependencies between companies and other internal or external actors (for example, trade unions, consumers, public authorities, NGOs), has promoted CSR as a way to overcome conflicts between business and other sectors of society. The core idea is that CSR-related stakeholder management systems allow companies to take those affecting or being affected by their business activities into account.[12] Going one step further, the main advocate of the 'stakeholder management' concept, Edward Freeman, promotes the development of 'stakeholder capitalism', where voluntary contractual arrangements between companies and their stakeholders are to replace the regulation of corporate conduct by the state.[13]

However, critics argue that stakeholder management actually puts companies at the centre of 'business–society' relations while relegating other actors to the periphery. In particular, stakeholder management would undermine the vertical

---

[9] See, for instance, the handbooks edited by Crane, McWilliams, Matten, Moon, and Siegel (2008) and Gond and Moon (2011).

[10] See, for instance, Moriarty (2008), Brenkert (2012), and Crane and Matten (2016).

[11] See, for instance, Salmon (2009), Abend (2014), Kaplan (2015), and Lampert (2016).

[12] See, for instance, Freeman (1984), Mitchell, Agle, and Wood (1997), and Bhattacharya, Sen, and Korschun (2011). Other strands of stakeholder theory exist, which militate for deeper changes in corporate governance law that would give effective and democratic control of companies to other 'stakeholders' than shareholders (for example, Moriarty 2014). However, these normative positions have remained peripheral both in the literature and in terms of concrete impacts on the CSR phenomenon.

[13] Freeman, Martin, and Parmar (2007).

authority of the democratic state by treating public authorities as a 'stakeholder' among others.[14] Moreover, the managerial systems of conflict prevention and conflict resolution promoted by stakeholder theory would obfuscate the uneven power relationships between mighty companies and weaker members of society. In short, stakeholder management would help companies address their own problems, with little genuine concern for the interests of 'stakeholders' and of society at large.[15]

The contribution of CSR to 'collaborative governance' is another contested dimension of this phenomenon. According to some CSR scholarship, complex societal problems arising from globalized economic activities would outgrow the regulatory capacities of territorially bounded national states. Against this backdrop, CSR would provide opportunities to involve companies in private and multi-stakeholder governance structures, including labour and environmental standards (for example, SA8000, ISO14001, ISO26000, Forest and Marine Stewardship Councils), as well as multilateral initiatives (for example, UN Global Compact, UN Guiding Principles on Business and Human Rights, EU CSR Strategy 2011–2014), in the pursuit of the common good. Thanks to these CSR-related governance structures, CSR would help palliate the deficiencies of national states by mobilizing companies' resources in collaborative problem-solving.[16]

Critical commentators find this claim dubious.[17] According to them, the growing involvement of companies in collaborative governance would rather reinforce the political power of companies under the guise of 'CSR', 'partnerships', and 'corporate citizenship'. In so doing, collaborative governance would weaken society's ability to protect collective interests when they are threatened by the pursuit of profitable business opportunities. More specifically, by promoting self-regulation and 'soft' law as an alternative to legally binding norms, CSR would undermine the ability of democratic public authorities, workers, activists, citizens, and other bearers of collective interests to oppose corporate malpractice and enforce rights.

---

[14] Banerjee (2008), Cazal (2009), Mansell (2013).

[15] See, for instance, Cooper and Owen (2007), Derry (2012), and Helin, Jensen, and Sandström (2013).

[16] Ruggie (2007), Vandenbergh (2007), Vogel (2008), Scherer and Palazzo (2011), Moon, Crane, and Matten (2011).

[17] Fuchs (2007), Sum (2010), Daugareilh (2010), Shamir (2010), Jacobsson and Garsten (2012), Fleming and Jones (2013), Kaplan (2015), Marchildon (2016).

Finally, CSR has triggered heated debates regarding companies' development impacts in developing and emerging countries from the Global South. Over the past two decades, the 'private sector' has been increasingly promoted as a partner for development by actors such as the United Nations, the World Bank and its bilateral counterparts, and governments of developing/ emerging countries.[18] CSR is closely associated with this trend. For instance, according to CSR approaches based on the 'triple bottom line' (TBL: people, planet, profit), companies can develop business practices that combine profit-making with socio-economic development and environmental sustainability across the world.[19] In the same vein, the 'bottom of the pyramid' (BoP) concept put forward by Coimbatore Krishna Prahalad envisages CSR as an opportunity for companies to design business models that alleviate poverty while opening up profitable market opportunities.[20] By implementing such approaches in concrete CSR projects located in the Global South, companies would increasingly compensate governments' inability to provide adequate public goods such as livelihood opportunities, education, health and sanitation, or access to water.[21]

Critics have highlighted inconsistencies and ideological biases characterizing these claims. In particular, concepts such as the TBL and the BoP would focus on synergies between 'business' and 'development', while overlooking structural contradictions between the two – for example, cost-cutting at the expense of unprotected workers, tax avoidance at the expense of the welfare state, resource extraction and mass production at the expense of the environment.[22] Moreover, studies of concrete CSR projects implemented in the Global South suggest that companies often put words into practice only when it benefits their financial prospects, and that the limited development outcomes of CSR projects do not make up for the negative effects of core business operations.[23] Ultimately, according to Dinah Rajak, CSR would not aim to advance 'development' as such, but 'to authenticate and extend the authority of corporations, not only

---

[18] See, for instance, Scheyvens, Banks, and Hughes (2016).

[19] Elkington (1998).

[20] Prahalad (2005). Williams (2015) makes a similar argument by pointing at untapped synergies between business development and environmental sustainability.

[21] See, for instance, Valente and Crane (2010).

[22] Norman and MacDonald (2004), Arora and Romijn (2012), Karnani (2011).

[23] Jeppesen and Lund-Thomsen (2010), Blowfield (2010), Sikka (2010), Gilberthorpe and Banks (2012), Jamali, Lund-Thomsen, and Khara (2017).

over the economic but over the social and political order, as transnational corporations are elevated as both agents and architects of development'.[24]

The limits of straightforward definitions of CSR

Notwithstanding their valuable contributions, both the mainstream managerial approaches and the critical approaches tend to take sides for or against CSR, and hence to produce competing homogeneous depictions of this phenomenon. Peter Utting and Jose C. Marques have once criticized the CSR literature for being 'largely ahistorical, empirically weak, theoretically thin and politically naïve'.[25] This hard-hitting assessment might be a little harsh, and it certainly applies only to a part of the CSR scholarship. But it points at important challenges for the study of CSR.

Abstract, general, and ideologically tainted definitions of CSR fail to account for the empirical characteristics of this concrete historical phenomenon. Indeed, the CSR phenomenon has developed out of a particular historical context, which is the controversial rise of large modern corporations in North America in the late nineteenth and early twentieth centuries.[26] From there on, CSR has gradually expanded geographically to become a 'transnational' phenomenon. A recent study on the spread of CSR in Venezuela (1962–1967) and in Great Britain (1977–1981) illustrates the intricate processes underlying this transnational expansion, in which business elites and CSR business associations have played a key role.[27] Besides, the CSR phenomenon has developed and changed historically in terms of its form and social significance. It has been enriched over time with new ideas, with new CSR-related norms, certifications and labels, as well as with new CSR-related corporate structures and activities. The CSR phenomenon has also expanded in terms of the number and type of participating actors. While religious actors, business schools, and business associations played a key role initially, CSR now involves a vast array of other actors such as experts and consultants, specialized auditing firms, financial investors, international organizations, national states, and NGOs.

This historic formation of the CSR phenomenon has been all but homogeneous. Distinct cultural traditions, institutional settings, political-

---

[24] Rajak (2011, 231).
[25] Utting and Marques (2010b, 3).
[26] See Carroll, Lipartito, Post, Werhane, and Goodpaster (2012) and Abend (2014).
[27] Kaplan and Kinderman (2017).

economic conjunctions, market positions, and technological systems have created regional and sectoral variations.[28] For instance, CSR tends to be more restricted to voluntarism in liberal market economies, such as the United States and United Kingdom, while coordinated market economies such as the Nordic countries have adapted CSR to their national political-economic models, in which the state plays a stronger role.[29] With regard to sectoral variations, Western multinational companies (MNCs) in the garment and sportswear industries are likely to use CSR to protect and enhance their brand value, while engineering companies involved in business-to-business (B2B) transactions might use CSR to address different concerns. Similarly, CSR in the banking industry does not resemble CSR in the mining sector. The diversity of CSR also shows up within multinational companies, whose subsidiaries do not share the same policies and practices, depending on the political-economic contexts in which they operate. In short, while the expansion of CSR has been primarily the work of globally active entities (for example, multinational companies, international organizations, and norm-setting agencies), and while many CSR-related norms and governance initiatives have a transnational scope, CSR remains embedded in multiple contexts that produce a diversity of characteristics and outcomes.[30]

Besides its historical and socio-spatial variations, the CSR phenomenon is deeply ambiguous. While companies and business-friendly actors (for example, business associations, consultants, business schools) seem to be prominent, CSR involves actors whose goals and *modi operandi* are not always aligned with business interests. For instance, some protagonists promote CSR-based 'soft' regulatory norms not to support business-as-usual, but to enrol companies in an incremental dynamic that starts with voluntary mechanisms to prepare the ground for more binding regulatory constraints.[31] Similarly, CSR policies adopted by national states are not always designed by business-friendly policy-makers, as other political forces sometimes gain the upper hand.[32] More generally, CSR mixes up diverse elements such as self-regulation and regulatory constraints, economic and political logics, as well as cynical uses of

---

[28] See, for instance, Matten and Moon (2008), Chen and Bouvain (2009), Brammer, Jackson, and Matten (2012), Gjølberg (2010), and Bansal, Gao, and Qureshi (2014).

[29] See Gjølberg (2010) and Brammer, Jackson, and Matten (2012).

[30] On global CSR, see in particular Dashwood (2012) and Tsutsui and Lim (2015).

[31] See, for instance, Vogel (2008), Hofferberth (2011), and Utting (2015).

[32] See Bernhard and Christian (2010), Kinderman (2013), Vallentin (2015), and Krichewsky (2017).

CSR and genuine beliefs in its proclaimed virtues. In other words, the concrete institutionalization of CSR is an open and ambiguous process that involves a plurality of actors, interests, goals, and institutional logics.

Finally, the CSR concept itself resists any attempt to pin down its meaning with a simple definition. Following Adaeze Okoye, CSR can be considered an 'essentially contested concept', that is, a concept whose intrinsic properties trigger ongoing contention about its proper meaning by its different users.[33] As companies have a direct interest in describing themselves as 'socially responsible' entities, their claims raise scrutiny. However, the actual 'social responsibility' of a company can be assessed in many different ways, on the basis of many different conceptions of what is socially responsible or irresponsible. Hence, agreement on the actual social responsibility or irresponsibility of a company is tedious. The contested character of CSR is strengthened by the fact that CSR can be used both aggressively and defensively: when activists criticize a company for being socially irresponsible, the company is likely to react by putting its social responsibility forward. As both claims are opposite depictions of the same entity, they are poised to generate controversies. Moreover, controversies on the meaning of CSR attract public attention, which reinforces controversies in return. Mainstream approaches and critical studies tend to get caught in these dynamics of contention. By depicting CSR as 'window dressing' or 'green washing', critical studies defend one 'true' meaning of CSR against the meanings put forward in mainstream managerial approaches, such as 'doing well by doing good', which they reject as false and misleading.[34] These

---

[33] Okoye (2009, 616). This was acknowledged earlier by other authors, such as Dow Votaw, who wrote in 1973 that

> the term ... is a brilliant one: it means something, but not always the same thing, to everybody. To some it conveys the idea of legal responsibility or liability; to others it means socially responsible behaviour in an ethical sense; to still others, the meaning transmitted is that of 'responsible for,' in a causal mode; many simply equate it with a charitable contribution; some take it to mean socially conscious; many of those who embrace it most fervently see it as a sort of fiduciary duty imposing higher standards of behaviour on businessmen than on citizens at large. Even the antonyms, socially 'irresponsible' and 'non-responsible' are subject to multiple interpretations. (Quoted by Carroll, Lipartito, Post, Werhane, and Goodpaster 2012, 7)

[34] Such controversies are perfectly illustrated by the debate in the *California Management Review* (2011, vol. 53, no. 2) between Aneel Karnani on the one hand ('"Doing Well By Doing Good": The Grand Illusion'; 'CSR Stuck in a Logical Trap: A Response to Pietra Rivoli and Sandra Waddock's "First they Ignore You...: The Time-Context

controversies, which tend to pit abstract and general definitions of CSR against one another, fail to provide a distanced and nuanced account of the essentially contested CSR phenomenon.

Developing a new approach to CSR: perspectives from social systems theory (SST)

Given the multifaceted, variegated, ambiguous, and contested character of the CSR phenomenon, studying *how CSR changes the structural tensions between corporate profit-making and competing collective values and interests* is challenging both in terms of theoretical conceptualization and in terms of empirical research. The present book does not intend to put an end to controversies between CSR advocates and CSR critics. Our aim is to attempt to develop a new analytical framework to study CSR, and to apply this framework in an empirical investigation of the development of CSR in India.

This analytical attempt draws in particular on the social systems theory (SST) developed by the German sociologist Niklas Luhmann and his followers.[35] Several aspects speak for this theoretical option. First, SST is a *theory of society*, which it defines as an all-encompassing system of communication in which various 'sub-systems' (interaction systems, organizations, function systems such as politics, law, the economy, science, or mass media) can be distinguished and analysed. As a theory of society, SST can 'describe society as a whole'.[36] This feature of SST is particularly relevant for CSR research, as it allows us to grasp the many – cultural, organizational, political, legal, economic, moral, and so on – dimensions of the CSR phenomenon. By doing so, SST avoids putting one dimension of CSR forward, such as the organizational dimension, and treating the other dimensions as external contexts.

A second advantage of SST is its ability to account for historical and spatial variations of complex social phenomena such as CSR. In particular, SST provides a sociological theory of modern 'world society' (as opposed to the idea of national societies) which is propitious for the study of interactions

---

Dynamic and Corporate Responsibility"'), and Pietra Rivoli and Sandra Waddock on the other hand ('The Grand Misapprehension: A Response to Aneel Karnani's "'Doing Well By Doing Good', The Grand Illusion"').

[35] For an introduction into this body of theory, see, for instance, Lee and Brosziewski (2009) and Stichweh (2015), and for German-speaking readers, Baraldi, Corsi, and Esposito (1997).

[36] Luhmann (2012, 4).

between global and more localized institutions, organizations, networks, processes, and events.[37] This perspective is helpful in capturing interplays between *various scales* in CSR. For instance, transnational CSR norms can be articulated with national CSR policy-making, regional cultural representations of how a 'socially responsible' company should behave, companies' contingent organizational dynamics, and protest movements that rely on networks of activists to translate local events embedded in particular contexts (for example, an industrial accident) into scandals receiving international media coverage.

Last but not least, according to SST, there is neither an 'objective reality' nor a 'true meaning' of collective phenomena. Social reality and social meaning are contingent constructs of social systems.[38] For instance, religion and science construct different realities by selecting and processing information in different ways, on the basis of different bodies of knowledge and structures – for example, religious doctrines, and scientific theories and methods. This *constructivist perspective* allows SST to analyse the dynamics of contention about the 'meanings' of CSR, without having to take sides by selecting one 'true' definition against the others (see Chapter 2).

In spite of these conceptual resources, only a few contributions have mobilized SST to analyse CSR so far. For instance, in his book on morality in society, Luhmann casts doubts on business ethics, which he envisages both as an ineffective attempt by the moral sphere to colonize price-driven economic operations, and as business executives paying lip service to abstract moral principles that *cannot* guide corporate conduct.[39] Jens Beckert also emphasizes the limited scope for non-economic rationalities in the guidance of corporate conduct. According to him, CSR supplies corporate managers with business-compatible symbolic answers to growing expectations of 'social responsibility', which are too complex, uncertain, and demanding to be met in practice.[40] In an essay on governance in contemporary society, in which religious morality and the modern state have subsequently lost their preeminent position, Helmut Willke refers to CSR as a form of contingent and flexible morality, which remains subordinated to the functional logic of the economic system.[41] For Susanne Holmström, CSR helps companies perceive and manage

---

[37] Luhmann (2012), Stichweh (2007a 2009).
[38] Luhmann (1995), Besio and Pronzini (2008), Lee and Brosziewski (2009), Fuchs (2013).
[39] Luhmann (2008).
[40] Beckert (2010).
[41] Willke (2009).

their interdependence with a plurality of contexts – economic, political, legal, moral, and so on – in a crisis-ridden global order.[42] In a recent article, Vladislav Valentinov and his co-authors have argued in the same vein by interpreting CSR in general and stakeholder management in particular as multifunctional devices, which allow companies to increase *their* sustainability by becoming more sensitive to the non-economic dimensions of their environment.[43]

This nascent stream within CSR research has outlined new analytical perspectives, which rely in particular on Luhmann's theory of modern society as a functionally differentiated social order (see Chapter 2). However, contributions from SST have remained highly abstract and general so far. Business ethics and CSR are analysed on the basis of theoretical reasoning, and empirical references are used mostly for illustrative purposes, if at all. This lack of empirical grounding limits the robustness of available interpretations of CSR based on SST. Moreover, by situating their argument solely within the 'big picture' context of global functional differentiation, authors fail to account for regional and sectorial variations of the CSR phenomenon.

On the contrary, the present book further develops the systems-theoretical analysis of CSR on the basis of thorough empirical research. It combines macro-sociological perspectives (for example, the differentiation of India's modern economy since the late eighteenth century) and detailed insights into the concrete formation and *modi operandi* of CSR (for example, CSR in India's cement industry; CSR public policy-making). By focusing on the Indian context, the study also allows us to grasp how global institutions of CSR, such as voluntary CSR reporting guidelines, interact with social structures and cultural patterns that are specific to a non-Western region of world society (for example, India's tradition of business philanthropy).

Outline of the argument

The theoretical framework and the empirical approach underlying the present analysis of CSR in India are spelled out in the next chapter. In line with previous CSR scholarship based on SST, the development of CSR is envisaged in this framework as an outcome of the increasing *functional differentiation of the economy* in modern society. As we will see, in Luhmann's theory, functional differentiation refers to the gradual historical shift from pre-modern

---

[42] Holmström (2010).
[43] Valentinov, Roth, and Will (2018).

hierarchical social orders, such as Europe's feudal society or India's caste system, to a modern 'world society' characterized by the primacy of a dozen functionally differentiated social systems: the economic system, the political system, law, mass media, science, education, health, religion, morality, arts, love, and sports. The accentuation of functional differentiation over the past decades has confronted society with new structural challenges, in particular with regard to interdependencies and disruptions between the economic system and other social systems (for example, politics, law, morality). The CSR phenomenon has developed historically in response to these challenges.

To understand more precisely *how* CSR has arisen from and acted upon these structural challenges, the theoretical framework proposes to study CSR as an *intermediary institution*.[44] Following Poul Kjaer, intermediary institutions are a specific kind of phenomenon in modern society. They emerge in reaction to tensions and conflicts between the economy and other social systems, such as the structural tensions between profit-making and competing collective values and interests outlined earlier. Intermediary institutions attempt to address these tensions by increasing the compatibility of economic processes with the logics and needs of other social systems. As in the case of CSR, intermediary institutions do so by operating *in between* social systems, rather than by relying solely on state interventions and the development of legally binding constraints.

As our empirical study of CSR in the Indian context will show, the specific performance of CSR as an intermediary institution is to increase the *responsiveness* of profit-driven economic processes vis-à-vis non-profit values and interests. By definition, profit-driven economic operations are oriented towards the economic system itself: they consist in monetary payments geared towards expectations of monetary returns. This self-referential orientation of profit-making, which increases the functional autonomy of the economy, has ambivalent consequences for the ability of the economic system to observe and address problems located in its environment. On the one hand, profit-making makes the economy responsive to social problems that appear as solvable needs on markets. On the other hand, the more profit-making dominates corporate conduct, the less the economy can be responsive to social problems located outside this market mechanism. Put under pressure to deliver high financial returns, companies are less inclined to take non-profit concerns into account, such as public health hazards due to industrial pollution or the detrimental effects of corruption on democracy. At some point, this restriction of economic

---

[44] Kjaer (2014, 2015a).

responsiveness creates tensions and conflicts which end up undermining profit-making itself. The development of the CSR phenomenon over the past few decades can be attributed to its ability to attenuate this contradiction by reinforcing the responsiveness of profit-driven economic processes.

One way for CSR to increase economic responsiveness is to introduce changes in companies' organizations: CSR-related organizational structures and practices enhance the ability of companies to selectively observe and address non-economic problems by *translating* these problems into parameters of economic risks, and by managing these risks according to profit-driven calculations. But CSR also introduces changes in other social systems, such as political systems, while these social systems contribute to the shaping of the CSR phenomenon in return. Does it mean that CSR mixes up different – economic, political, moral, and so on – rationalities? Findings from our empirical study suggest that the social systems involved contribute to CSR on the basis of their own operating logics. For instance, notwithstanding lobbying by industrial interest groups, India's CSR public policies were driven primarily by electoral concerns. Nonetheless, paradoxically, while as an intermediary institution, CSR involves multiple social systems, it ends up reinforcing the autonomy of the economic system vis-à-vis other social spheres. Thanks to CSR, the economy can better anticipate and undermine the development of constraints that would otherwise be imposed by other social systems, such as politics or morality. Furthermore, by enhancing economic responsiveness, CSR can reinforce the role of profit-driven calculations in the way tensions between corporate profit-making and competing collective values and interests are selectively observed as problems and addressed in society.

This analysis of CSR as an intermediary institution is developed, contextualized, and substantiated empirically in the subsequent chapters of the book. This empirical part articulates three areas of investigation: a *macro-sociological analysis of processes of functional differentiation underlying business–society interplays and the development of CSR in India*, an *in-depth case study of CSR in India's globalizing cement industry*, and *a detailed study of CSR public policies adopted recently by India's central government*.

The macro-sociological part of the analysis (Chapters 3 and 4) shows how CSR in the Indian context has been shaped by peculiar processes of functional differentiation, which involve both the global function systems of world society and India-specific social structures and cultural patterns. Three historical periods can be distinguished, each of them being characterized by a peculiar set of prevailing social structures. The first period, which spans from the late eighteenth century to the mid-twentieth century, corresponds to the gradual differentiation of India's economy as a modern capitalist system. As part of this process of differentiation, modern business corporations developed out of complex interactions between pre-modern institutions, in particular a division of labour structured primarily by the stratified system of castes, and modern institutions introduced by the British colonial ruler to exploit capitalist opportunities in the Indian colony. The resulting social structures and cultural patterns have had long-lasting impacts on the role of companies in relationships between the economy and other spheres of social life (for example, Indian forms of paternalism and business philanthropy).

The second period started in the late 1940s with the constitution of the federal Republic of India as a democratic sovereign national state. While pre-existing social structures did not disappear overnight, the formation of India's functionally differentiated political system was followed by a deep restructuring of business–society interplays. In particular, the central government controlled by Jawaharlal Nehru initiated a state-led interventionist development strategy. With instruments such as five-year plans, massive investments in public enterprises, price control for selected commodities, production licences and quotas, as well as tightly regulated labour relations, this strategy attempted to subordinate the economy to politically defined development goals. As a result, the self-steering of the economy through market prices and profit-driven investments was limited by numerous political interventions and legally binding regulations, which companies could hardly ignore – though rules imposed by the state were far from being systematically implemented. In a context where the state was clearly in charge of steering the country towards modern development, attempts of reformist activists and liberal business actors in the 1960s and 1970s to introduce CSR in India failed to gain traction.

This constellation changed with the economic reforms introduced by the central government from the mid-1980s onwards, which ushered a third period that is still ongoing. The state has repositioned itself from being a dominant controller to becoming an active supporter of economic dynamics. Overall, socio-economic development policies are now less about steering economic operations with regulatory constraints than about setting up 'investor-friendly' conditions for the economy to prosper according to its own operating logic. This shift has provided companies with new leeway vis-à-vis non-economic function systems, in particular politics. Conversely, enhanced market competition and changes in corporate governance, which are also related to India's increasing economic integration within global capitalism, have strengthened the role of financial performance objectives in the organizational steering of corporate conduct. As the present study shows, the rapid development of CSR in India since the late 1990s emanates from this structural reconfiguration. The more the purely self-referential economic value of monetary accumulation has dominated corporate conduct, and thereby the productive sector of the economy, the more tensions have accumulated between the economic system and other spheres of society. CSR has gained momentum in India over the past two decades in response to this tension-ridden intensification of functional differentiation.

The second part of the empirical analysis, which consists of an in-depth study of CSR in India's cement industry, provides more detailed insights into the links between the increased functional differentiation of India's contemporary economy, the rise of CSR in the subcontinent, and the impacts of this intermediary institution on tensions between profit-making and competing collective values and interests (Chapter 5). As the historical development of India's cement industry reflects broader changes characterizing the country's political economy, it is a particularly suitable case to study trends whose significance exceeds this particular sector. Indeed, the commissioning of India's first cement plants in the first half of the twentieth century is part of a broader process of indigenous industrial diversification and growth. Under India's interventionist regime, the cement sector grew rapidly thanks to massive public investments in the Cement Corporation of India Ltd (CCI), while price and distribution controls hampered investments of private cement manufacturers. As part of India's economic reforms of the 1980s and 1990s, the government gradually deregulated the cement sector. It also divested from the CCI and introduced incentives to encourage private investments in this industry. Since the early 2000s, India's cement industry has been increasingly integrated in global capitalism through foreign direct investments (FDIs) conducted by the world's leading multinational cement manufacturers, including the French company Lafarge, the Swiss company Holcim, and the Mexican company Cemex.[45]

The social and environmental impacts of cement production further enhance the relevance of this industry for the present study.[46] In the mid-2000s,

---

[45] Lafarge and Holcim merged in 2015, but they entered the Indian market and invested on the subcontinent as separate entities long before this merger, in 1999 and 2005 respectively.

[46] For an overview, see CSE (2005).

large cement plants (above 0.2 million tons of production capacity per year) employed on average about 1,000 skilled and unskilled workers. While labour relations used to be regulated by the Indian Cement Wage Board on the basis of national tripartite agreements, the past two decades have witnessed a shift towards company-level agreements that provide more autonomy to employers. Simultaneously, new tensions have arisen around issues such as growing pressures on productivity, harsh working conditions, layoffs induced at least partly by increasing mechanization and the sub-contracting of tasks, and the increasing use of casual workforce at the expense of permanent employees.

Cement production is also prone to conflicts between companies and local village communities. Because the production of cement requires limestone, factories are usually located in rural areas where limestone can be extracted. As a consequence, villagers usually have to give up large tracks of fertile agricultural land that companies need to set up their production facilities and for mining purposes. Local communities are also often exposed to decreasing water resources, as blast mining induces cracks in the groundwater tables. In addition, air pollution (dust, SO_x, NO_x) generally reduces the productivity of fields located near the plant, and it triggers respiratory diseases among neighbouring populations. Such a concentration of conflict-ridden social and environmental issues provides a fertile ground to study how CSR changes the way social systems observe and process tensions opposing profit-making and competing collective values and interests.

In terms of empirical scope, the analysis of CSR in the Indian cement industry combines sector-wide data with an in-depth study of Lafarge India Pvt. Ltd, which is a subsidiary of the French multinational company Lafarge S.A. (since 2015: LafargeHolcim). At the time when the fieldwork on Lafarge India was conducted, between January 2008 and January 2011, Lafarge was one of the world's largest companies: it had about 84,000 employees working in 79 countries, and in 2010, it was ranked by *Forbes* as the world's 390th largest company by revenue. Since the Rio Earth Summit of 1992, Lafarge has also been considered a front-runner in the field of CSR and sustainable development. In the aftermath of this landmark event, which according to a former CEO of Lafarge 'revealed' the strategic significance of global societal challenges to the company,[47] a new department for CSR and sustainable development was created at the Parisian headquarters, and Lafarge's CEO took up the position of President of the World Business Council for Sustainable

---

[47] Interview conducted by the author on 18 November 2009.

Development – a powerful business think tank of which Lafarge is a founding member. Lafarge maintained its vanguard position in the field of CSR, as illustrated by its early participation in the United Nations Global Compact, its partnerships with major NGOs (WWF, CARE, Habitat for Humanity), its listing on the sustainable stock market indexes FTSE4Good and the DJSI STOXX, and the publication of annual CSR reports that adhere to the guidelines of the Global Reporting Initiative and are reviewed by two internal stakeholder committees.

Lafarge entered into the Indian cement market in 1999 with the incorporation of its subsidiary Lafarge India and the acquisition of two factories owned by Tata Steel: the Sonadih cement plant, located in the state of Chhattisgarh, and the Jojobera cement plant, located in the state of Jharkhand.[48] In 2001, Lafarge India strengthened its position with the acquisition of the Arasmeta cement plant from Raymond Cement, also located in Chhattisgarh. Over the course of the 2000s, in addition to the installation of a second production line in Sonadih, Lafarge India invested in several new cement plants: Mejia (West Bengal) and Jaintia Hills (Meghalaya) in 2002, Alsindi (Himachal Pradesh) in 2006, Nimbahera (Rajasthan) in 2007, and Ravoor (Karnataka) in 2009.[49] For the present study, extensive qualitative fieldwork was conducted in and around the plants of Sonadih and Arasmeta in Chhattisgarh, as well as on the cement plant project of Alsindi, which was used by Lafarge India as a laboratory to design a new CSR strategy. This empirical work informs a detailed analysis of how changes in India's post-reform political economy have generated new tensions between the economy and other spheres of society at the interface between companies and their societal environment, how companies have mobilized CSR in response to these tensions, and how the resulting CSR-related organizational structures and activities have changed the way these tensions are observed and processed.

Because the study of India's cement industry focuses on companies' use of CSR, it falls short of apprehending how other social systems participate in the formation of this intermediary institution, and how CSR contributes

---

[48] Lafarge had already invested in India in the mid-1990s with a transborder cement plant project involving a limestone mine located in the Indian state of Meghalaya and a cement plant located in Bangladesh. However, this project was accomplished only in 2006.

[49] In July 2016, LafargeHolcim agreed to sell the cement activities of Lafarge India Pvt. Ltd. to the Indian conglomerate Nirma Ltd. for US$1.4 billion. The transaction is still to be approved by the Competition Commission of India.

to changing these systems in return. While covering the multiple function systems involved would exceed the scope of the present study, a third part of the empirical analysis takes this functional dimension into account by examining the role of India's political system (Chapter 6). In fact, since 2007, India's state authorities have been increasingly involved in CSR through a series of dedicated public policies that mobilize CSR as a regulatory instrument. These public policies have directly contributed to the formation of the CSR phenomenon. They selected and institutionalized distinct meanings of the contested CSR concept, and by formulating normative expectations towards corporate conduct, they introduced new coordination mechanisms between the economy and other spheres of society. Conversely, studying the making of these public policies provides insights into how CSR has contributed to changing India's regulatory politics by opening up distinct horizons of political intervention. For the purpose of the present study, the empirical analysis focuses on India's two major CSR public policies: the National Voluntary Guidelines for the Social, Environmental and Economic Responsibilities of Business (NVGs), which were introduced in 2011 by India's Ministry of Corporate Affairs, and the CSR clause of the new Companies Act, which was adopted in Parliament in 2013.

The main findings of this theory-driven empirical study of CSR in India are presented in a concluding chapter (Chapter 7). By combining insights gained from the various parts of the empirical analysis, this chapter attempts to provide plausible contributions to better understand how the intermediary institution of CSR changes patterns of economic responsiveness in a society confronted with growing tensions and conflicts between profit-making and competing collective values and interests.

With regard to empirical material, the analysis is informed by a combination of various bodies of literature and a large corpus of first-hand and second-hand data, which was gathered between 2007 and 2014 over the course of several field visits. This data comprises 189 semi-structured interviews with a variety of actors (for example, business executives, government officials and elected representatives, workers, trade union leaders, journalists, activists, villagers), in situ observations, and a number of documentary sources including reports, policies and other official documents, minutes of parliamentary debates, laws, files extracted from legal proceedings, press articles, petitions, as well as letters and e-mail exchanges.

Chapter 2

✠

CSR, Functional Differentiation, and the Problem of Economic Responsiveness

CSR as a product of functional differentiation

A key hypothesis in CSR research based on SST is that the CSR phenomenon exists in relation to a much broader phenomenon, which is the historical development of modern society as a world society based primarily on functional differentiation.[1] To grasp this idea of functional differentiation, one has to consider a broad overview of modern world history.

Before functional differentiation unfolded, western Europeans were living in a feudal social order. This order was characterized by the primacy of hierarchical (also called 'stratified') differentiation: in most domains of social life, people's life chances and ways of life were conditioned by their inherited position in a stratified structure, which stretched from royal families and the high nobility down to families of landless peasants, vagrants, and serfs. From the sixteenth century onwards, this stratified order was progressively disrupted by the formation of functionally differentiated subsystems – a contingent evolutionary process that gained momentum in the late eighteenth century and that reached far into the twentieth century.

To illustrate the emergence of functional differentiation, the monetization of the economy and the development of markets increasingly decoupled access to ownership from one's inherited social position in a hierarchical order. The rise of constitutional states transferred political decision-making from the heights of royal dynasties and aristocratic families to self-organized political systems, in which people are included in a political demos under conditions of formal

---

[1] See in particular Luhmann (2012 and 2013).

equality through the status of citizenship. Religious or natural laws gave way to a system of positive law, whose legitimacy is based on internal procedures and rules. Science progressively asserted itself as a system of knowledge production that is guided by the autonomous pursuit of truth. Religion receded from its role as an all-encompassing provider of order in society, to constitute itself as a distinct sphere of social life that entails multiple belief-systems.

This gradual process of functional differentiation, whose unfolding has been much less neat and linear than it appears in the sketch above, has participated in the constitution of a contemporary 'world society' by way of an increasing globalization of function systems. Common parlance still refers to 'society' as a collection of national 'societies', whose boundaries would more or less match the political boundaries of national states. But following SST, this vision misses the fact that all human beings have become included as participants in an integrated entity called world society.[2] In this world society, life chances and ways of life depend less on one's inherited social position than on the dynamics of global function systems. For instance, the economy became global on the basis of convertible currencies and integrated price-making markets. A global political system emerged, composed of national states and transnational structures of governance. A global legal system developed, of which the positive law of sovereign countries is an integral part. In the global system of science, scholars exchange with colleagues and refer to scientific publications from across the world. Information is generated in a global system of mass media, which reports on events located all over the world. And a number of world religions and more localized belief-systems must coexist with one another.

This functionally differentiated global order has to face a number of structural challenges. Five such structural challenges can be identified, which seem to participate in the emergence and ongoing expansion of the CSR phenomenon.[3]

First, society's continuous expansion (for example, more economic transactions, more political decision-making, more laws and trials, more scientific research), combined with the 'setting-in-motion of the material, the social and the cultural world at an ever increasing speed',[4] has put human beings and society's bio-physical environment under increasing strain. However, function systems have a limited sensitivity towards such impacts,

---

[2] See Luhmann (1997), Stichweh (2007b), and Holzer, Kastner, and Werron (2014).
[3] The following analysis builds mostly on the work of Holmström (2010).
[4] Rosa, Dörre, and Lessenich (2017, 58).

as they only process information that seems directly relevant from their own viewpoints.[5] For instance, electoral stakes and political strategies condition the way politics takes work-related suffering or the loss of biodiversity into consideration. Similarly, the economic system observes such issues when they affect costs, prices, and profit. Science considers work-related suffering or the loss of biodiversity as data that can inform the development of scientific knowledge. These multiple and fragmented sensitivities lead society and social systems within it to react selectively but often with intense emotional moods. Working conditions in Apple's Chinese suppliers or the fate of whales triggers international outcry: modern society underreacts and overreacts at the same time. With concepts such as 'business ethics' or the 'triple bottom line', CSR provides social systems with positive perspectives to address structural problems of antagonism, as it promises to attenuate the destructive impacts of society's economic growth and to support policies and practices promoting collective and consensual solutions.

Second, as a result of functional differentiation, cultural visions of the world that were based on a given religious order, such as Christianity, have given way to a heightened recognition of society's ontological contingency. Our 'common future', to paraphrase Gro Harlem Brundtland's landmark report of 1987, lies not in the hands of God or deities, but in ours. This relativistic cultural perspective confronts social systems with collective concerns for risks, as the decisions they produce become as many gambles on the future. More specifically, problems of discrepancies between the benefits decision-makers can expect to reap and the potential harmful consequences of their decisions for others have gained salience. Companies are directly exposed in this situation to the risk-taker versus victim dichotomy. Many of their profitable business operations might imply negative outcomes for others – for example, burned out workers, consumers poisoned by noxious products, households impoverished by financial speculation, citizens disempowered by effective lobbying, indigenous communities uprooted for the sake of resource extraction, future generations threatened by climate change. These concerns lead non-economic function systems and organizations to call for 'socially responsible' business conduct (aggressive use of CSR), which companies answer by developing CSR-related organizational structures, managerial tools, and practices (defensive use of CSR).

The third structural challenge arises from tensions between the operational autonomy of function systems and their complex web of interdependence.

---

[5] See in particular Luhmann (1989).

On the one hand, function systems are driven by an existential compulsion towards operational autonomy: a system can only exist and reproduce itself if it maintains its difference from its environment. For instance, science needs to prevent politics or religion from controlling the production of scientific knowledge, or it would cease to be science and melt into political propaganda or religious faith. Similarly, a political system whose collectively binding decisions can be openly bought would be absorbed in the economy as a traded commodity – a reason why corruption must remain a discreet and illegitimate practice.

However, a paradox needs to be underlined: the more function systems are autonomous, the more they become interdependent. For instance, not only do political decisions impact the economy, but a functioning economy requires political and legal systems to fulfil a number of functions, such as the management of conflicts and the enforcement of contracts. Similarly, political systems are structurally dependent on a functioning economy, as building up political power requires sufficient tax revenue. Because of this mutual reinforcement of autonomy and interdependence, functional differentiation 'increases the sensitivity and motivation [of systems] to develop self-restrictions and coordinating mechanisms in recognition of [their] interdependence'.[6] In our case, CSR attempts to support self-restriction and inter-systemic coordination. While the primary guiding value of capitalist firms remains the production of wealth through monetary accumulation, companies are expected to avoid 'socially irresponsible' practices that would corrupt justice, undermine democratic decision-making, hijack science and education, or threaten the guiding values of other function systems such as mass media, health provision, religion, art, and sport.

Fourth, global functional differentiation challenges the ability of national state politics to address collective problems by producing and enforcing collectively binding decisions.[7] As traditional policy instruments, such as 'command and control' regulations, fail to control complex problems involving multiple systems interacting at various socio-spatial scales, politics must consider alternative instruments to govern society. One such alternative, which has proved particularly popular over the past two decades, consists in 'multi-stakeholder' collaborative governance settings, which rely on incentive structures that mobilize the internal logics of other function systems.

---

[6] Holmström (2010, 147).
[7] See also Willke (2009).

Environmental governance is a typical case.[8] The growing use of CSR as a governance instrument participates in this trend: 'the political system', writes Susanne Holmström, 'relieves the pressure on own risky decision-making and increasingly sends on the responsibility, in particular to the economic system, by means of political initiatives aimed at internalizing the societal horizon within the business community'.[9]

Finally, globalization creates structural challenges when the functionally differentiated global normative order (democracy, market economy, independent justice, religious tolerance, free press, autonomous science, and so on) encounters a variety of regional social structures and cultures. Indeed, regional contexts are characterized by different degrees of functional differentiation (for example, theocracies), as well as by social structures whose mode of differentiation follows other logics (for example, stratified caste system, lineage-based ethnic groups). Such regional diversity has consequences regarding the normative expectations vis-à-vis the economy in general and corporate conduct in particular. In a context of globalization, practices that used to be regionally legitimate are suddenly questioned by the global norms of functional differentiation. The intermingling of politics and business within family structures, for instance, raises new suspicions of cronyism, nepotism, or even corruption. Moreover, globalization confronts companies – especially MNCs – with legitimacy conflicts between regional and global norms. Managing these conflicting expectations requires new resources of organizational sensitivity, cultural intelligence, and legitimation strategies. CSR contributes to providing such resources. For instance, as the study of CSR in India's cement industry will show, CSR provides companies with legitimizing scripts whose underlying principles are general and flexible enough to allow subsidiaries to adapt them to local institutional arrangements and cultures (see Chapter 5).

The CSR phenomenon as an 'intermediary institution'

The ways by which the CSR phenomenon deals with these structural challenges can be further specified with the concept of 'intermediary institution'.[10]

---

[8] See, for instance, Meadowcroft (2007), Andonova and Mitchell (2010), Voß and Bornemann (2011), and Newell, Pattberg, and Schroeder (2012).

[9] Holmström (2010, 150).

[10] On the concept of intermediary institutions, see Kjaer (2014, 2015a, 2015b).

Following Poul Kjaer, intermediary institutions are distinct social phenomena that have developed precisely to help functionally differentiated social systems sort out and stabilize their interplays, in particular with regard to relationships between the economy and non-economic spheres of society.

Kjaer identifies three such intermediary institutions, which have succeeded one another over the past two centuries: European corporatism of the nineteenth and early twentieth centuries (for example, the Catholic model of trade unionism; Italian fascism), neo-corporatism of the post-war period (for example, national tripartite labour agreements between employers' associations, trade unions and governments), and contemporary global governance (for example, climate change governance). These historical intermediary institutions differ from one another in certain respects. For instance, corporatist arrangements were local and mostly informal, neo-corporatism was based on more formalized national frameworks, while contemporary governance involves transnational and often highly formalized structures. Nonetheless, these intermediary institutions share a number of defining properties, which also characterize the CSR phenomenon.

One common characteristic is that intermediary institutions have accompanied the growing intervention of state authorities in society, while at the same time offering alternatives to such intervention. Many classical contributions in the political sociology of the state have emphasized how, over the past two centuries, national states have grown not only in number but also in terms of areas of policy-making – from the core sovereign domains of foreign policy, internal security, justice, and money, to infrastructure development, trade, production, labour, education and research, health provision, family planning, housing, social insurance, environmental protection, arts and culture, sports, and so on.[11] Across these areas, the state has been busy regulating – with more or less success – the complex interplays between, on the one hand, society's functionally differentiated economic system and, on the other hand, other domains of collective life that are both supported and disrupted by the *Eigendynamik* (internal dynamics) of the economy.[12]

However, state authorities have not been the sole performer of this function. A great number of other actors have intervened collectively on problems

---

[11] For an overview, see, for instance, Wimmer and Feinstein (2010).

[12] For a more detailed theoretical conception of the dependence of non-economic spheres of society towards the economy, and the development of state interventions – in particular through social policy – to regulate this dependence, see Schimank (2015).

arising from interplays between the economy and non-economic spheres of society. These include private economic actors and their representative bodies (for example, trade associations, employers' associations), religious bodies, international organizations (for example, International Labour Organization, World Health Organization), trade unions, foundations, NGOs, and a vast collection of other more or less formally organized interest groups. While in some circumstances, the involvement of these actors has supported or complemented state-based regulation, in other cases, such as the development of private environmental standards, non-state actors have mobilized against state intervention through the development of alternative regulatory arrangements. Intermediary institutions have developed out of these dynamic interplays.

A further common characteristic of intermediary institutions is their inter-systemic dimension. While conventional state interventions originate from the political system, which tries to act upon the functioning of other social systems by way of collectively binding decisions, intermediary institutions span across the boundaries of social systems. More precisely, their development involves contributions from public and private actors who are embedded in multiple social systems; their formal institutional structures and the ideas on which they are based transect social system boundaries; their functioning activates the participation of several systems; and their effects can be observed in many spheres of society. This inter-systemic dimension of intermediary institutions allows them to articulate different social systems: they act as 'the hinges of modern society insofar as they serve as central sites for the stabilization of relations between multiple social spheres, most notably between the economic and the non-economic spheres of society'.[13] Intermediary institutions are 'simultaneously oriented towards *internal stabilization* of economic processes and establishment of *external compatibility* with non-economic segments of society'.[14]

Poul Kjaer refers succinctly to CSR as an integral part of global governance. But CSR can be envisaged and studied as an intermediary institution in its own right, which is part of the broader intermediary institution of global governance. CSR has developed historically both as an alternative to conventional state intervention (self-regulation versus state intervention) and as a complementary structure of societal problem-solving (CSR as corporate contributions to

---

[13] Kjaer (2014, 117).
[14] Kjaer (2014, 119), emphasis added.

sustainable development).[15] CSR is also clearly an inter-systemic phenomenon, whose formation and functioning has mobilized a variety of social systems: CSR is altogether an area in which companies invest to pursue economic objectives, a policy field in which state authorities intervene, a set of more or less juridical norms and standards, a theme on which mass media generates information, an area of scientific research, and a topic in both religious and moral discourse. Furthermore, CSR is directed towards the coordination and stabilization of problem-ridden interplays between the economy and other spheres of society.

With regard to peculiar characteristics of 'governance', they also apply to the CSR phenomenon. CSR involves public and private participants in collaborative settings (for example, the United Nations' Global Compact); it is composed of a loosely coupled collection of decentralized initiatives and norms (as referred, for instance, in the overarching CSR norm ISO 26000); these norms are generally non-binding, flexible, and geared towards adaptive learning processes; CSR is institutionalized through consensus-building rather than through agonistic decision-making processes; and the legitimacy of CSR-based regulatory institutions relies primarily on output criteria such as 'efficient problem-solving', as opposed to input criteria such as democratic representation.[16]

CSR and the problem of economic responsiveness

On the one hand, we can relate the development of CSR to functional differentiation. On the other hand, we can envisage CSR as an intermediary institution. But this useful analytical construct does not sufficiently circumscribe the concrete mechanisms and activities through which CSR can become an operational intermediary institution responding to the structural challenges arising from functional differentiation. To conceptualize more precisely how CSR changes tensions between profit-making and competing collective values and interests in a context of functional differentiation, we propose to add 'economic responsiveness' as a third key component of the analytical framework.

---

[15] In the terminology of neo-institutionalist CSR research, CSR can both 'mirror' and 'substitute' the involvement of the state in the governance of economic processes (Jackson and Apostolakou 2010).

[16] On these shared characteristics of governance and CSR, see, for instance, Jessop (1997), Graz and Nölke (2007), Willke (2009), Shamir (2010), Jacobsson and Garsten (2012), Lievens (2015), and Kjaer (2015a, 2015b).

The concept of responsiveness is not new to CSR research. It was popularized as 'corporate social responsiveness' in the 1970s by a series of contributions to management studies.[17] One of them, formulated by S. Prakash Sethi, defines social responsiveness as a level of corporate performance vis-à-vis social needs which goes beyond what common sense or managerial conceptualizations of CSR can achieve.[18] For Sethi, 'social responsibility' is a prescriptive idea, according to which companies' behaviour *should* be congruent with the prevailing norms, values, and expectations of society, which exceed market pressures and legal obligations. 'Social responsiveness' would be about companies proactively anticipating societal problems, either related or unrelated to their own activities, and taking measures to prevent these problems from occurring, even at the expense of profit-maximization.

Unlike Sethi, Robert W. Ackerman and Raymond A. Bauer envisage corporate social responsiveness not as a complement of CSR, but as an alternative to it.[19] Writing in 1976, the authors observed a context in which Anglo-Saxon companies were facing growing social demands beyond the provision of goods and services for a profit. Companies were increasingly expected to respect and foster consumer rights, occupational health and safety, civil rights, peace, environmental protection, and other non-economic collective values and interests. Ackerman and Bauer argued that in such a context, the idea of 'corporate social responsibility' does not bring much, as it circles around endless debates on *which* expectations companies should fulfil and *why* they should do so. For Ackermann and Bauer, speaking of 'corporate social responsiveness' usefully sets the focus on *how* companies and their managers can identify social demands (for example, labour welfare, diversity, consumer safety, environmental protection) and respond to them.

In a landmark paper, William C. Frederick further developed this view by opposing the 'supreme vagueness' of CSR_1, understood as some sort of social obligation, to the pragmatic usefulness of corporate social responsiveness (CSR_2), understood as 'the capacity of a corporation to respond to social pressures'.[20] Leaving the quagmire of moral speculations on 'social responsibilities' behind, the concept of corporate social responsiveness would

---

[17] Apart from the specific stream of literature on 'corporate social performance', contemporary CSR research has partly forgotten and oversimplified the concept of corporate social responsiveness. See Acquier, Daudigeos, and Valiorgue (2011).

[18] Sethi (1975).

[19] Ackerman and Bauer (1976).

[20] Frederick (1994 [1978], 154).

allow management scholars and practitioners to explore and improve the micro-organizational and macro-institutional arrangements that can help companies detect and manage demands arising from their socio-political surrounding.

Around the same period, Archie B. Carroll contributed yet another conceptualization of corporate social responsiveness.[21] For him, social responsiveness is neither a proactive complement to prescriptive CSR nor is it a managerial approach that breaks away from normative considerations. It is rather a description of what companies *do* in response to the economic, legal, and ethical responsibilities that society expects them to fulfil. According to Carroll, these expectations – or 'social responsibilities' – find expression in a number of concrete social issues related, for instance, to labour conditions, to consumer health, or to industrial pollution. Companies would be more or less 'responsive' depending on whether they ignore these expectations, whether they react to them defensively by accommodating demands, or whether they are proactive, for instance, through planning and forecasting, organizing for social response, and controlling social activities and their outcomes. In this perspective, corporate social *performance* would be an outcome of the interplay between corporate social *responsibility* (what society expects from companies) and corporate social *responsiveness* (how companies respond to these expectations).

This brief overview of the concept of responsiveness in the managerial CSR literature illustrates the common model underlying this line of thinking. While authors differ in the way they relate 'responsibility' and 'responsiveness', they all envisage responsiveness on the basis of a stimulus–response schema applied to the distinction organization/environment. On the 'environment' side of the distinction, society and the various interest groups it entails would have actual or potential demands that companies would be expected to fulfil. On the 'organization' side of the distinction, companies would be more or less able to identify and process or even to anticipate and prevent these demands, depending mainly on their organizational structures and the influence of broader institutional settings.

This conception of responsiveness is congruent with the purpose of the authors mentioned above, which is to produce managerial doctrines that can help managers improve the responsiveness of their organization. However, by focusing on organizational (corporate) responsiveness, the managerial outlook

---

[21] Carroll (1979).

envisages business–society interplays without taking society's functional differentiation explicitly into account. The result is an imprecise view of the contexts in which companies operate. For instance, processes that are specific to function systems (for example, policy-making, consumption, moral judgement) are mixed up in unspecific categories such as 'social pressures', 'social demands', or 'social needs'. Another shortcoming of this model is the tendency to envisage CSR as an open-ended collection of expectations towards corporate behaviour and as companies' efforts to match these expectations. This conception of CSR does not fit the sociological outlook on the CSR phenomenon developed in the present study. CSR is conceived here as a concrete and historically situated intermediary institution, whose multiple dimensions are reducible neither to social expectations nor to companies' response to these expectations.

Given these shortcomings, the systems-theoretical analysis of CSR calls for an alternative conception of responsiveness. Building on SST, we propose to use the concept of responsiveness to describe a *specific type of operations* at work in social systems. This type of operations consists in the *selective observation* and the *solution-oriented processing* of *social problems*.[22] The key ideas of 'selective observation', 'processing', and 'social problems' need to be briefly developed.

The idea of selective observation is a core element of SST. Social systems operate on the basis of communication, which takes place between participants. Whenever a participant A selects a piece of information, makes an utterance (for example, speaks, writes, gesticulates), and other participants (B, C, D, ...) infer an information from the utterance, a communicative event occurs.[23] Social systems consist of such communicative events, which they connect selectively

---

[22] To our knowledge, 'responsiveness' has not been integrated into the conceptual vocabulary of SST so far. The definition and explication of the term proposed here builds on ongoing discussions conducted within the *Forum Internationale Wissenschaft* of the University of Bonn.

[23] SST conceives of communication as the very substance of society. Of course, communication requires the cognitive and physical participation of human beings to happen. But social systems operate *between* human participants. They remain exterior to the latter's respective minds (psychic systems) and bodies (biological systems): no one knows what people think or what happens in their body when they communicate with one another. Social systems can only communicate about this, for instance, by attributing certain thoughts to certain persons, or by describing behaviours as 'actions' performed more or less intentionally by 'actors'. See Luhmann (1995) and Lee and Broszewski (2009).

to one another in communication flows. To give but a few examples, the economic system operates on the basis of interrelated monetary transactions; political systems operate on the basis of communication directed towards the production and implementation of collectively binding decisions; law operates through legal proceedings; scientific research involves communicative operations, such as discussions in seminars and conferences or the writing and reading of publications; and organizations operate through communicative decision-making processes.

Each communicative event that flows into these communication processes can be described as an *observation*, that is, the indication of something which is distinguished from something else.[24] Social systems are observing systems. For instance, the exchange of a commodity involving a salesman and a customer will distinguish 'this commodity' from any other commodity that could have been bought with the customer's money, as well as 'this price' from any other sum of money that could have been expected as payment for this transaction to occur. The salesman and the customer observe the commodity and the price in the thought processes of their respective mind. But when the transaction occurs, it is the economic system that *observes* the commodity (and not another) in the monetary language of prices. Similarly, if a Member of Parliament (MP) invokes 'rising unemployment' in a parliamentary debate, and if this distinction is integrated into the communicative process taking place in this debate, one can say that the political system has *observed* 'rising unemployment'. The observation of a 'piece of evidence' in a trial, or of 'data' in scientific research, would be further examples of observation by social systems.

While observations occur as single communicative events, they are not isolated. Social systems *process* information by relating observed distinctions with one another in *meaningful* ways. 'Rising unemployment', for instance, would have little meaning if it was uttered out of the blue in a parliamentary assembly, without triggering any ensuing sequence of communication. The meaning of this distinction in a given parliamentary debate depends on the preceding distinctions it is related to (for example, 'last year'), and on the ensuing distinctions that political communication observe in relation to it (for example, 'calls for a policy change').

Both the observation and the processing of information in social systems are necessarily *selective*: as communication cannot refer to everything simultaneously, nor establish all possible meaning-generating connections,

---

[24] On the concept of observation, see in particular Luhmann (1995) and Fuchs (2010).

distinctions must be selected and processed one step at a time. It is through this selective production and processing of information that social systems observe and thereby construct social reality. Whatever is distinguished in communication exists in the eyes of social systems. Whatever is not communicated about is socially non-existent.[25]

In this context of communication and selective observation, responsiveness requires two conditions to occur. First, it requires a social system that selectively observes a *social problem*. Problems are distinctions of past, present, or future alternative states of things, where one alternative is thought of or described as being better or worse than the other. To exist as problems in society, problems must be described by social systems.[26] For instance, a customer might be disappointed by the quality of the product he or she bought, and think 'it should be more solid' or 'it was definitely over-priced'. But to become a problem in society, and not just in the mind of the disappointed customer, the poor quality/price relation of the commodity must be thematized as a problem in communication. Similarly, 'rising unemployment' is not a social problem as such – though many people might experience it that way. It becomes a social problem and can be processed as such only when it is referred to as a problem in communication. In this perspective, social problems are not given, nor are they constructed by more or less rational 'actors' who would interact in a functionally undifferentiated social space. Social problems are

---

[25] This is why the psychic systems of human beings and the social systems of society are distinct realities. Each human being lives in his or her own reality, which consists of what is being distinguished by the thought-processes of his or her conscious mind. Human beings can communicate *about* their thoughts, but thoughts cannot be transferred from one mind to another through social communication. A speaker, for instance, never knows what his speech triggers in the minds of his audience. He or she can only think about it, and wonder. For the same reason, social communication can hope to change the state of mind of human beings, but communication cannot penetrate human minds: society never knows how human minds react to what is being said, written, paid, painted, or indicated through any other medium of communication. Society can only communicate about it.

[26] This acceptation of the 'social' quality of problems seems more accurate than the usual distinction in the CSR literature between 'social' and 'environmental' problems. Child labour is a social problem not only because it refers to a social state of things (people are involved) but also because it is described as a problem in social communication. And climate change is a social problem because it is described as such in social communication, even if it refers to an ecological state of things which, as such, involves not people but climatic conditions.

communicatively observed (constructed) by social systems over the course of their operations.[27]

The second condition for responsiveness to occur is that a social system must selectively process the observed problem in a way that is *directed towards solutions*. A political system that observes rising unemployment as a problem, but that decides that nothing can or should be done in this regard, is not responsive. Conversely, if the observation of this problem triggers further communication on public policies aiming to curb unemployment, the political system can be said to be responsive. Similarly, the economic system is responsive to problems whenever payments intended to help solving these problems occur. Such problems can be internal, such as when a company buys more productive machinery to increase returns on investments: a transaction occurs in response to the economic problem of achieving high returns on investment as opposed to low returns. But as for other social systems, the economy can also be responsive to problems located in its environment, such as perceived needs of customers (for example, hunger, social prestige), political objectives (for example, public spending in social welfare programmes), or religious beliefs (for example, Islamic finance).

This revisited concept of responsiveness allows us to shed new light on CSR and the underlying structural tensions between profit-making and competing collective values and interests. These structural tensions arise from the fact that profit-making in a functionally differentiated economy is both an *engine* of economic responsiveness and a *constraint* on economic responsiveness.

As already suggested above, the functionally differentiated economic system which prevails in modern society is a communication system that operates through monetary transactions.[28] Its operations consist in monetary payments. Material aspects that are usually conceived of as being an integral part of the economy, such as resource extraction, the installation of factories, labour, the

---

[27] This constructivist perspective on problems in society differs from the structural-functionalist approach to social problems, which was influential in particular in the United States, according to which sociology can diagnose and prescribe treatments for social problems, understood as objective disruptions and deficiencies in the effective functioning of society (for example, Merton and Nisbet 1971). It also differs from the symbolic-interactionist perspective, which envisages social problems as deviant behaviours that are socially constructed through norm-setting and the labelling of deviant groups (Becker 1966).

[28] For details on the theory of the economy in SST, see Luhmann (1988). A discussion of this part of SST can be found in Beckert (2002).

exchange of commodities, or consumption, are envisaged by SST as a 'derivative reality' ('*derivativen Sachverhalt*') of economic communication.[29] These concrete activities are economic only in terms of their monetary dimension, such as the cost of resource extraction, the salary being paid in exchange for work, the monetary added value that can be extracted from labour, or the money which changes hands when a commodity is sold on the market.

As a system of monetary transactions, the modern economic system is *self-referential*: each payment has an economic meaning, which is that the one who pays loses his/her capacity to use this money for other payments, while the one who receives the money can now use it to make other payments. However, economic self-reference is generally coupled with *external reference*, that is, with references to the environment of the economic system. In the case of consumption, for instance, one pays a certain amount of money (self-reference) to get a commodity that one perceives as valuable because of its relevance in non-economic circumstances, such as the need for food or the need for social prestige (external reference). The transaction has both an economic meaning expressed in the language of prices – a certain amount of money changes hands – and a non-economic meaning that the economy observes in the form of 'needs': the need for food to sustain living organisms, the need for luxury cars as status symbols, the need for electoral chances related to given public expenses, the need for legality through the payment of fines, and so on. The economic system observes itself through self-referential prices, and it observes its environment in the form of needs by processing information on what is being paid for.

In a capitalist market economy, *profit-making is a driver of economic responsiveness* inasmuch as it motivates producers to observe social problems in the form of needs, and to address these needs by supplying relevant goods and services for a profit. Whether these needs have already been formulated or whether they are anticipated or even created by innovative entrepreneurs makes little difference here. The economic processes set in motion by the profit-driven decision of owners to produce useful commodities are responsive economic processes. Situations of shortage, such as those triggered by the disruptions of war, make the importance of this mechanism of economic responsiveness for everyday life visible. This profit-driven mechanism of economic responsiveness can also be responsive to societal issues, as illustrated by the development of fair-trade products or the provision of financial services to fund investments that reduce industrial pollution.

---

[29] Luhmann (1988, 54–55).

However, *profit-making also constrains economic responsiveness* inasmuch as it directs economic processes towards monetary accumulation. Profit-driven payments are primarily self-referential: one pays money according to calculated expectations of monetary returns. With profit-making, the economy 'orients itself to itself', and actual or potential 'needs' located in the system's environment are only considered inasmuch as they seem economically relevant for profit-driven cost–benefit calculations.[30] In other words, the significance of profit-making as a guiding value in economic processes makes these processes less sensitive to non-economic meaning contexts. To quote a few examples, profit-driven payments consider the activities of politics, justice, art, science, education, health, or morality in terms of their consequences for financial returns on investments. Hence, profit-making constrains economic responsiveness vis-à-vis problems which might be relevant in other meaning contexts, but which seem to be either irrelevant for profit-making or sources of additional economic costs.

In short, profit-making conditions economic responsiveness, that is, the selection of needs and problems which the economy can observe and process. By directing economic payments towards expectations of monetary gains based on cost–benefit calculations, profit-making introduces an asymmetry in the relationships between the economic and non-economic spheres of society. It leads economic transactions to observe and process collective values and interests such as social welfare, public health, democracy, or environmental protection, only inasmuch as these collective values and interests are relevant for monetary gains. As the empirical study of CSR in India will show, the development of the CSR phenomenon is directly related to this conditioning of economic responsiveness by profit-driven calculations.

Translating the analytical framework into empirical CSR research

While the theoretical framework outlined above opens up perspectives for the study of CSR, it requires further specifications regarding its application in empirical CSR research. In particular, investigating CSR as a concrete historical intermediary institution requires us to define how this object of inquiry can be empirically identified and circumscribed. The essentially contested character of CSR makes this step particularly crucial, as the plurality of definitions of CSR that circulate in society prevents the empirical research process from using a consensual understanding of CSR as a starting point.

---

[30] Luhmann (1988, 56).

A strategy to circumscribe the essentially contested CSR phenomenon consists in tracing the use of the CSR concept in society. Doing so avoids a pre-configuration of the empirical analysis through one or the other of the common abstract definitions of CSR, such as 'corporate conduct that fulfils social expectations beyond market and legal constraints', 'doing well by doing good', or 'window-dressing'. More importantly, this approach enables us to account for the multiple meanings that 'CSR' actually has in and for society. The same CSR programme of a company can be described as 'a substantial contribution to sustainable development' by the company, and as 'green washing' by critical activists. None of these two meanings is truer or falser than the other: they are both expressions of the essentially contested character of CSR. How, then, can we proceed?

While the multiple meanings given to CSR by social systems are not more or less true, each meaning makes differences, as its occurrence in social communication contributes to shaping the concrete CSR phenomenon. The prevailing meaning given to CSR in corporate meetings, for instance, will directly impact the characteristics and outcomes of CSR-related practices in companies. Similarly, the meaning given to CSR in public policies and legal norms will directly impact the political and legal forms of the CSR phenomenon. And the CSR phenomenon will not have the same economic characteristics if CSR is related to small business expenses or to massive investments in improved labour conditions or pollution abatement. In this perspective, investigating how social systems selectively use the CSR concept and relate it meaningfully to other distinctions enables an empirical analysis of the institutionalization processes, the concrete properties, and the changes induced by the intermediary institution 'CSR'.

According to the SST framework, to study this meaning-generating formation of the CSR phenomenon, three interrelated dimensions of social systems can be considered: the *semantic* dimension of concepts, the *operational* dimension of social communication, and the *social-structural* dimension of institutions.

The *semantic dimension of social systems* comprises the concepts which social systems have created and memorized over the course of their socio-cultural evolution, such as 'the state', 'business', 'development', 'biodiversity', 'rationality', 'globalization', and many more.[31] What this cultural reservoir of concepts entails at any given point in time and space impacts the functioning of social systems and of society at large. As it supplies social systems with certain

---

[31] See in particular Luhmann (2012 and 2013), Stichweh (2006), and Andersen (2011).

distinctions and not others, the semantic dimension conditions the categories with which social systems observe and thereby construct social reality. As a concept, CSR is a constitutive element of this semantic dimension. Since it appeared in the United States towards the late nineteenth century, 'CSR' has progressively spread into the cultural reservoir of an increasing number of social systems, thereby enabling a growing number of social systems such as business organizations, NGOs, politics, law, mass media, or morality, to observe and thereby to construct corporate entities in terms of the basic distinction: 'socially responsible'/'socially irresponsible'.

However, as for other concepts, 'CSR' has no standalone social meaning. Its meaning is (re)produced and transformed in *the operational dimension of social systems*, depending on the way social systems relate it with other concepts and distinctions. More precisely, whenever a concept is selected in the communicative operations of a social system, it opens up a horizon of potential other distinctions that could be selected as a meaningful 'next step' to pursue the sequence of communication. The actual social meaning of the concept depends on which of the potential 'next steps' is selected. For instance, the moment 'CSR' is mentioned in a meeting, it introduces the distinction 'social responsibility'/'social irresponsibility'. But the meaning of this distinction in the meeting is still open. CSR could be related in a number of ways with a number of ensuing distinctions such as 'child labour', 'our suppliers', 'protest movements', 'partnering with NGOs', 'competitors' CSR policy', 'effective lobbying', or 'sustainable development'. Depending on the distinctions that are selected from within this horizon of potential meanings, the actual meaning given to 'CSR' in this meeting will be different.

This operational process of meaning construction reproduces and transforms the culture of social systems. In the words of Luhmann, concepts 'condense' meaning, in the sense that they store the meaning which is generally given to them in the cultural context in which they are employed, and keep this general meaning available for social communication. Concretely, at the operational level, the meaning-generating relations of concepts with distinctions establish general meanings that become associated to the concepts. For instance, if CSR is generally related to distinctions about stakeholder management, the mention of 'CSR' in a communicative process will implicitly refer to how companies manage their stakeholders. However, the general meaning of concepts is not fixed. It can evolve as a result of displacements in the way concepts are actually related to other distinctions. For instance, if 'CSR' is increasingly associated with distinctions about 'window-dressing', the general meaning of this concept might shift accordingly. In other words, while the general meaning of concepts is culturally conditioned, it is not determined, as the horizons of potential meaning introduced by concepts are always open to a certain extent. This indeterminacy of meaning is all the more pronounced in the case of essentially contested concepts such as CSR. As there is no established consensual understanding of CSR, but a plurality of competing general acceptations of the term, social systems can use CSR in a great variety of meaning contexts, and the horizon of potential meanings CSR opens up in the construction of social reality is particularly wide (see Chapter 5).

This meaning-generating process, which takes place in the operative dimension of social systems, is interrelated with their *socio-structural dimension*. SST defines social structures (institutions) as more or less formalized normative expectations regarding how social systems should normally operate. Informal social structures are institutionalized by repetition. For instance, the repeated association of CSR with stakeholder management practices will institutionalize a normal (expected) pattern of operation whereby companies will develop stakeholder management systems in the name of their corporate social responsibility. The more companies repeat this expected pattern, the stronger it will be. Conversely, social systems which deviate from established social structures contribute to weakening or to displacing them: what used to be expected or considered normal progressively fades away (for example, using philanthropic donations to secure political support), and what used to be a deviant pattern is repeated often enough to become a new norm (for example, managing politicians as stakeholders). While this institutional process applies to informal structures, formal structures such as CSR laws, guidelines, and standards involve different mechanisms of (re)production and change. Formal structures are established according to specific procedures, and this formalization ensures that expectations remain valid in spite of recurring occurrences of deviance. For instance, even a CSR-related law that is poorly implemented remains a valid norm until it is changed through formalized law-making procedures.

To sum up, the empirical study of the CSR phenomenon and its consequences for economic responsiveness can be conducted under the guidance of the following framework:

- Step 1: Under which conditions and how has the essentially contested concept of CSR been introduced in the communication processes of social systems? In relation to which preceding distinctions?
- Step 2: Whenever CSR was selected, how did social systems exploit the possibilities of meaning construction it provides? Which distinctions

were selected out of the meaning horizon opened up by CSR in any given sequence of communication? To which extent did these selections reproduce or displace institutions and cultural meaning patterns? What is underlying such processes of institutional and cultural reproduction and change?

• Step 3: How is the development of the CSR phenomenon changing business–society interplays? How does it change the social structures and the cultural meaning patterns on the basis of which social systems observe, process, and regulate tensions opposing profit-making and competing collective values and interests?

An empirical study of CSR in the Indian context

India provides favourable conditions to investigate the development of CSR as an intermediary institution of world society, and to analyse empirically how CSR changes economic responsiveness in a context of structural tensions between profit-making and competing collective values and interests.

First, the Indian case provides opportunities to analyse how CSR, understood as a global phenomenon emerging out of functional differentiation, operates outside of the Western world. Initially, Luhmann conceived his theory of modernity as functional differentiation almost exclusively with reference to western Europe. The validity claim of this theory was extended afterwards to other regions and cultures. According to this claim, modern society emerged precisely in the western European context, before it expanded to become a world society by gradually overtaking the pre-modern social orders of other regions. While this historical sketch is plausible,[32] the socio-

---

[32] Plausible, but not unchallenged. Lars Eckstein and Christoph Reinfandt, for instance, criticize the distinction in SST between modernity of the Global North and massive exclusion in the Global South, for Luhmann's impressionistic accounts of the Global South would bear 'chilling proximity ... to the characteristic ideological projections of colonial travel writing (bare life, threatening physicality, disease, primitive sexuality, and so on), a proximity that places Luhmann in an uncomfortable continuity with imperial epistemologies' (Eckstein and Reinfandt 2016, 160). As the present study illustrates, this critic of Luhmann's writings does not preclude the use of SST to investigate concrete processes of functional differentiation that unfold in countries such as India, in a way that accounts for local specificities without falling prey to exaggerated dichotomies between a modern 'North' and a post-traditional modernizing 'South'.

cultural evolutionary process it describes has not been as linear as suggested here. Functional differentiation, along with other typical social structures and cultural systems of modern world society, did not simply expand out of Europe and erase pre-existing structures and cultures across the globe. Modern world society gradually emerged out of a variety of ancient structures and cultures, overlaying some of them, reconfiguring, displacing, or undermining others.[33]

As a consequence, historical processes of functional differentiation and related phenomena such as CSR have unfolded under various regional conditions. They have been shaped by contingent interactions between, on the one hand, world society's global structures and culture and, on the other hand, regional institutions and cultural patterns. Peculiarities of the Indian context, such as the active role of the caste system, the presence of indigenous tribes, Hinduism, or the country's colonial past, provide fruitful opportunities to investigate the role of these global–regional interactions in the formation and the *modi operandi* of the intermediary institution of CSR. In so doing, the present study will examine P. Sundar's claim that 'Indian CSR has an organic evolution from within its own history and culture which sets it apart from that in the West'.[34]

A second propitious feature of the Indian case is the country's contemporary phase of 'emergence'. Since it was coined by Goldman Sachs in the late 1990s, the description of BRICS (Brazil, Russia, India, China, and South Africa) as 'emerging' countries has become a popular way of describing countries that are neither developing countries of the Global South nor advanced industrialized countries of the Global North.[35] As an emerging country, contemporary India has a particular mix of general characteristics that are directly relevant to CSR. Its political-economic trajectory was marked by major economic reforms, which dismantled state interventionism and import-substitution to make room for a deregulated market economy that is increasingly integrated into global economic structures and flows. These reforms triggered a gradual but far-reaching political-economic reconfiguration, as part of which the role

---

[33] Social structures and related cultural patterns that are specific to world society entail, for instance, formal organizations, deterritorialized networks, integrated markets, transnational epistemic communities, a global public sphere, as well as events of global significance such as World Exhibitions or the Olympic games. On interactions between world society's global and regional social structures and cultures, see in particular Stichweh (2007a), and with reference to Latin America, Mascareño (2012).

[34] Sundar (2013, 11).

[35] Fourcade (2013). See also Jaffrelot and Schoch (2008).

of the primary engine of 'development' was shifted to a great extent from the state to the private sector.[36] This political-economic reconfiguration has ushered a phase of rapid economic growth, which culminated in the 2000s with annual growth rates of 7 to 9 per cent. However, both the material benefits (for example, income, education, health) and the harmful consequences (for example, expropriation of land, pollution) generated by this rapid economic growth have been distributed highly unequally within the Indian population.[37] Overall, notwithstanding a rising upper-middle class, many of the country's 1.3 billion inhabitants still face acute poverty-related hardships: India was ranked 135th on the World Human Development Index of 2014.

This constellation has been prone to salient controversies and socio-political conflicts regarding interplays between profit-driven business expansion and India's uncertain development prospects. To what extent should companies be unbridled and actively supported to generate jobs and income that the country desperately needs to overcome its development deficits? To what extent should their profit-driven processes be contained to protect labour welfare, the life chances of expropriated farmers and indigenous groups, the balance of fragile ecosystems, and the democratic quality of Indian politics? As CSR has gained increasing significance in relation to these public debates and conflicts, India provides contrasting opportunities to observe how CSR, as an intermediary institution, changes the way society observes, processes, and regulates tensions between profit-oriented business expansion and competing collective values and interests.

---

[36] See Reed and Mukherjee (2004), Rodrik and Subramanian (2005), Rajakumar (2011), Kohli (2012), Krichewsky (2011), Ruparelia, Reddy, Hariss, and Corbridge (2011), and Kennedy (2014).

[37] See Sen and Dasgupta (2009), Mehta and Sarkar (2010), Bardhan (2012), Drèze and Sen (2013), Banerjee-Guha (2013), and Suryanarayana and Das (2014).

Chapter 3

✠

Economic Differentiation and the Rise of India's 'Embedded' Corporate Capitalism

To investigate the hypothesis that CSR is an intermediary institution arising from processes of functional differentiation, these processes must be identified. This chapter focuses on the functional differentiation of the Indian economic system. It describes how monetization and the development of markets and incorporated firms under British colonial rule created the conditions for a modern capitalist economy to develop. As the chapter shows, this process of functional differentiation remained partial. A significant part of the economy remained 'embedded' in functionally undifferentiated social structures, in particular with regard to the rural agrarian economy. And economic transactions and non-economic spheres of society remained enmeshed within the core of India's modern capitalism.

In particular, large Indian industrial companies were not driven by the sole axiom of profit maximization, but by a blend of economic and non-economic logics. After independence, the adoption of state-based economic development policies triggered significant structural reconfigurations in India's political economy. However, while the functional differentiation of the economy progressed under this new setting, extensive regulation and political interventions restricted the role of profit-driven calculations in the economy.

In the following pages, the institutions and processes underlying this partial functional differentiation of India's corporate capitalism are analysed in four domains of business–society interplays: corporate governance, labour relations, relations between companies and politics, and companies' non-business activities that are formally directed towards the common good, in particular corporate philanthropy.

Economic relations in pre-modern India

The formation of a functionally differentiated economic system in India is tightly connected with European colonialism, which asserted its power on the subcontinent from the mid-eighteenth century onwards. At that time, following the death of Emperor Aurangzeb in 1707, the Mughal Empire had already disintegrated into several hundreds of kingdoms and local chieftains. These feudal political units were more or less bounded into an unstable and war-prone system of allegiances and alliances, which was dominated by a few groups such as the Marathas, the Rajputs, the Bundelas, the Jats, and the Sikhs. A few foreign powers – in particular the British, the Portuguese, and the French – had already set foot on the subcontinent to develop trade and gain control over new territories, mostly around strategic coastal cities and ports (for example, Calcutta, Madras, Kochi, Bombay). But their political as well as economic significance was still peripheral if one considers India as a whole. With regard to the economy, for instance, colonial trade involved mostly the export of textile to Europe, and in the late eighteenth century, this represented no more than 1–2 per cent of India's total textile production.[1]

In this pre-colonial setting, production and exchange of goods and services was organized mostly on the basis of a stratified system of caste, which structured the overall division of social labour. While the concept of 'caste' is the most commonly used, it actually refers to two distinct categories.[2] One is the normative Hinduist view of society as an organic hierarchical order composed of four *varna*s: the Brahmins (priests, teachers, scholars), who are supposed to constitute the 'head' of society, the Kshatriyas (ruling nobility, administrators, and warriors), who are viewed as the arms of society, the Vaishyas (merchants, artisans, farmers) who are society's stomach, and the Shudras (servants), who are the legs supporting the superior parts of society – Dalits or 'untouchables' being considered too impure to be included in this representation of the social body. But caste also refers to *jati*s, which are the concrete endogamous ethnic groups that define one's 'caste' identity. Unlike the *varna*s, the *jati*s are not positioned vis-à-vis one another according to a fixed normative classification, but according to complex dynamics of mutual positioning. These dynamics, which have always been regionally diverse, involve many variables such as the *jati*s' respective religious practices, their demographic strength, their material wealth, and their political clout.

---

[1] Roy (2000, 30).

[2] For an overview, see Jodhka (2012) and Vaid (2014).

It was on the basis of the institution of *jati*s that production and exchange of material goods was organized in pre-modern India. Most of the *jati*s were specialized in agricultural activities, such as livestock farming or the cultivation of certain grains, fruits, or vegetables. Some *jati*s were cultivators entitled to a share of the village's grazing or agricultural land (*patta*), while other *jati*s worked as tenants or as agricultural labourers. Other *jati*s were in charge of handicraft and cottage industry or providing services in villages and towns (for example, carpenters, blacksmiths, barbers, tailors, scavengers). *Jati*s from upper castes, including Brahmins who performed religious rituals and acted as scholars and teachers, the ruling aristocracy, and holders of administrative offices, were generally meeting their material needs through donations to temples and through taxation of a share of agricultural production – about 30 to 50 per cent of land revenue.[3] Among this mosaic of groups, those who acted as *zamindar*s had a particular status: as holders of hereditary or acquired land ownership, they managed their estates, performed administrative-political functions locally in the name of the ruler, and collected revenue from farming which they transferred as a tax to the ruler.

This division of labour based on ethnic-occupational groups was often extremely accurate,[4] and it was stabilized by strong institutions, including customary rights and duties, and the expectation that one should only perform occupations whose purity corresponds with the purity of one's *jati*. But it also entailed a certain degree of flexibility. Some *jati*s covered several occupations. Moreover, it was not unusual for non-agricultural *jati*s facing economic hardship to turn to cultivation to make ends meet. For instance, when the flow of manufactured goods imported from Europe in the nineteenth century suddenly decreased the demand for Indian handicraft, a number of *jati*s of artisans shifted to agriculture, which had been simultaneously expanding thanks to improved irrigation systems. Certain *jati*s would also succeed in

---

[3] This sketch overlooks the existence of significant regional variations, including, for instance, the existence of *jati*s of Brahmins who were involved in agricultural production.

[4] As Tapan Raychaudhuri narrates,

> The dagbar who made leather bags for holding ghee and sugar-cane juice was socially and occupationally distinct from the chamar manufacturing shoes, leather ropes and drumheads. The yoghurt-makers of Bihar were clearly distinguished into two mutually exclusive sub-castes, the guriyas who first extracted the butter and the majrotis who first curdled the milk. (Raychaudhuri 1983, 9–10)

collective strategies of upward mobility such as Sanskritization, which consists in improving the group's status by adopting rituals and other practices of superior castes.

As the production and the exchange of goods was 'embedded' in this stratified social order, monetary exchanges as part of market transactions played little role. In fact, the bulk of India's population was living in isolated villages or village clusters in which the production and circulation of goods was regulated by a customary system called *jajmani*:

> There was a unity between agriculture and village industry. While agriculture supplied food and raw material to artisans, the latter supplied and repaired implements, ornaments, pottery, cloth, shoes, furniture, etc. There was very little use of money in the process of exchange in rural areas. It was the barter system which prevailed.[5]

Only limited commodities were supplied through local or regional town markets, such as salt, sugar, ghee, or quality cloth. More generally, trade was hampered by poor inland transport infrastructure, highly unsafe roads and waterways, and countless custom barriers (*chowki*s) between and within territories controlled by rulers and local chieftains. Moreover, trade was suffering from the absence of an integrated monetary system. Multiple currencies were circulating, including sea shells (cowries), copper coins, silver coins, gold coins, and from the late eighteenth century onwards, paper notes issued by private or government-supported joint-stock banks, such as the Bank of Hindostan or the Bank of Calcutta. These currencies were issued under various political authorities, and they were not related to one another by a unified system of exchange. In fact, the value of metallic coins was quite uncertain, as it was determined in different terms depending mostly on metal content, weight, prevailing price of the metal in a given market, and the age of the coin.[6] As for paper notes, their use was limited to trade, and their value was correlated to the banks issuing them, in a context where many such banks proved to be short-lived.

In spite of these hurdles for trade, a number of *jati*s were active as merchants.[7] In north India, the main merchant communities were the Hindu Marwaris from Rajasthan, the Hindu and Jain Banias from Gujarat, the Zoroastrian

---

[5] Mishra (1994, 30).

[6] See Roy (2000) and Tripathi and Jumani (2007).

[7] For an overview, see, for instance, Lachaier (2003).

Parsis who had migrated from Persia from the seventh century onwards and were established mainly on the western coast, the Hindu Bhatias and Lohanas from Maharashtra, the Hindu and Sikh Khatris, Aroras, and Aggarwals from Punjab, and the Muslim Memons, Khojas, and Bohras. In south India, the dominant merchant communities were the Chettiars and the Nagarattars from Tamil Nadu, and the Kamma Naidus from Andhra Pradesh. Most of them were involved in local and regional trade, though long-distance trade in the form of caravans started to pick up in the eighteenth century. Merchants were also operating as financiers, bankers, and tax collectors. Concerning the latter activity, some merchants had acquired collection rights that allowed them to collect the part of the agricultural production that was levied by the ruling authorities on a given territory, to sell it in town markets, and to pay the due tax to the ruler in monetary form. A few Indian businessmen, such as Jagad Seth or Abdul Gafur, were commanding large-scale inter-regional and foreign trade operations. They also exerted considerable power over aristocratic rulers through the provision of credit and other financial services.

As European business – in particular through the East India Company – was gradually developing, an increasing number of Indian merchants started working as partners or agents for European companies. Their role involved mainly intermediation with local suppliers, conversion of currencies, and logistics. This provided a new source of income for the merchants involved, such as the Marwaris, who partly migrated from Rajasthan to Bengal to seize this economic opportunity. But the scope and capitalist orientation of these activities remained limited:

> There are not many instances where trading and banking firms became involved in industry before the nineteenth century, whether as direct producers or as financiers. Artisans remained distant from professional traders and bankers. The latter did finance industry in the case of exportable goods such as textiles in certain regions. But these industries were more exceptions than the rule. Commercial and financial capital, thus, found relatively little use outside commerce and banking. A great deal of trading and banking profits went into the purchase of idle assets such as gold jewellery, such spiritual assets as building temples, construction of ghats in Kashi, or charity and relief during famines.[8]

---

[8] Roy (2000, 177). The Kashi *ghat*s are wide steps of stones descending to the Ganga river, which were constructed in the sacred city of Varanasi.

Taken together, these characteristics of India's pre-modern social order point at a cultural and institutional setting in which production and exchange of material goods was deeply 'embedded' in and mixed up with other dimensions of social life. This setting corresponds to Karl Polanyi's ideal-typical depiction of economic activities in traditional societies, where 'man's economy, as a rule, is submerged in his social relationships'. In such settings,

> [man] does not act so as to safeguard his individual interest in the possession of material goods; he acts so as to safeguard his social standing, his social claims, his social assets. He values material goods only in so far as they serve this end. Neither the process of production nor that of distribution is linked to specific economic interests attached to the possession of goods; but every single step in that process is geared to a number of social interests which eventually ensure that the required step be taken. These interests will be very different in a small hunting or fishing community from those in a vast despotic society, but in either case the economic system will be run on noneconomic motives.[9]

In fact, even speaking of an 'economic system' is partly inaccurate here, as people living in such circumstances do not perceive or describe production and exchange as a distinct and internally coherent economic sphere of social life. As long as price-making markets remain peripheral,

> each single event necessarily contains a bundle of economic items. Yet for all that, the unity and coherence of those facts is not reflected in men's consciousness. For the series of interactions between men and their natural surrounding will, as a rule, carry various significances, of which economic dependence is only one.[10]

Or, in the terms of SST, the economic problems of possession and satisfaction of material needs were addressed through social structures that were primarily differentiated through kinship and stratification, not through functional differentiation. Material possession was directly coupled with one's status in the stratified social order of *jatis*, including through the attribution of certain occupations, through customary rights to use common property resources, and/or through customary or acquired rights to a share of the goods produced by others. The *jajmani* system is typical of this primacy of stratification over functional differentiation: for most Indians, production and

---

[9] Polanyi (1957 [1944], 46).
[10] Polanyi (1957, 71–72).

exchange of material goods was enmeshed in inter-caste relations that involved all domains of social life.

Functional differentiation under colonial rule: the rise of India's corporate capitalism

From the late eighteenth century onwards, this pre-modern social order was disrupted by a gradual process of functional differentiation of the economy. British colonial authorities played a key role in this process as they developed new institutional frameworks and technical infrastructures that provided favourable conditions for functional differentiation to unfold. But this process also interacted with pre-colonial social structures, which either limited or delayed functional differentiation, or which were absorbed and integrated into the institutions of India's modern economy.

Such interactions between indigenous social structures and the colonial expansion of western European modernity shaped the gradual monetization of the Indian economy.[11] Until the nineteenth century, exchanges in kind (for example, grains, animals, services) were the most prevalent form of exchange, and monetary transactions involved multiple currencies that were not integrated into a united monetary system. In this context, a first step towards the institution of a unified monetary system was taken in 1807, when the East India Company decided to refuse the payment of land revenue in kind or in non-metallic currencies such as the cowries. This decision pushed monetization in rural areas forward, as cultivators and *zamindars* had to take credits and to sell a share of the crop on markets to accumulate enough money to pay the taxes to the Company. Towards the same period, British authorities progressively phased out bimetallism by demonetizing gold and imposing silver coins in the territories under their control. In 1835, a further step was taken with the Coinage Act, which defined the silver coins of the East India Company as the only legal tender for transactions involving British authorities. However, India's economy was still far from having a unified monetary system. Independent native rulers continued to mint their own coins, and older currencies such as the *toras* of Farrukhabad or the *hallee sicca* rupees of Hyderabad continued to circulate up to the 1860s.

---

[11] On the monetization of the Indian economy, see in particular Rothermund (1970), Chandavarkar (1983), Bagchi (1985), Roy (2000), and Sivramkrishna (2017).

While British authorities had imposed silver, they were not exercising any control on the volume of monetary supply. Coins were minted by autonomous mints based in Bombay, Calcutta, and Madras. As Europe shifted to a system of gold standard, and with the discovery of new silver ore deposits, the supply of silver coins in India increased rapidly: in 1877, India was absorbing 84 per cent of the world's production of silver. This trend provoked a rapid depreciation of silver rupees. While this depreciation was benefitting Indian exports to Europe, it was costly for the colonial Government of India,[12] whose incomes were in silver while it had to pay home charges in gold to the British crown. To act against the depreciation of the rupee, the Government of India closed the independent mints in 1893, took over the control of the minting of coins, and decoupled the value of the currency from its metallic content: the Indian rupee became a token coin. In 1898, India shifted to the gold standard, and in 1931, the value of the rupee was coupled with the British sterling.

A similar process of gradual monetary integration took place for paper currencies. The first bank to issue paper notes in India was the Bank of Hindostan, which was set up in 1770. A few other banks followed, such as the Bank of Calcutta, which was founded in 1806, and the three Presidency banks that were set up by the East India Company in Bengal (1809), in Bombay (1840), and in Madras (1843). But with the Paper Currency Act of 1861, the Government of India put an end to this privilege and became the sole provider of paper notes. These notes had a limited spatial validity, as they could only be used within so-called currency circles around Calcutta, Bombay, and Madras. From 1910 onwards, new currency circles were added. And in 1935, the Government of India created a central bank, the Reserve Bank of India, which took over the function of monetary supply.

This progressive institutionalization of a unified monetary system was accompanied by a growing monetization of economic transactions. The shift from the payment of land revenue in kind to its payment in currencies was a powerful driving force in this regard. Another driving force underlying monetization was the gradual extension of markets and trade. In particular, the growing exports of agricultural products (for example, grains, spices, tea) and other goods, such as indigo and saltpetre, pushed monetization in and around the supply chains of European and Indian companies.

---

[12] In 1858, following the massive anti-colonial rebellion of 1858, the government of British territories in the Indian subcontinent was transferred from the East India Company to the Government of India, which was controlled by the British crown.

While the development of markets spurred the monetization of economic transactions, the gradual emergence of a unified monetary system also facilitated the development of markets. Already in the mid-eighteenth century, markets for inter-regional trade connected the coastal zones of Bengal, Gujarat, and the Coromandel: prices of certain commodities in one region were reacting to price variations in the other regions.[13] Moreover, regional and local markets existed for certain commodities, such as coarse cloth, which were produced in cities and sold in rural areas. But as suggested earlier, at that time, markets were still a rather peripheral institution in terms of its outreach in the organization of Indian society. From the mid-nineteenth century onwards, this changed by way of a growing commodification and marketization of the Indian economy.

Besides monetary integration, a key condition underlying this trend was the development of railways across the subcontinent.[14] Railways were of strategic importance to British colonial authorities: not only would they extend the administrative and military control of this vast territory but they would also support colonial capitalism by providing access to new raw material and by opening up new market opportunities for imported British goods. The first railway line was laid in 1853 between Bombay and Thane. From there on, thanks to British know-how, capital, and machinery, India's railway network grew exponentially. By 1890, 25,495 kilometres had been laid, and in 1947, the network comprised 65,217 kilometres. In terms of geographic scope, by 1867, the 19 most populous Indian cities were connected to the network, and by 1947, railway lines reached into all but a few remote districts of the subcontinent. This network proved a crucial infrastructure for the development of trade into the hinterland: the net metric tonnage of freight carried by railways grew from 3.6 million in 1871 to 143.6 million in 1947. As noted by Elisabeth Whitcombe,

> just as railways were responsible for expanding India's overseas trade and changing its orientation, they also promoted internal trade. In so doing, they were instrumental in transforming the structure of prices in India. Before railways, inter-regional price differences were pronounced, and the local prices of grain, cotton, and other agricultural commodities fluctuated with the changes in local supply conditions, particularly rainfall. As the railway network expanded, and with it trade in commodities, price differences between regions narrowed dramatically.

---

[13] Raychaudhuri (1983).
[14] For an overview, see Whitcombe (1983).

Moreover, 'by transporting raw materials at lower cost and carrying finished goods to internal markets, railways played a major role in the growth of India's modern industry'.[15]

Monetization and marketization of India's economy created favourable conditions for a further change to unfold, namely the partial shift of manufacturing from household production and small workshops operated by caste-based guilds of artisans to industrial capitalism.[16] In terms of labour, a significant part of this shift took place at the level of small-scale industry, which comprises small labour-intensive production units characterized by a simple organizational structure and a low level of mechanization. But in terms of contribution to the gross domestic product (GDP), it was large-scale industry that pushed the development of India's industrial capitalism forward.

The rise of modern corporate capitalism in India's production sector first required the legal institutionalization of the business corporation.[17] This process, which replaced the use of British and Indian customary law, followed closely the development of corporate law in Great Britain. After Great Britain adopted the Joint Stock Companies Act in 1844, a series of legislations were introduced in India to regulate and incorporate joint-stock companies and banks. These laws were welded together in the Indian Companies Act of 1866, whose blueprint was the English Companies Act of 1862. Thanks to this legal framework, registered companies could secure rights attached to legal personhood, such as the right to ownership and the right to form contracts. Moreover, thanks to limited liability, entity shielding, and the possibility to transfer shares without the consent of other shareholders, entrepreneurs could raise capital more easily and reduce their personal exposure in case of bankruptcy.

Indian corporate law and governance arrangements also entailed specific features. In particular, until the mid-twentieth century, Indian corporate governance was characterized by a set of institutions known as the managing agency system. Under this system, the management of a company could be handed to a managing agent firm, which would provide professional management and other business services against a share of the company's benefits. This was used by European entrepreneurs to facilitate the creation of

---

[15] Whitcombe (1983, 745–46 and 48).

[16] Roy (2000).

[17] See, for instance, Mukherjee-Reed and Reed (2004), Gollakota and Gupta (2006), Tripathi and Jumani (2007), and Roy and Swamy (2016).

new undertakings on the Indian subcontinent, as they would benefit from the experience and networks of established managing agencies. But the managing agency system also became popular among Indian business families, which could set up and control publicly listed companies without owning a majority of the companies' shares.

Overall, until the 1860s, India's corporate landscape remained concentrated in trade-related activities, which were conducted by both European businessmen and Indian members of traditional merchant communities. British colonial authorities were encouraging this prominence of trade over industrial production, as custom barriers and tariffs were discouraging indigenous manufacturing and promoting imports of British goods. However, contingent circumstances disrupted this configuration and kick-started a move of Indian merchants from trade to industrial entrepreneurship.[18] The trigger of this shift was the outbreak of the Civil War in the United States. As this war disrupted the supply of raw cotton to British mills, India experienced a short-lived but intense boom of Indian cotton exports. Once the American supply was re-established, India found itself with massive stocks. Some Indian merchants who had accumulated considerable wealth over the past decades, such as Jamshedji Tata, Morarjee Gokuldas, and Karamchand Premchand, saw these stocks of cotton as an opportunity to invest in Indian textile mills. During the last decades of the nineteenth century, the native textile industry spread first in the states of Maharashtra and Gujarat, and later on in other economic centres such as Delhi. Towards the same period, businessmen of the Marwari community and a few others started investing in jute production around Calcutta, as the international growth of trade had created a flourishing market for jute to pack transported goods. Around the turn of the century, other Indian entrepreneurs such as the Godrej brothers, Walchand Hirachand Doshi, Lal Shri Ram, and Kasturbhai Lalbhai, started developing new lines of business. Of course, European businessmen were also seizing these new opportunities, and a number of companies controlled by Europeans, such as the Sasson Spinning & Weaving Company, Killick Nixon & Co., Birds & Co., and Andrew Yule & Co., contributed to developing industrial manufacturing in the subcontinent.

From the First World War onwards, India's industrialization accelerated and diversified in both sectorial and geographical terms. Industrial production

---

[18] For an overview, see, for instance, Bagchi (1972), Kurien (1994), Mukherjee Reed (2001), and Tripathi and Jumani (2007).

experienced a 50 per cent growth in the 1920s, and a 200 per cent growth between 1930 and India's independence in 1947.[19] The contribution of large-scale industry to real national income jumped from about 15 per cent in 1900 to about 45 per cent in 1947.[20] Over this period, industry controlled by Europeans remained dominant. In 1939, the 57 largest business groups operating in India comprised 38 European groups (713 companies amounting to a capital of about 2 billion rupees), and 19 Indian groups (196 companies amounting to a capital of 550 million rupees).[21] But these figures mask a strong dynamism of native industrial entrepreneurship in the inter-war period:

> The Indian investments were no longer confined to just a few industries such as cotton textiles and cotton gins and presses, in which they had established a competitive advantage before the war, but had also expanded into new lines such as sugar, paper, starch, shipping, engineering, chemicals, air transport, and many others. In fact, the native investments in these new lines were growing at a much faster pace than in the more traditional industries. Also, the Indian challenge to the British monopoly in industries such as jute and coal had become much more pervasive and determined.[22]

As part of this trend, new names of Indian industrial families appeared on the country's business scene, such as he Singhanias, the Bajajs, the Dalmia Jains, the Thapars, and the Modis. Industrial entrepreneurship also spread in south Indian cities, such as Hyderabad, Madras, and Coimbatore, among merchant communities including the Nagarattar and the Kamma Naidu. Nevertheless, Indian industrial entrepreneurship remained concentrated within a few families: in 1947, 18 families were controlling most of the companies that were not controlled by European firms.[23]

Taken together, the processes outlined earlier contributed to the formation of India's economy as a functionally differentiated sub-system of society.[24] Currencies were integrated into a unified monetary system, and markets turned from being spatially situated places of exchange into becoming institutionalized social spaces of transaction that are segmented not according

---

[19] Markovits (2002).

[20] Roy (2000, 157).

[21] Tripathi and Jumani (2007, 111).

[22] Tripathi and Jumani (2007, 93).

[23] Sundar (2000, p. 17).

[24] At the level of theory, see the constitutive elements of functionally differentiated economic systems identified by Luhmann (1982, 1988, 2013).

to spatial location, but according to the commodity being exchanged. Under this setting, a significant share of the goods and services produced in India could be sold for/acquired against money on markets, and markets also existed for the three 'fictitious commodities' that are natural resources, labour, and money.[25] Besides the provision of commodities, monetization and markets had also introduced a function-specific system of economic coordination based on prices. Wherever transactions were monetized, prices had become the unit of economic calculation. As such, prices would convey information either on amounts of money that had been paid in previous transactions or on amounts of money that were expected to be paid for a certain transaction to happen. In other words, prices were mirroring the economic behaviours and expectations of participants. But they also acted as programmes that would steer the behaviour of participants: depending on prices, natural and legal persons would decide whether to buy or not buy a certain commodity, whether to save or not save money, whether to work or not work for a certain employer, whether to invest or not invest in the production of certain commodities, or whether to distribute or not distribute money to someone else.[26]

Previous institutions that had been guiding production and the circulation of goods and services, such as the caste system, were not internal structures of the economy, but multi-functional institutions. Conversely, market prices were and continue to be a *self-referential* system of economic coordination. Under this system, *economic* behaviour (paying/not paying; selling/not selling) is steered by price-mediated observations of the economic behaviour of others. Moreover, this self-referential system is *autopoietic*, that is, each payment operation regenerates the capacities of the economic system to operate. Indeed, whenever a payment takes place, the one who paid money must replenish her/his payment capacities by securing new incomes (for example, wages, credit, profit, gifts, theft), while the one who got paid must decide what to do with the money she/he received (consuming, saving, investing, giving). Finally, in such a system, *profit-making* becomes a peculiar guiding value that makes production

---

[25] Fictitious commodities are things which were not produced as commodities, but which are transformed into commodities through a legally supported process of appropriation, commodification, and marketization. See Polanyi (1957 [1944]).

[26] Polanyi makes the same argument when he writes that in a market economy,

[production] will then be controlled by prices, for the profits of those who direct production will depend upon them; the distribution of the goods also will depend upon prices, for prices form incomes, and it is with the help of these incomes that the goods produced are distributed amongst the members of society. (1957 [1944], 68)

a self-referential operation of the economy. In the words of Luhmann, with profit-driven investments in productive undertakings,

> the autopoiesis of the system becomes a reflexive process. It orients itself on itself. One pays to replenish and if possible to increase one's payment capacities (rather than to obtain the object or the service one is paying for). Only when the system accepts this criteria of profit as the perspective for its own steering does it become independent in the productive sector from 'private' motives and values, namely from the fact that someone would rather operate a perfume factory than a tannery, or that someone feels obliged or inclined to pursue his father's line of business.[27]

Functional differentiation is not a comprehensive switch from one institutional setting to another, but a gradual and non-linear process. If one considers the period stretching from the late nineteenth to the mid-twentieth century, in the Indian context, functional differentiation of the economy remained limited in several respects. First, the monetized economic system only covered part of the production and exchange of goods and services: according to estimates, the non-monetized sector of the Indian economy in the early 1950s was still about 43 per cent in rural areas and about 10 per cent in urban areas.[28] Second, prices were not the sole mechanism of economic coordination: caste-based division of labour and exchanges governed by the *jajmani* system persisted far into the twentieth century.[29] And third, profit was not the only guiding value that oriented the behaviour of producers, including within large companies – the core institutions of India's rising corporate capitalism. This last point, which is crucial for the analysis of CSR as an intermediary institution, requires further elaboration.

India's 'embedded' capitalist firms

To what extent was the guiding value of profit driving decision-making in India's large companies of the late-nineteenth to mid-twentieth century? It is difficult to provide a clear-cut answer to this question. Unlike what authors such as Pushpa Sundar seem to believe,[30] one cannot rely on claims made by business

---

[27] Luhmann (1988, 56), my translation.
[28] Chandavarkar (1983).
[29] See, for instance, Ishwaran (1966) and Lachaier (1999).
[30] Sundar (2000, 2013).

executives of that time. As it is the case with CSR today, such claims were not external observations of corporate conduct, but self-descriptions that were likely to be part of legitimating narratives.[31] An alternative is to rely on the work of historians. The historiography of decision-making processes governing India's large companies towards the late nineteenth and early twentieth centuries is rather thin. But to complement insights provided by historians, one can analyse the institutional frameworks underlying companies' decision-making processes, and show how the norms entailed in these institutional frameworks were more or less favourable to subordinating corporate conduct to the guiding value of profit maximization.

The following analysis covers four domains of observation that are particularly relevant in this regard: corporate governance, labour relations, relations between companies and the political system, and activities conducted in the name of non-business purposes. The analysis focuses on large native companies which have had a long-lasting influence on India's political economy and CSR. It leaves companies controlled by European business groups aside, as most of these companies were sold or diluted before or shortly after India's independence.

With regard to corporate governance structures (first domain), which define relations between ownership and control in business organizations, the prevailing model among Indian companies was combining the managing agency system (the control of companies by professional managing agent firms) and the institution of the joint family.[32] While family structures could vary along religious and regional lines, joint families usually comprised all male descendants of a common ancestor, their wives, and unmarried daughters. The joint family constituted a legal entity, which had rights to ownership and to form contracts. Under this model, the different businesses, assets, and incomes of the business house were the shared property of the family members, also called coparceners in this respect. The patriarch (*karta*), who was heading both the family and the business house, would inter alia decide on the distribution of dividends among the coparceners, according to their position in the family structure and their legitimate needs. Managerial positions in the companies

---

[31] See in particular Abend (2014), whose findings on the construction of business ethics in the United States are also relevant for the Indian case, all the more when one considers the fact that Indian discourse on business ethics, such as Mahatma Gandhi's doctrine of trusteeship, was directly inspired by American figures such as John Ruskin or Andrew Carnegie.

[32] See, for instance, Goody (1996) and Lachaier (2003).

controlled by the business house were also distributed among family members according to their position in the family tree. As a rule, the *karta* would give the control of new companies promoted by and/or under management contract with the business house first to his brothers, then to his cousins, then to his sons, and then to his nephews. Close associates of the family, such as friends belonging to the same caste, were also positioned in the boards of directors of the companies controlled by the business house. In the boards, age was a further parameter, as elders would usually occupy more prominent positions then their younger counterparts.

This family-based distribution of executive positions, coupled with cross-investments between companies under the control of the business house, strengthened the family's control over its businesses. It was also conducive to decisions that aimed at the long-term development of the company, rather than at short-term profit maximization. Beyond wealth accumulation, business houses were key to develop the social reputation and prestige of the family, and hence the life chances of family members. As suggested by Thomas Timberg in reference to Marwari businesses, 'their goal was a rather more complex one than simply maximizing their firm's growth or profit – they were concerned, perhaps, with maximizing its name'.[33] Claude Markovits makes a similar statement by pointing at practices such as the creation of companies for the endowment of family members, without much calculation about expected profits: like their merchant ancestors, India's industrial families were mixing up business and family affairs, and 'serious doubts are in order regarding a definition of the firm as a profit-maximizing agency in the Indian context'.[34]

To some extent, this blending of economic and non-economic considerations was extending beyond the boundaries of the joint family, to include the larger caste community. Indeed, business houses were integrated into dense community-based business networks. For the most part, their partners, suppliers, and providers of financial capital were not just other market actors, with whom they had contract-based commercial relationships. They were members of the same ethnic group. These intra-community networks had a clear economic function, as they reduced transaction costs through trust and social control. For instance, inappropriate behaviour could be punished by ostracism, which meant potential economic and social ruin.[35] But community

---

[33] Timberg (1978, 6).

[34] Markovits (2008, 154).

[35] See Lachaier (2003), Damodaran (2008), and Wolcott (2010).

ties also induced caste-based solidarity beyond economic calculation: business actors conceived of themselves as important members of their community, and they were significantly involved in its economic, social, and cultural development. For instance, the Marwari Association, which was created in 1898 by a group of business families, aimed to 'promote and advance the moral, intellectual, commercial, economic, political and social interests of the Marwari community and to protect its rights and status.... [And] to found and support establishments for disseminating commercial, technical, and general education in different branches of art and science in the Marwari community'.[36]

With regard to labour relations (second domain), at the level of managerial positions, caste solidarity could also be observed, as applicants originating from the same *jati* as the one of the business family had better chances to be recruited than candidates with a different ethnic background.[37] In the lower levels of the hierarchy, the blending of economic and non-economic considerations in labour relations rested upon two interrelated phenomena: trade unionism and paternalism.

The development of trade unionism among Indian industrial workers[38] goes back to protest movements that started from the 1880s onwards among workers of the Bombay textile industry.[39] These eruptions of protest were still local and spontaneous: when a company announced wage restrictions, higher expectations of productivity, and/or layoffs, leaders among workers or external political activists sometimes tried to organize actions such as slowdowns and strikes. Such protests were often violently repressed by the police force under orders of British authorities. Progressively, these local dynamics developed into more stable alliances between workers and political activists of the independence movement, which started gaining momentum after the return of Mohandas Karamchand ('Mahatma') Gandhi to India in 1915. Leaders of the independence movement would help workers create unions, such as

---

[36] Statutes of the Marwari Association, as cited by Kochanek (1974, 135).

[37] See Damodaran (2008).

[38] Workers employed in India's manufacturing sector were about 600,000 individuals in 1900, and about 3 million in the mid-twentieth century (Krishnamurty 1983). This increase in absolute terms corresponds to a stable share of manufacturing in the occupational structure of the working population during this period. Besides demographic growth, while new jobs were created in new sectors such as pulp and paper, food processing, steel, and mining, mechanization in sectors such as the textile industry destroyed large numbers of jobs.

[39] See, for instance, Bhattacherjee (2001) and Candland (2007).

the Girni Kamgar Union and the Bombay Textile Labour Union, which were also used as platforms to mobilize workers for the nationalist struggle for independence. The formation of the International Labour Organization (ILO) in 1919, which required member states to facilitate the organization of tripartite labour negotiations, was a further driver underlying the rise of Indian trade unionism.

In 1920, trade union leaders who were also active in the Congress founded the first pan-Indian federation of trade unions, the All India Trade Union Congress (AITUC). Six years later, another step in the institutionalization of trade unions was taken with the Trade Union Act, which provided trade unions with a legal status as legitimate bodies representing employees in negotiations with employers and the state. While AITUC was gaining momentum, with already 250,000 members in 1930, a second trade union movement emerged during the inter-war period under the leadership of Mahatma Gandhi. Unlike AITUC, which was directly supported financially and otherwise by Moscow, Gandhi developed a paternalistic movement that preferred pacific and collaborative negotiations over class struggle: 'Indeed, Gandhian trade unionism was explicitly modelled on the family. Industrialists were to treat workers as benevolently as they would treat their own children; and workers were to treat industrialists as respectfully as they would treat their own parents.'[40]

These two streams of trade unionism encouraged a number of Indian companies to develop paternalistic forms of labour relations. The case of Tata is well known, in particular because Tata companies provided many social rights to their workers long before these rights were introduced in labour law (see Table 3.1). But paternalistic relationships were also common in other companies controlled by Indian business houses. The core workforce generally enjoyed life-long employment, and positions were often handed over from father to son. Moreover, workers would benefit from subsidized housing facilities as well as free education and healthcare for their families. Companies often also conducted cultural and sport programmes for the benefit of their employees. Casual workers such as the *badli* (substitute) workers, who accounted for up to 30 per cent of the workforce in some industries, had no access to these services. Their employment relation was too flexible to be integrated into the paternalistic system. But as argued by Arjan de Haan on the basis of a study of *badli* workers in the jute industry,[41] the use of such casual workforce in

---

[40] Candland (2007, 26).
[41] de Haan (1999).

companies was not just the expression of profit-driven managerial strategies. The *badli* system rather perpetuated a pre-existing form of employment which served the need of flexibility both of companies and of *badli* workers, who combined seasonal agricultural occupation in their village of origin and periods of waged labour in the manufacturing sector. In fact, according to de Haan, *badli* workers generally left their job in the factory not because they were forced to do so by the management, who would have used them as a convenient adjustment variable, but because they had things to take care of in their village, such as helping in the fields or attending a family function such as a wedding.

Table 3.1 Tata Steel's social policy

Social rights	Year	Year when it was introduced in labour law
Eight hours working day	1912	1948 (Factories Act)
Free health care	1915	1948 (Employees State Insurance Act)
Social department	1917	1948 (Factories Act)
School for employees' children	1917	-
Committee for complaints and redressal	1919	1947 (Industrial Disputes Act)
Paid leaves	1920	1948 (Factories Act)
Social aid fund	1920	1952 (Employees Provident Fund Act)
Compensations for work-related accidents	1920	1924 (Workmen's Compensation Act)
Training for apprentices	1921	1961 (Apprentices Act)
Maternity benefits	1928	1946 (Maternity Benefit Act)
Bonuses	1934	1965 (Bonus Act)
Pension fund	1937	1972 (Payment of Gratuity Act)

Source: Singh (2008a, 124).

As emphasized by Sudhir Kakar,[42] paternalism was extending employment relations beyond price-driven transactions on the labour market. Paternalism was strengthening and stabilizing employment relations through an exchange of integration and social welfare against loyalty and subordination. Such an exchange presented obvious economic advantages to companies. It was conducive to cooperative behaviours that would limit the influence of AITUC among workers. Moreover, it was not only *badli* and other casual workers

---

[42] Kakar (1971).

who remained attached to rural life and family-related obligations. Many permanent (registered) workers too had similar ties. Thanks to the provision of social services, companies could somewhat limit uncertainties arising from the resulting high rates of absenteeism and turnover, and constitute a stable pool of workforce that would accumulate skills and integrate industrial discipline. Besides this economic rationality, paternalism might also have resonated positively with the socially progressive mind-set of many Indian industrialists, in a context of rising economic nationalism spurred by the struggle for independence. Though the extent of this motivation is hard to assess, this is at least what many industrialists claimed, and we know that Mahatma Gandhi's doctrine of cooperation between the different segments of Indian society was influential among the country's rising business elite.[43]

The struggle for independence that marked Indian politics (third domain) in the first half of the twentieth century influenced Indian companies beyond the domain of labour relations. Before the First World War, members of the Congress movement and businessmen from merchant communities had little contact with each other. But their ties developed rapidly during the inter-war period. Within the Congress, the idea that political independence also required a strong indigenous industry, as a condition for independence from colonial capitalist interests, gained traction. Conversely, many Indian businessmen were unhappy with colonial economic policies that provided advantages to their European competitors, as well as with racist discourses on the cultural inability of Indians to develop an industry on their own.[44] Against this backdrop, the political rise of the Congress under the leadership of Mahatma Gandhi was welcomed and actively supported.

In fact, a number of business families provided significant financial support to the Congress. Gandhi's close relations with prominent Indian industrialists, such as Kasturbhai Lalbhai, Jamnalal Bajaj, and G.D. Birla, played a role in this regard. But support to the independence movement also came from other corners of India's business community, such as from a network of smaller industrialists from Bengal, who were moved by strong nationalist sentiments.[45] In 1927, ties between Indian industrialists and the independence movement were further strengthened with the creation of the Federation of Indian Chambers of Commerce and Industry (FICCI). By federating the multiple regional and caste-based associations of Indian businesses, FICCI

---

[43] See Markovits (2008) and Sundar (2013).

[44] Bagchi (1972), Kochanek (1974).

[45] Mukherjee Reed (2001).

was to act as a counterweight to the Association of Chambers of Commerce (ASSOCHAM), which was controlled by Europeans. In FICCI's first annual report, its Director G.D. Birla emphasized that 'Indian commerce and industry are intimately associated with, and are indeed a part of the nationalist movement – growing with its growth, and strengthening with its strength'.[46]

As this quote suggests, economic calculations were not entirely absent from this alliance. Supporting the Congress was a way of building up leverage on British colonial authorities, so as to obtain more favourable economic and trade policies. Moreover, developing ties with Mahatma Gandhi and other business-compatible forces within the independence movement was also an attempt to counter the rise of other political currents, in particular, leaders who were connected to AITUC and/or who were envisaging a communist future for the country. Concretely, individual businessmen and FICCI would sometimes use their connections in the Congress to weaken trade union leaders and political activists who were perceived as being too radical. The proximity between industrialists and the Congress also proved advantageous as it helped a group of prominent businessmen to define the blueprint of India's post-independence economic policies, the Bombay Plan of 1944, which combined state interventionism with a capitalist economic order.[47] The fluctuation of relations between business actors and the Congress during the 1930s also suggests that economic considerations were not ignored: while Gujarati industrialists remained steady supporters of Mahatma Gandhi, members of the Marwari community started oscillating between the Congress and the British ruler, while west coast Parsi businessmen, in particular the Tata business house, cultivated good relationships with the British to facilitate access to European capital and markets.[48]

Nonetheless, authentic nationalist sentiments should not be underestimated. In the effervescent atmosphere of the independence struggle, many industrialists identified with the nationalist cause, and conceived of their enterprise not only as a means to accumulate wealth but also as a contribution to the development of a politically free and economically prosperous nation.[49] The following account of the foundation of the Godrej conglomerate by the General Director of Godrej Industries illustrates this point:

---

[46] Cited in Mukherjee Reed (2001, 64).

[47] See in particular Lokanathan (1945), Kochanek (1974), and Markovits (2008).

[48] Markovits (2008).

[49] See Mukherjee (2002) and Tripathi and Jumani (2007).

In fact, the group started its existence because my grandfather was one year younger than Mahatma Gandhi, he knew Mahatma Gandhi, and one day, in a casual conversation, he told Gandhi: 'We cannot have an independent country if we don't have an independent economy', and Gandhi replied: 'What are you doing about it?'

So my great-uncle, who by chance was a lawyer, started a business. Actually, he also was a self-taught scientist, and he personally developed new products, including vegetable oil based soap, for the first time in India, and a fire-proof safe. His motivation was to prove that industrial products could be made in India, and everything didn't need to be imported from the UK, because that was the colonial practice.[50]

The entanglement of profit-related and non-profit logics in the conduct of Indian industrial companies can also be observed in relation to extra-commercial activities (fourth domain), which at that time became increasingly described as business 'philanthropy'. Practices performed by Indian companies under this label can be traced back to practices of the industrialists' merchant ancestors. In addition to their commercial activities, it was common for merchants to redistribute part of their wealth in activities such as the building of wells and temples, the funding of religious festivals, or the relief of victims of famines and natural calamities.

These practices were nested in multiple institutions and meaning contexts. They were altogether a religious act performed to please the deities, a way of improving the status and social prestige of oneself and one's family within one's community, an occasion to create useful bonds with religious and political authorities, a means to legitimate profit-making by turning private accumulation of wealth into a source of public goods, and a way of shaping one's public image as an influential and trustworthy businessman – a key asset in an economy based on social status and reputation rather than enforceable contracts.[51] Religious gifts were particularly important to ensure one's respectability in the community by publicly displaying one's adherence to values of faith and frugality. The funding of infrastructures and public services, as well as the payment of tributes, were rather directed to the ruling nobility and imperial elites, as a means to favour supportive patronage and limit political decisions that would hurt economic prospects.

---

[50] Interview conducted by the author, 3 October 2007.
[51] See Haynes (1987) and Sundar (2013).

By and large, the native industrial entrepreneurs of the late nineteenth and early twentieth centuries carried out these redistributive practices. The fact that they were themselves (former) merchants or members of merchant communities was obviously conducive to such continuity. The interrelationship between business development and the social prestige of the families controlling the business houses was also a favourable condition in this regard. But philanthropic donations were also stimulated by the colonial and anti-colonial socio-political context. While religious business philanthropy continued, as illustrated by the construction of Birla's famous temple Laxminarayan Mandir in Delhi in the 1930s, British cultural influence favoured the development of more secular forms of philanthropy, which were attached to modern values of progress such as individual freedom, access to education and health, or science and technology. Concretely, Indian business houses started funding orphanages and schools, dispensaries and hospitals, as well as universities, art schools, and research institutes. Simultaneously, business philanthropy became a way for India's industrialists to support anti-colonial nationalism:

> [the nationalist movement] had a dimension broader than the merely political. It encompassed economic, social and cultural issues like women's emancipation, nationalist education, revival of Indian art, building a strong technological base for the economy to take it into the modern era, and so on.... In the extraordinary circumstances of the times, the line between politics and philanthropy had become blurred because social reform, cultural revival, economic development and political emancipation were very closely enmeshed.[52]

Building on his good relationships with the native business community, Mahatma Gandhi actively promoted business philanthropy as a contribution to the independence movement. Besides direct interventions, such as asking business leaders to support specific projects or welfare organizations, Gandhi formulated and promoted a doctrine of business philanthropy based on the concept of trusteeship.[53] This doctrine, which combines ideas of Western thinkers and philanthropists, in particular John Ruskin and Andrew Carnegie, and religious ethics formulated in classical Hindu texts such as the Bhagavad Gita, conceives of wealth as a gift of God that needs to be used for improving the welfare of all (*sarvodaya*). In this perspective, once the wealthy members

---

[52] Sundar (2000, 169).
[53] See Chakrabarty (2011) and Sundar (2013).

of society have covered their basic material needs, they must employ the resources that have been entrusted to them for advancing social welfare and economic equality. In the words of Gandhi, who addressed the rich sections of society, 'You should regard yourselves as trustees and servants of the poor. Your commerce must be regulated for the benefits of the toiling millions and you must be satisfied with earning an honest penny.'[54]

Taken together, the empirical observations presented here show that in the early phase of India's corporate capitalism, which flourished thanks to and participated in the growing functional differentiation of the economy, native large companies were not solely guided by profit-driven calculations. Expectations of a monetary return on investment were certainly not absent from the premises and values guiding decision-making processes. However, family-based structures of corporate governance, the embedding of industrial entrepreneurship in caste-based merchant communities, socio-political dynamics underlying labour relations and the development of paternalism, anti-colonial economic nationalism, and institutionalized forms of business philanthropy were introducing other parameters and guiding values in the steering of corporate conduct. In short, modern industrial companies were not just a means to increase the financial capital of business owners but also a means to enhance the social prestige and life chances of the family to develop the cultural and social welfare of the community, and to advance the project of a modern and sovereign Indian nation.

The growing economic role of the state during the interventionist era

> At the stroke of the midnight hour, when the world sleeps, India will awake to life and freedom. A moment comes, which comes but rarely in history, when we step out from the old to the new, when an age ends, and when the soul of a nation, long suppressed, finds utterance.[55]

With these solemn words, Jawaharlal Nehru declared the official end of India's colonial era and the beginning of her journey as an independent nation on 15 August 1947. Though the formation of India's modern political structures

---

[54] Cited in Sundar (2000, 177).

[55] Jawaharlal Nehru, 'Speech On the Granting of Indian Independence, 14 August 1947', Modern History Sourcebook, Fordham University (https://sourcebooks.fordham.edu/mod/1947nehru1.asp).

was already quite advanced at this moment in time, it was of course a crucial moment, as India's political system could be integrated and reorganized on the basis of a sovereign constitutional national state. After more than two years of work, the Constituent Assembly adopted the Indian Constitution in November 1949, and on 26 January 1950, India became a 'sovereign democratic republic'.[56]

Obviously, India's independence did not preclude significant continuities between politics under colonial rule and the newly founded post-colonial state. Furthermore, social structures characterizing Indian society in and across other spheres of society prevailed long after the 'stroke of the midnight hour'. Nonetheless, the constitution of a new sovereign state marked the beginning of a new era, including with regard to the country's political economy and business–society interplays. In particular, under the powerful leadership of Prime Minister Jawaharlal Nehru, India's central government adopted a series of policies that reorganized the economy according to a mix of capitalism and socialism.

While private property and freedom of contract were maintained, the state took a central position in economic development, both as an economic actor and as a political regulator of the private sector. By investing massively in public enterprises, the government thought to accelerate economic development by compensating the inability of the private sector to shoulder all required investments. Given the limited fiscal resources of the state, a strong public sector would also help fund the development of social welfare programmes. More generally, Nehru envisaged economic growth not as an end in itself, but as a means that had to be directed according to democratic political objectives.[57] This view included a certain distrust vis-à-vis large private companies. At the annual meeting of FICCI in 1952, Nehru declared: 'We are not willing to give private enterprise the high place which some countries have given it. We are ready to view it with suspicion.... If you imagine that we should keep private enterprise before us as an axiom or presumption you are mistaken.'[58]

The principle of a mixed economy was already laid down into the Industrial Policy Resolution of 1948. This policy resolution divided the productive sector

---

[56] Preamble to the Constitution of India, 1949.

[57] For more details, see, for instance, Kochanek (1974), Parekh (1991), Khilnani (2012 [1997]), Roy (2007), and Mukherji (2009).

[58] Jawaharlal Nehru quoted in Kochanek (1974, 217).

into four categories. The first, which entailed arms and ammunition, atomic energy, and railways, was reserved to state monopolies under the control of the central government. The second category entailed sectors in which only the state could start new ventures, but where existing private production facilities were tolerated (coal, iron and steel, aircraft manufacture, shipbuilding, telecommunications, and minerals). The third category comprised sectors in which private companies would have to operate within a tightly regulated framework (for example, machine tools, chemicals, fertilizers, cement, paper, automobiles, electric engineering). Finally, the fourth category designated all other sectors, which were left open to the private sector. In addition to this division of the economy, the Industrial Policy Resolution of 1948 stressed that while foreign investments were needed, they would be subject to close scrutiny and formal approval by the government, who would control their compatibility with the country's public interest. Moreover, managerial control and the majority of the capital of companies had now to stay in the hands of Indian citizens. Coupled with trade policies based on import-substitution, this measure encouraged the departure of a number of foreign – in particular European – investors and companies, and helped insulate the country's corporate capitalism from foreign competition.

In 1950, the role of the state was further strengthened with the creation of a Planning Commission, whose role would be to formulate and implement five-year plans. The main goals of planning were to achieve modernization and poverty reduction through coordinated industrialization and the orientation of investments towards the so-called backward regions. To do so, a complex bureaucratic system of production licenses and quotas was developed under the Industries (Development and Regulation) Act of 1951. Known as the 'licence-permit raj', this system enabled the state to control – with more or less success – the nature, the level, and the location of private investments in production facilities. Under the planning system, the state also regulated production volumes, prices, and the geographical distribution of goods in selected sectors. The state was also empowered to take over the managerial control of any private company who would be found to operate against the nation's interest. With the second plan, which extended from 1956 to 1961, the Planning Commission became the main body in which India's economic policies were crafted. It was put under the personal direction of the prime minister, and Nehru populated the commission with economists and technocrats who were selected 'for their broad agreement with his political project: committed to "socialistic" and reformist ideals, in the Indianized version of social democracy, and above all to a scepticism about the market and a belief that the state had to take responsibility for allocating resources in the economy'.[59]

In 1956, the role of the state in the economy was developed further with the formulation of a new Industrial Policy Resolution, according to which the goal of social and economic policies should be to establish a 'socialist pattern of society'.[60] Under this new policy, the list of industries reserved for the public sector increased from six to seventeen. In a second list called 'concurrent', which entailed twelve industries, private investments were expected to complement the dominant public sector enterprises. The rest of the economy was left to the private sector. This policy resolution became the guiding framework for economic development policies up to the late 1970s, and during this period, the actual share of the public sector in industrial investment grew significantly (see Table 3.2).

Table 3.2   **Sector-wise allocation of industrial investment (in per cent)**

Plans	Public sector	Private sector
Plan I (1951–56)	19.7	80.3
Plan II (1956–61)	53.8	46.2
Plan III (1961–66)	59.1	40.9
Plan IV (1969–74)	57.5	42.5
Plan V (1974–79)	58	42

Source: Rajakumar (2011).

Besides this division of the productive sector, the government also intervened in investment flows through a number of public financial institutions, including the Industrial Credit and Investment Corporation of India, the Industrial Finance Corporation of India, the Industrial Development Bank of India, Unit Trust of India, the Life Insurance Corporation of India, and the Infrastructure Development Finance Company. These institutions enabled the government to channel investments in strategic sectors, and to supply cheap credit to companies under financial stress.

Following the death of Nehru in 1964, after a short interlude, Indira Gandhi came to power in 1966. Lacking the aura, popular support, and strong position within the Congress that Nehru had enjoyed, Indira Gandhi became obsessed

---

[59] Khilnani (1997, 85–86).
[60] Government of India (1956, Art. 6).

with centralizing power to strengthen her own position in Indian politics. As part of this strategy, she transferred authority from the technocratic Planning Commission to the political Ministry of Finance, and increasingly politicized the administration in charge of devising and implementing economic policies by using appointments to seal alliances and reward loyalty. Indira Gandhi also counter-balanced a lack of support from within her own party by seeking the support of the left parties, which she obtained at least partly thanks to an emphatic 'pro-poor' and 'anti-capitalist' rhetoric. This rhetoric shift was accompanied by a further expansion of the role of the state in the economy, including with regard to the regulation of private companies. Among other decisions, the nationalization of banks in 1969 strengthened the role of politics in finance. The same year, the Monopolies and Restrictive Trade Practices Act of 1969 was adopted to counter the growing concentration of the private sector in the hands of a few industrial conglomerates (see below). One year later, an Industrial Licensing Policy was introduced to tighten the licence and quota system, with the objective to favour the development of small and medium enterprises.

The political regulation of private companies

How did the new institutional setting underlying India's interventionist period change the role of companies in interplays between the economy and other spheres of society? In particular, how did it change the way corporate conduct articulated profit-making with competing collective values and interests?

With regard to corporate governance, family structures continued to play an important role. In fact, most of the industrial families that had prospered in the inter-war period continued to control large shares of India's private sector. And business houses which were created after independence, often by acquiring assets sold by British companies that were divesting from India, were also controlled by families.[61] This domination of family business prevailed despite political and regulatory changes. For instance, a new Companies Act was adopted in 1956 to phase out the managing agency system, in order to reduce the concentration of capital controlled by the country's business elite as well as to protect the interests of investors in general and of small shareholders in particular. During the 1960s and 1970s, the state also provided financial support and training programmes to promote entrepreneurship on the basis of

---

[61] Khanna and Palepu (2005).

business plans, without formally taking the ethnic identity of applicants into account. But in 1965, almost half of the non-governmental and non-banking assets of the country were controlled by 75 business houses, most of which were originating from India's traditional merchant communities – in particular the Marwaris, the Parsis, and the Gujarati Banias.[62] Deeply entrenched cultural representations might have contributed to this enduring pattern. For instance, while managers of public financial institutions were supposed to avoid any ethnic discrimination, in fact, they were often 'quite reluctant to extend financial assistance to persons not belonging to traditional business communities and/or families with long-standing business experience',[63] as such origins were perceived as a precondition for having the qualities required for business success.

Notwithstanding these elements of continuity, several major changes occurred in the governance of corporate conduct under the interventionist period. First, the above-mentioned investments of the state in public sector enterprises partly decoupled entrepreneurship in the productive sector from traditional community and family structures. Like traditional business houses, which had blended profit-making with other objectives such as social prestige and economic nationalism, public enterprises were not focused on profit-maximization. As an instrument of the state's socio-economic development policies, they were governed to serve broader purposes. They were altogether a means to support overall economic development by complementing private industrial investments in strategic sectors (for example, transport infrastructures, energy, heavy machine tools), an opportunity to reduce regional inequalities by developing economic activities in the so-called backward regions, a way to fund the state in a context of meagre fiscal revenue, and a way to enhance national sovereignty by making India economically less dependent on foreign powers.

Second, while traditional communities remained a relevant context for India's private industrial conglomerates, their relative significance decreased as corporate conduct became increasingly informed by national structures and events. With regard to financial capital, for instance, the role of intra-community networks receded, while public financial institutions and stock markets became the main providers of credit and investments. This shift made companies less dependent on community ties. Companies also remained quite independent from their new providers of capital. Small shareholders had little

---

[62] Kochanek (1987).
[63] Oza (1988, 74).

means to interfere in corporate decision-making, and financial institutions were also rather lenient:

> Because financial institutions were themselves not accountable for the profitability of the investments they made, there was no incentive for them to exercise a level of control that would have been commensurate with the level of their equity interests. Instead, control was usually left to the family members who ran the businesses and who held relatively little equity compared with that held by public financial institutions.[64]

While the formal control of private companies remained in private hands, corporate conduct became increasingly oriented by political-bureaucratic regulations and interventions. Under the 'license and permit raj', key business decisions such as about investment in fixed capital, the geographical location of factories, production levels, product prices, the price of shares issued on stock markets, or the remuneration of directors were not defined by business strategy in response to market fluctuations. They were defined by bureaucrats according, at least formally, to political decisions and rules oriented towards the common good. In this setting, competition and the economic success of companies depended less on economic efficiency and market position than on the ability of companies to secure advantages through political connections, corruption, and unrecorded transactions carried out in the black economy.[65]

National politics and regulatory norms also gained significance in the domain of labour relations. In fact, as a former leader of AITUC, Jawaharlal Nehru conceived of labour relations as a key part of the country's development strategy. In the predominating view of that time, the agrarian-rural economy would soon be replaced by an industrial-urban order, in which 'industrial employment would shape a future in which employers, workers and the state would accommodate their separate interests for the common good'.[66] Moreover, as per Articles 41–43 of the Directive Principles of State Policy, the Indian Constitution expected the state to play a key role both in the institutional design and in the functioning of this accommodation.[67] In other words,

---

[64] Gollakota and Gupta (2006, 189).

[65] Mukherjee Reed (2001).

[66] Breman (1999, 3).

[67] Article 41 states, 'The State shall, within the limits of its economic capacity and development, make effective provision for securing the right to work, to education and to public assistance in cases of unemployment, old age, sickness and disablement, and in other cases of undeserved want'; Article 42 states, 'The State shall make provision

while industrial workers represented no more than six per cent of India's total workforce in the early 1950s, labour policies and regulations were highly relevant in political terms.

Against this backdrop, in the wake of independence, the state adopted a series of major labour laws that gradually superseded the prevailing paternalistic employment relations. For instance, the Industrial Disputes Act was adopted in 1947 to define the legal procedures of labour disputes settlement, and to provide for the creation of national and regional administrative bodies dedicated to the regulation of labour relations. Inter alia, the act also introduced an obligation for companies employing more than 300 workers to seek permission from public authorities before proceeding with any layoff.[68] In 1948, the Factories Act was adopted to regulate working conditions in production units comprising 10 employees or more. Among other measures, this act forbade the employment of children under the age of 14, defined requirements regarding the workplace (for example, hygiene, light, ventilation, temperatures), and empowered labour departments to conduct inspections in companies' premises. Other labour laws followed, such as the Minimum Wage Act of 1948, the Payment of Bonus Act of 1965, and the Payment of Gratuity Act of 1972. The state also created a social security system based on the Employees' State Insurance Act of 1948 and the Employees' Provident Funds and Miscellaneous Provisions Act of 1952. This general legal framework was complemented with the Contract Workers (Regulation and Abolition) Act of 1970 and the Contract Labour and Inter-State Migrant Workers Act of 1979, which provide rights to temporary and migrant workers. Among other provisions, the Contract Workers Act allows public authorities to prohibit the use of temporary workforce in any establishment.

Within this institutional setting, national and regional public authorities became much involved in the regulation of labour relations and the settlement of disputes. For instance, the state encouraged the formation of trade unions,

---

for securing just and humane conditions of work and for maternity relief'; and Article 43 states, 'The State shall endeavour to secure, by suitable legislation or economic organization or in any other way, to all workers, agricultural, industrial or otherwise, work, a living wage, conditions of work ensuring a decent standard of life and full enjoyment of leisure and social and cultural opportunities and, in particular, the State shall endeavour to promote cottage industries on an individual or co-operative basis in rural areas.'

[68] In 1982, this obligation was extended to any company employing more than 100 workmen. Managers, as well as contract workers who worked less than 240 days in the year for the company, are not considered 'workmen' in this law.

whose number jumped from 3,522 in 1949–50 to 13,248 in 1965.[69] While not all of the registered unions were part of national federations, the latter also gained momentum. AITUC, which had been created in 1920 in relation to the Congress, had already joined hands with the Communist Party of India (CPI) in 1945, while the Trade Union Federation, which had been created in 1929, became affiliated to the Congress Party in 1947 under a new name, the Indian National Trade Union Congress (INTUC). After independence, other party-affiliated trade union federations were constituted, including the Hind Mazdoor Sabha (HMS) in 1948, which was related to the Janata Dal; the United Trade Union Centre (UTUC) in 1949, which was affiliated to the Communist Party of India – Marxist Leninist (CPI-ML); the Bharatiya Mazdoor Sangh (BMS) in 1955, which was associated with the Bharatiya Janata Party (BJP); and the Centre for Indian Trade Union (CITU), which was carved out of AITUC in 1970 following the split between the CPI and the Communist Party of India – Marxist (CPI-M).

This strong connection between trade unions and political parties strengthened the ability of trade unions to push for labour-friendly policies in Indian politics, while providing parties with an organizational platform to mobilize electoral support. Beyond such collaboration, trade unions were supported by the state as part of the above-mentioned 'accommodation':

> A strong trade union movement was central to the project of uplifting the poor and working classes. 'The attitude towards trade unions', according to the government's first Five-Year Plan (1950–55), 'should not just be a matter of tolerance but they should be helped to function as a part and parcel of [the] industrial system.' The second plan was theoretically explicit. It recognized the 'utter necessity of a strong trade union movement for safe-guarding the workers' interest and achieving the targets of the plan', declared that the 'creation of industrial democracy is a pre-requisite for our cherished goal of establishing a socialist society', and stressed that industrial democracy would not be possible without a 'strong and healthy' trade union movement.[70]

Following this political line, which prevailed up to the social unrests and the state of emergency of the mid-1970s, the state tended to favour labour rather than employers in the national tripartite negotiations that were conducted under the various Industrial Wage Boards.[71]

---

[69] Bhattacherjee (1999).

[70] Candland (2007, 70).

[71] See, for instance, Bhattacherjee (2001), Candland (2007), and Thakur (2008).

The dominant role of the state in the economy after independence significantly altered relations between companies and Indian politics. In the late 1940s and early 1950s, overall, these relations were still consensual. Building on the close ties that had developed in the inter-war period, India's business elite and the Congress were envisaging economic development policies based on a complementarity between the state and the private sector.[72] Massive infrastructure and industrial investments by the state were key for private companies to develop their own business. For instance, it would provide access to raw material and supply companies with machinery and intermediary goods. Public financial institutions were also welcome, as they provided cheap loans with flexible repayment schedules in a context of scarce capital. The import-substitution policy was providing useful protection from foreign competition. And a strong welfare state would support the development of interior demand. In an international context where communism was strong, supporting the government of Jawaharlal Nehru was also a way for business actors to keep more radical political factions at bay, so as to secure the capitalist organization of India's economy. Such support was particularly strong in the first few years following independence, as the powerful presence of Sardar Patel in the Congress provided for economic policies that were rather liberal and in line with the preferences of India's business elite.

The death of Sardar Patel at the end of 1950 freed Nehru from the necessity to constantly compromise with the conservative factions of the Congress. This political change allowed for the gradual strengthening of economic regulation by the state, as described above. This trend divided India's business community. On the one hand, most of the west coast business leaders, in particular the Tatas and other members of the Parsi community, reacted by publicly criticizing the overload of rules and political interventions. In 1956, a group of them created the Forum of Free Enterprise, whose purpose was precisely to lobby for less restrictive economic policies. On the other hand, the Marwari and other businessmen from the east coast maintained their public support to the Congress, including through the FICCI. This support prevailed even under the rule of Indira Gandhi, as the Congress was perceived by many as a factor of political stability. But Indira Gandhi's growing anti-capitalist rhetoric, combined with her decision to nationalize banks and to act against the concentration of capital, undermined this support and motivated an increasing number of companies to leave FICCI.

---

[72] Kochanek (1974), Mukherjee Reed (2001), Mukherji (2009).

Besides their contributions to public debate, Indian companies developed various strategies to cope with and to take advantage of the political-bureaucratic regulation of the economy. Most of India's large companies developed new organizational structures, such as Delhi branch offices known as 'industrial embassies', to deal with the innumerable licences and clearances that had to be obtained from public administration. Inter-personal contacts with relevant ministers and bureaucrats were an important asset in this regard, both to secure advantages and to minimize the extent of so-called red tape – the illicit payment of bureaucrats to obtain the due processing of files. Companies also contributed to the funding of political parties. In 1967, for instance, 74.72 per cent of the Congress's funds were coming from the country's four largest business conglomerates (Tata, Birla, Khatau, and Martin Burn).[73] And from the late 1960s onwards, an increasing number of young businessmen started running for parliamentary elections to strengthen the voice of the business community in national and regional politics. While this latter strategy yielded poor electoral results, overall,

> the system grew increasingly into an exchange relationship between business and government. Business (the buyer) went to government (the seller) for benefits, and in return paid in the form or resources such as campaign contributions, political donations, and jobs for relatives. The political leadership came to depend very heavily on the system as a quid pro quo for securing campaign contributions, and the bureaucracy depended on it for payoffs, employment, power, prestige, and patronage.[74]

With regard to the extra-commercial activities of companies, they receded and their function changed during the interventionist period. Business philanthropy had been closely associated with traditional patterns of redistribution and the social prestige of businessmen, and it had been galvanized by economic nationalism during the freedom struggle. But during the interventionist period, as revealed in 1959 by an Enquiry Committee of the Direct Taxes Administration, company-related philanthropic trusts and foundations increasingly became empty shells used for purposes of tax avoidance. According to Pushpa Sundar, this decline of India's tradition of business philanthropy was due in part to cultural changes characterizing the new generation of businessmen, as well as to a new division of roles between business actors and the state:

---

[73] Mukherjee Reed (2001)
[74] Kochanek (1987, 1284).

Religious faith was less intense, and the [business] class as a whole was less inclined to involve itself in civic affairs or in public charities. It believed that public works and welfare of the poor were principally the responsibility of the government which collected taxes from business for the purpose.[75]

The gradual decoupling between business development and the socio-cultural life of businessmen's community might also have played a role, but this hypothesis requires empirical examination.

While traditional business philanthropy was losing ground, the concept of CSR started appearing in India's public sphere in the mid-1960s. Inspired by George Goyder's book *The Responsible Company*,[76] the former independence activist Jayaprakash Narayan joined hands with a few companies and the Indian International Centre to organize a conference on CSR in New Delhi in 1965, which was inaugurated by Prime Minister Lal Bahadur Shastri. A few public seminars followed, and in 1966, the three business leaders J.R.D. Tata, Rahul Bajaj, and Arvind Mafatlal launched the Fair Trade Practices Association (FTPA) to promote the self-regulation of 'socially responsible' businesses. An offshoot of the Forum of Free Enterprise, the FTPA was a direct reaction to reports of several public expert committees that incriminated the excessive concentration of capital in India and the undesirable consequences of such concentration both for consumers and for democracy.[77] However, the FTPA failed to gather broad support among Indian business actors, and it had little impact on the growing regulation of corporate conduct by the state.

In the following years, explicit references to CSR remained limited to other short-lived attempts to initiate change. For instance, in a report released in 1978, the High-Powered Expert Committee appointed by the central government to review issues of corporate governance stated that any company 'must behave and function as a responsible member of society just like any other individual' and 'accept obligation to be socially responsible and to work for the larger benefits of the community'.[78] The expert committee proposed the introduction of a legal obligation for companies to report on the social and environmental impacts of their operations, as a means to 'test' the level of their corporate social (ir)responsibility. But unlike most of the other proposals

---

[75] Sundar (2000, 230).

[76] Goyder (1961).

[77] The Mahalanobis Committee in 1964, the Monopolies Inquiry Commission in 1965, the R.K. Hazari Committee in 1969, and the Dutt Committee in 1969.

[78] Sacher Committee (1978, 95).

made by the expert committee, CSR-related reporting was discarded in the subsequent law-making process.

Overall, when compared with the former period, business–society interplays during the interventionist era were characterized by a number of changes. The Indian state partly subsumed companies into a broad political project of social modernization. As part of this project, the state adopted economic development policies that progressively weakened the institutional 'embedding' of corporate capitalism in family structures, ethnic communities, paternalistic employment relations, and traditional cum nationalist business philanthropy. This loosening of institutional ties to non-economic spheres of society was accompanied by the development of alternative institutions, which either replaced, displaced, or superseded the previous setting. While family and community life remained a variable of corporate conduct, decision-making in Indian firms became strongly oriented by (or against) political-bureaucratic regulations and interventions. Labour relations became structured primarily by labour laws and national tripartite negotiations, in which employers were facing strong trade unions and state authorities that were primarily concerned with labour welfare. Interactions between companies and the political system became increasingly structured by the national formal institutions underlying the interventionist regime. And pre-existing patterns of business philanthropy receded, as contributions of companies to social welfare became increasingly channelled by the state through taxation and social policies.

Taken together, these institutional and cultural changes were favourable to two trends. On the one hand, the partial disembedding of business organizations from non-economic structures was prone to a greater focus of companies on the guiding value of monetary gains. On the other hand, India's functionally differentiated political system took over the main role of regulating interplays between companies' primarily profit-driven operations and competing collective values and interests. More specifically, politics was to enable and to promote the development of profit-driven business operations that it observed as being beneficial for higher collective values and interests – for example, national sovereignty, poverty reduction and social welfare, the 'modernization' and 'development' of the so-called backward areas, and so on. Conversely, wherever the primarily profit-driven operations of companies seemed to contradict such collective values and interests, politics was to intervene by elaborating and implementing regulatory constraints.

Chapter 4

✠

Increasing Functional Differentiation and the Rise of CSR

As the previous chapter has shown, until the early 1980s, the role of corporate profit-making in the functioning of the Indian economy was limited by various institutional settings. After peculiar conditions during the emergency rule under Indira Gandhi (1975–1977), followed by two years of ineffective policy-making under a government based on a heterogeneous coalition, the return to power of Indira Gandhi in 1980 marked the beginning of a new period for India's political economy. This period, which is still ongoing, is characterized by four interrelated trends:

1. A gradual shift from the interventionist regime to 'pro-business' economic development policies
2. A greater operational focus of companies on financial returns on investment
3. Growing contention on the impacts of corporate conduct on non-profit values and interests framed under the essentially contested concept of 'development'
4. A rapid expansion of the CSR phenomenon

The present chapter provides an empirical analysis of these four interrelated trends, which are investigated in more detail in Chapters 5 and 6.

Economic reforms and the 'pro-business' tilt of India's economic development policies

Indira Gandhi is known as a political leader who was obsessed with securing her own power and position both within the Congress Party and within the state apparatus. In the late 1960s and early 1970s, this motive had led her to assert her autonomy against rural elites, which exerted significant control over the Congress Party, as well as over regional and local politics. To counterbalance this loss of a powerful support base, Indira Gandhi had crafted a rhetorical – and partly political – alliance with left-wing political forces.[1] Under the slogan *garibi hatao* (war on poverty), this alliance was framed as a 'pro-poor' movement that would defend the masses against predatory agrarian exploitation and big-business capitalism.

After the emergency rule (1975–1977), followed by a massive electoral defeat of the Congress and two years of ineffective coalition government under the Janata Party, Indira Gandhi returned to power in 1980. At this point, however, *garibi hatao* was not a suitable political strategy anymore. The authoritarian turn of Indira Gandhi and her ruthless oppression of trade unions and political activists during the emergency had alienated the support of left-wing political forces. Moreover, because Indira Gandhi had centralized and personalized the exercise of power, the large-scale economic and social crises that marked the mid-1970s were largely perceived as being *her* failure to deliver on her promises: the 'pro-poor' rhetoric without tangible outcomes had backfired as a political strategy. The international context, marked by economic globalization and a rise of neoliberal economic policies, had also changed in a way that was favourable to a shift from redistributive state interventionism to supply-side economic policies.

Against this backdrop, Indira Gandhi put *garibi hatao* and related talks of redistributive justice on the backburner, and crafted a new alliance between the central state and India's corporate capitalists.[2] Improving production and boosting the country's economic growth were declared a top political objective, and the Nehruvian model of state interventionism was now considered a handicap in this regard. Public enterprises were seen as being too ineffective to accelerate industrial development. Instead, the state was to unshackle the

---

[1] In fact, political decisions made by the government of Indira Gandhi were not always guided by this rhetorical alliance:

> Indira Gandhi lacked the political instruments – a well-organized party and/ or a lower-level bureaucracy that would respond to central directives – needed to implement her antipoverty policies, and she certainly did not try very hard to push against entrenched interests. On the contrary, when difficult choices had to be made, she often made concessions to propertied classes, reserving the worst of her wrath for her political opponents. (Kohli 2012, 29)

[2] See, for instance, Kohli (2012) and Hasan (2012).

private sector from the licence–permit system, and to support economic growth through investment-friendly policies. Similarly, trade unions and labour militancy were increasingly envisaged not as a vehicle for social welfare and redistributive justice, but as an impediment for higher productivity and private investment growth.

This 'pro-business tilt'[3] was concretized in a first series of policies that introduced changes in the institutional framework underlying India's political economy.[4] In particular, the central government started reducing investments in public sector enterprises, while encouraging private investments in sectors that used to be dominated by the state. For instance, restrictions on investment and production volumes were eased in industries such as chemicals, drugs, and cement. Measures such as tax reliefs or temporary guarantees of minimum profit rates for new industrial investments were also adopted to incentivize private productive investments in these sectors. With regard to labour relations, the description of labour protests as 'anti-social demonstrations' by Indira Gandhi and other political leaders became more widespread, and was accompanied on the ground by increasing political support to employers – for instance, by directing the police to contain or to deter strikes.[5]

These first measures were recognized by most observers as the beginning of a much broader and significant change of direction in the country's economic development policies. Hence, these small changes received much attention and triggered fierce debates and controversies both within the Congress Party and in the wider public sphere. Liberal reformists, who often belonged to the younger generation of political leaders, were calling for more ambitious changes. Conversely, many among the Nehruvian old guard were ideologically opposed to a 'pro-business' strategy and concerned about its potential electoral consequences. A number of bureaucrats and business actors were also worried about reforms that might unsettle established rents and privileges.[6] In 1985, bad electoral results for the Congress in eleven regional state elections galvanized internal opposition to reforms, as these results were interpreted as a reaction of the poor masses against a shift from redistributive justice to 'pro-rich' economic policies.[7]

---

[3] Kohli (2012, 1).

[4] For an overview of the economic reforms introduced in the 1980s, see Panagariya (2008, ch. 4).

[5] See Kohli (2012, 103), Thakur (2008), Candland (2007), and Bhattacherjee (2001).

[6] See in particular Jenkins (1999).

[7] See Hasan (2012, 50).

Following the assassination of his mother in relation to the insurgency of Sikhs in Punjab, the new prime minister, Rajiv Gandhi, adopted a cautious strategy that combined a discrete continuation of piecemeal reforms with increased spending in social welfare programmes. Until 1989, private investments were increasingly allowed in sectors that used to be reserved for the state, a growing number of industries were partly or completely removed from the licence–permit system, controls on prices and distribution were lifted in most sectors, and restrictions imposed by the Foreign Exchange Regulation Act were softened. But the assassination of Rajiv Gandhi in 1989 and the ensuing electoral defeat of the Congress interrupted the reform process by putting a heteroclite coalition in power.

In 1991, the economic reform agenda experienced a breakthrough under Narasimha Rao, who became prime minister in the context of a severe crisis of payment. The International Monetary Fund (IMF) and the World Bank provided financial assistance, but they were expecting structural reforms in return. Narasimha Rao placed reform-oriented politicians and experts in key decision-making positions, including by putting the Finance Ministry under the leadership of the economist Manmohan Singh. Using the crisis as a political window of opportunity, Rao's government pushed unpopular reforms through Parliament and conveniently blamed the Bretton Woods institutions for that matter.[8]

Beside short-term measures such as monetary devaluation and a massive reduction of public spending, structural reforms were progressively introduced as part of the government's New Economic Policy. Among other changes, most industries that were reserved to the public sector (energy, telecommunications, civil aviation, and so on) were opened to domestic and foreign private companies; the state partly divested from public sector enterprises; the licence–permit system was completely abolished; most of the remaining administrative controls on price and distribution were lifted; and the price of new shares issued by companies on stock markets was deregulated. India's new economic policies also shifted from the previous import-substitution strategy to a greater integration of the economy in global markets and production networks. Maximum tariffs were reduced from 300 per cent in 1990–1991 to 40 per cent in 1997–1998; other restrictions on imports were largely removed; restrictions

---

[8] See Mukherji (2013). Mirroring Margaret Thatcher's famous assertion 'There is no alternative', the Finance Minister Manmohan Singh stated in Parliament during his first budget speech that 'no power on earth can stop an idea whose time has come' – the 'idea' being economic deregulation and liberalization.

on foreign institutional investors (FII) and foreign direct investments (FDIs) were either scrapped or significantly lightened; the rupee was made convertible at market rates on the current account (but not on the capital account); and domestic companies were allowed to seek financial capital abroad, including through external commercial borrowings.

This overview of the economic reforms of the 1990s provides indications on the extent of the shift characterizing India's economic development policies during this period. The reform process was conducted to a great extent by technocrats, experts, and political actors outside the realm of mass democratic politics – which in the 1990s was preoccupied by other topics related mainly to caste politics, regionalism, and the rise of Hindu nationalism.[9] This discretion of the reform process is also a result of political strategies used by reformers to mitigate contention.[10] In particular, reformers used a gradual strategy that consisted in changing the institutional setting 'by stealth', one measure after another, and by keeping formal institutions while changing political practice when formal change was politically not feasible (for example, reforming labour laws). Reformers also pushed institutional change through backdoor negotiations between representatives of various interest groups, as well as by supporting the organization of reform-friendly interest groups such as the Confederation of Indian Industries (CII).[11] A further strategy consisted in using India's federal system to first move forward in reform-prone regions, before inducing change among regions that lagged behind through the organization of inter-regional competition for economic resources.[12]

While the change of direction in India's economic development policies took place in the 1980s and early 1990s, the reform process has been pursued in the same direction over the past decades, both at the national level and – with increasing significance – at the subnational level.[13] Two examples

---

[9] See Varshney (1998), Yadav (1999), Jaffrelot (2011), Hasan (2012), Mukherji (2013), and Corbridge, Harriss, and Jeffrey (2013, ch. 6).

[10] See Jenkins (1999).

[11] See Sinha (2005).

[12] On this particular point, see Kennedy (2014).

[13] This continuity of the reform process might seem puzzling in a country characterized by a high turnover in the national and regional governments – Indian voters having a pronounced 'anti-incumbent' behaviour. As noted by K.C. Suri, 'party or leaders who support and implement reforms while in power turn into opponents of reforms once they sit in opposition. Similarly, those who oppose reform policies of the ruling party while in opposition turn to be zealous pursuers of reforms once they come to power' (Suri 2004, 5405).

illustrate this trend. One is the changing role of the Planning Commission. Unlike other components of the Nehruvian interventionist system, the Planning Commission was kept operational until recently. But its role and orientation changed: it shifted from prescriptive planning, whereby the state acts as an overarching orchestrator of economic development, to indicative planning, whereby the state acts as a facilitator for the development of the market economy.[14] Facilitation through planning was carried out by providing information to autonomous private economic actors, but also by identifying areas in which the state should invest to bolster private sector–led economic growth. Between 2004 and 2014, this new function of indicative planning was performed under the chairmanship of Prime Minister Manmohan Singh and the deputy chairmanship of Montek Singh Ahluwalia – two key architects of India's economic reforms. In 2014, another step was taken by the newly elected prime minister, Narendra Modi, who dissolved the Planning Commission and replaced it with the Niti Aayog, a policy think-tank chaired by the prime minister and the economist Arvind Panagariya – a staunch supporter of neoliberal economic policies.[15]

The second example is the special economic zone (SEZ) policy, which was introduced by the government of Manmohan Singh in 2005 as 'a key instrument for achieving national economic goals, which included deeper engagement with global markets'.[16] Partly inspired by the Chinese experience, the SEZ policy was intended to overcome social and political impediments to economic reforms and industrial growth by providing business-friendly conditions to companies in selected portions of the territory – including cheap land, tailored infrastructures and utilities, simplified administrative procedures, tax holidays, and overall political support. SEZs would be created either by public authorities or by private developers who conceive SEZ projects and implement them after receiving formal approval from the Ministry of Commerce and Industry. In effect, the SEZ policy has not achieved the ambitious initial expectations of policy-makers and private investors so far.[17] By 2017, only 420 SEZ projects had received formal approval. While various sectors are represented, including pharmaceuticals, chemicals, biotech, and engineering, a majority of the projects are concentrated in information technology (IT) and IT-enabled services – a sector which is not particularly labour-intensive and which would

---

[14] See Bagchi (2007) and Nayar (2012).

[15] See Panagariya (2008) and Bhagwati and Panagariya (2012).

[16] Kennedy (2014, 79).

[17] See, for instance, Kennedy (2014).

not have required the public resources provided by the SEZ policy to expand. By December 2014, about 1.2 million people were employed in SEZs, for a national workforce of about 420 million individuals.[18]

The gradual opening of multi-brand retail and other restricted sectors to foreign direct investors, Narendra Modi's 'Make in India' initiative of 2014, and regional industrial policies in which state governments have offered extensive political support and various regulatory as well as material advantages (for example, land, tax breaks) to attract and retain investments, are further examples of the continuation of the economic development strategy that was initiated with the first generation of economic reforms in the 1980s.

Fostering the functional differentiation of India's corporate economy

Overall, the 'pro-business' political-economic reorientation has restructured relationships between companies and the state, in particular with regard to large companies of the formal economy. While the state used to operate as an overarching orchestrator of economic development and a guardian of national sovereignty, it has morphed into an underlying supporter both of private sector–led economic growth and of India's integration within the global economy. Conversely, companies have gained significant operational autonomy vis-à-vis non-economic collective values and interests, while facing increasing expectations with regard to their economic performance. This general trend, which has heightened the degree of functional differentiation of India's economic system, can be observed and analysed more systematically in the four domains of business–society interplays that were considered in the previous chapter. The present section focuses on the first three domains (corporate governance; labour relations; relations between companies and politics). Companies' non-business activities formally directed towards the common good are addressed in a later part of the chapter.

During the interventionist period, industrialization through public sector enterprises and the tight regulation of private companies by the state had overtaken and weakened the role of families and caste communities with regard to corporate governance (see Chapter 3). As the economic reforms put the emphasis back on the private sector, while lifting regulatory constraints associated with the licence–permit system and import-substitution, profit-

---

[18] Rahoof and Arul (2016).

making seems to have gained significance as a guiding value for corporate governance.

Several elements suggest that the financialization of corporate governance has been limited in the Indian context. For instance, a recent study of networks and interlocked directorate within large business groups in India shows that unlike the global trend, Indian liberalization and globalization have strengthened rather than weakened the role of homophilic ties based in particular on family membership, and to a lesser extent on caste, religion, and regional identity.[19] Most large Indian companies are still controlled by small and dense networks of family members and close associates, with a few family-business groups (for example, Tata, Birla, Adani, Jaypee, Godrej, Mahindra) occupying central positions in the country's corporate network. Conversely, banks and other institutional investors are not represented much on the boards of Indian companies. Other studies also indicate that market-enabling legal changes based on international corporate governance standards, as well as the growing weight of stock markets and institutional investors in the capital of firms, have not broken the ability of capitalist families and their associates to retain control in companies' boards.[20] However, the dominant position of families and allied directors on the boards of India's large companies is an element of continuity that does not preclude changes in other aspects of corporate governance.

First, following a number of reforms in the 1990s that deregulated and liberalized the financial system, corporate financing has relied increasingly on the issuing of shares in stock markets, and commercial banks have overtaken state-sponsored financial institutions as sources of credit.[21] Overall, while the financial system has become more competitive and more efficient in its function of allocating capital to fuel investments and economic growth, the pressure on companies to deliver sufficient returns on investments is likely to have increased when compared with the pre-reform period. Second, while most business families in control of large conglomerates used to own small shares of the companies' capital (15 per cent on average in the 1970s and 1980s), they increased their stakes significantly to secure control and avoid hostile takeovers.[22] As the families' wealth has become more tightly coupled with the shareholder value of companies under their control, financial performance is

---

[19] Naudet and Dubost (2017).

[20] See, for instance, Chandrachud (2011).

[21] See Rajakumar (2014).

[22] Rao and Guha (2006).

likely to have gained weight as a guiding value in the management of Indian firms. A third change is the end of import-substitution and the resulting increase in competitive pressures. To survive in competitive markets, Indian companies have changed the management of their organization. Business process reengineering, management of semi-autonomous units by objectives, mechanization, sub-contracting of non-core tasks, and other managerial changes have been deployed on a large scale to make business organizations economically more efficient.[23] Finally, India's integration into the global economy has strengthened the presence of foreign multinational companies on the subcontinent. Incoming FDI has increased exponentially: the annual average was US$104 million in the 1980s, US$1.5 billion in the 1990s, US$16 billion in the 2000s, and US$34 billion between 2010 and 2016.[24] Returns on investments are a core parameter guiding the management of the Indian subsidiaries that foreign companies have set up as part of this trend.

The combination of growing operational autonomy vis-à-vis non-economic concerns and an increasing focus of companies on efficiency and financial performance can also be observed in the domain of labour relations. While the state had been supportive of labour during the interventionist period, as part of its socialist development strategy, violent repression of trade unions during Indira Gandhi's emergency rule in the mid-1970s was followed by a general change in the state's attitude. The preventive arrest of 6,000 labour activists and the subsequent arrest of 25,000 trade union leaders and workers on the occasion of a general strike in 1982, which opposed economic adjustment measures, illustrate this shift.[25] More generally, reforming India's highly complex and rigid labour laws has been on the political agenda over the past three decades or so. While most of these laws only apply to formal employment, which represents about 7–8 per cent of the country's workforce, they have been identified by Indian policy-makers, business associations, experts, and international organizations such as the World Bank as heavy constraints on productivity gains and competitiveness, employment generation, and economic growth.[26]

---

[23] In the words of an Indian senior business executive, 'now everything is about "lean organization". If you want to survive, you have to do that. You have to externalize, to improve your processes' (interview conducted by author, 01 April 2008).

[24] These figures were taken from the database of the UNCTAD (http://unctadstat. unctad.org).

[25] See Candland (2007, 96–98).

[26] See, for instance, Candland (2007), Thakur (2008), Sen and Dasgupta (2009), and Guha (2009).

In 1999, a National Commission on Labour was set up to identify options to revamp the country's labour laws and adapt them to the dynamics of a globalizing economy. But a lack of consensus between the state, employers' associations, and trade unions hindered the implementation of the recommendations made by this commission.[27] Since then, at the national level, only piecemeal changes have occurred. For instance, the introduction of special provisions in SEZs ensure 'investor-friendly' labour relations, for example, by putting the political management of labour issues in the hands of the Development Commissioner, whose main duty is to make companies invest and stay in the SEZ.[28] In spite of a strong electoral mandate to put the country back on the track of reforms and rapid economic growth, the government of Narendra Modi has also failed to make big changes in labour laws so far, beyond a few measures associated with the 'Make in India' campaign, such as the introduction in 2014 of a self-certification platform for compliance with labour laws, intended to 'make it easier for businesses to comply with labour regulations and to end "arbitrary harassment" by the "inspector raj"'.[29]

However, while labour regulation has remained mostly untouched de jure, the constraining nature of the legal framework has been substantially weakened de facto. At the regional level, growing competition between state governments to boost investments on their territory has led them not only to soften formal constraints but also to assure potential investors that enforcement of labour rights would be handled in a business-friendly manner.[30] Interviews that were conducted with fifteen trade union leaders as part of the present study provided further evidence of this trend.[31] Several interviewees explained, for instance, how bureaucrats from the Labour Department, who used to be more concerned with labour welfare, increasingly tended to favour employers when writing inspection reports or during the intricate processes of dispute settlement. While the extent and evolution of the role of bribes in such processes is difficult to assess, corruption also plays a role in the weak implementation of labour

---

[27] See Bhattacherjee (2001), Jenkins (2004), and Hill (2009).

[28] Singh (2008b), Jenkins, Kennedy, and Mukhopadhyay (2014).

[29] Ruparelia (2015, 764). See also Rajalakshmi (2014).

[30] See Jenkins (2004) as well as findings from our study of Lafarge India's cement plant project in Himachal Pradesh, presented in Chapter 5.

[31] Two interviews were conducted in the national secretariat of the AITUC, one interview was conducted within the secretariat of the New Trade Union Initiative, and twelve interviews were conducted with various regional and local trade union leaders operating in the cement industry in Chhattisgarh.

laws. The experience of a trade union leader from the Pragatisheel Cement Shramik Sangh (Progressive Cement Worker's Union), which is affiliated to the Chhattisgarh Mukti Morcha (CMM – Chhattisgarh Liberation Front), illustrates this point:

> 80 members [of our union] had been terminated. So we approached the Labour Commissioner. When we started approaching him, the management bribed the Labour Commissioner. I know this, because he was not interested to follow the procedure and recommend the case further ahead. So we made an agitation in front of his office. A mass rally, a dharna. Under this pressure, he forwarded the case to the Chief Labour Commissioner. In Raipur, again they tried to bribe the Chief Labour Commissioner. We contacted the State Labour Minister. He gave direction to the Chief Labour Commissioner to refer the case to the Industrial Relations Court.... The Chief Labour Commissioner forwarded the case to the Secretariat. In the Secretariat, the Labour Department Superintendent and other colleagues directly asked us to put some 'weight of Gandhi-ji' on the file. You know, on our bank notes, there is the picture of Gandhi. Directly they asked me. I told them: 'We are very poor, we have been terminated for the past 5–6 years, so we are totally unable to do this.' They laughed and said: 'Then you go. We will work as we are usually working'. After one month, they issued the note 'Your case could not be referred, so it has been rejected'. They put the file in the dust bin.[32]

In addition to the 'pro-business' reorientation of the Indian state with regard to labour relations, which is part of the broader political-economic shift outlined above, labour-related constraints on corporate conduct have been weakened by the crisis of trade unionism on the subcontinent. While trade unions used to exert significant power, from national tripartite negotiations on wages and working conditions down to the organization of work at the factory level, this power has been undermined by a conjunction of factors. First, while the ties between trade union federations and political parties used to help unions put labour demands on the political agenda, the commitment of the Congress Party and other parties to a 'pro-business' development strategy has changed this relationship. In the present configuration, these ties often allow policy-makers and economic interest groups to use political parties to discipline trade unions.[33] A second factor is the gradual decentralization of bargaining,

---

[32] Interview conducted by the author, 10 May 2008.

[33] See Candland (2007). An informal discussion conducted in 2008 in New Delhi with a senior business executive from the Indian subsidiary of a large French company

from national tripartite agreements to plant-level agreements between the management and representatives of employees. This decentralization has led to a fragmentation of the Indian trade union landscape by opening up a space for the creation of new politically affiliated and independent unions.[34] This fragmentation lowers the plant-level representativeness of trade unions, and it creates divisions and instability. Because of harsh competition for members, local union leaders tend to criticize one another and to work against each other, rather than to join hands in negotiations and strikes. Fragmentation also makes it easier for the companies' managers to play unions against each other, as well as to pick and choose those with whom they accept to interact. Furthermore, decentralized bargaining coupled with plant-level instability of labour unions makes the bargaining processes less transparent, and therefore more prone to bribery. As a trade union leader from the New Trade Union Initiative claimed:

> Every trade unionist receives offers from companies all the time. So we have to be careful. It starts with a car to bring you to a meeting, the company paying a hotel bill, or inviting you for a meeting in a nice restaurant. If the person accepts those small offers, the company will know she can propose more and bribe the trade unionist. It is a widespread phenomenon, but it is difficult to quantify.[35]

Similar claims can also be found among managers, such as by the managing director of the Indian subsidiary of a French company:

> When we took over the plant, we were told to be careful with trade unions. Now we have good relationships with the union leaders. We take good care of them.... Taking care in the sense of ... giving a small envelope. It existed

---

provided a concrete example of this phenomenon, as the business executive mentioned how he was developing good relationships with high-level members of several political parties to be able to ask for their support in case of labour unrest in the company's factories.

[34] See Bhattacherjee (2001). This fragmentation is also due to the fragmentation of India's political party landscape since the 1980s, in a context where the Congress Party has lost its hegemonic position to the advantage of the BJP and a number of regional parties. Several of India's 1,761 political parties, which include 7 national and 48 large regional parties, have supported the creation of affiliated trade unions of their own.

[35] Interview conducted by the author, 23 April 2008.

before we came, and we think that we should not break what existed before. We just give a little more, to be on the safe side.[36]

In short, while the legal framework has not changed much, the business-friendly inclination of public authorities and the weakening of trade unions has given companies significantly more autonomy in the management of human resources than it was the case during the interventionist era. Overall, while wages and working conditions have improved for skilled employees in the organized sector, such as for engineers or managers, most companies have used their autonomy to reduce their low-skilled permanent workforce. To do so in spite of the harsh restrictions for layoffs and retrenchments that are still imposed by the Industrial Disputes Act of 1947, employers have made extensive use of the so-called voluntary retirement schemes (VRS). These schemes are formally based on a mutual agreement between the employer and the employee. However, employees are often put under pressure or threatened: no data allows us to quantify the extent of this phenomenon, but 'forceful VRS' has become a common category of labour relations in the Indian context, including within large companies.[37] Besides reductions in the permanent workforce of a given company, for instance, to compensate for mechanization and other sources of productivity gains, 'forceful VRS' also allows companies to discipline those who continue to work, as they fear they will become the next ones if they do not fulfil the expectations of their employer.

Part of the reduction of the permanent workforce is also related to a growing use of casual labour in the production process, including by companies from the organized part of the Indian economy: the share of informal workers in the organized sector has risen from 32 per cent in 1999–2000 to 54 per cent in 2004–2005, and to 67 per cent in 2011–2012.[38] While this trend is partly due to the rise of the construction industry as an employment provider in the 2000s, subcontracting and the use of low-skilled casual workforce provided by middlemen in the manufacturing industry and the service sector have also contributed to this trend. Unlike permanent employees, contract workers and other casual labourers provide companies with significant autonomy, so

---

[36] Interview conducted and translated from French to English by the author, 25 July 2007.

[37] See Jenkins (2004) and Chapter 5.

[38] Mehrotra, Parida, Sinha, and Gandhi (2014). Between 2009–2010 and 2011–2012, trends have started to change with a rapid increase of employment in industry and service, in particular in the construction industry.

that employment relations in India are de facto less rigid than what the legal framework suggests. As a plant-level human resources manager in a cement company explained:

> If we talk in financial terms, people are assets, they are assets as well as they can be liabilities. In the downturn, they can be liabilities for us, because they are fixed costs.... Whenever there is an industrial dispute, a misunderstanding or a difference in opinion between these people and us, we are the representation of the management. So if there is a dispute, there are different levels where the dispute is being heard and answered. There are tribunals: there are Labour Courts, Industrial Courts, Civil Courts, High Courts, Supreme Court. We have a hierarchy here. The dispute is going from one court to another.
>
> So to avoid those confusions in the long go, on the long term, we are trying to reduce the liabilities in a manner which will be beneficial to us, and to those people also. Because not everybody in the unionized category is against the management for a particular say. But if a majority or a chunk of them are opposing us for a particular matter, the others will have to come with them. I am speaking about permanent employees. So we have those things, and the intensity of a particular problem is louder if they are permanent employees.... Contract workers are a floating population, they keep coming and going. Say if you award a contract to a person for a period of one year, even during this one year, it is not necessary that the contractor employs the same people.... Contractors will also keep floating, according to the demand, if it increases or if it decreases. Or during our shut down and maintenance activities, we have a high demand, so we will employ 1,000 people for two months. For the 10 remaining months, we will not require more than 400 people altogether every day in the plant. It depends on the activity. Sometime there is a break down, so we need additional people, so contractors get more people. It is a demand and supply thing.[39]

With regard to interplays between companies and India's political system, structural changes pertaining to the 'pro-business tilt' of the country's economic development policies have been outlined here. They point not to a withdrawal of the state from the economy, as the neoliberal *doxa* would suggest, but to a gradual change from state-led economic development to state-supported economic development, in which the central protagonists are private companies operating on deregulated and open markets. The processes underlying this change have been everything but linear and consensual, both on the side

---

[39] Interview conducted by the author, 5 December 2008.

of state actors and among India's business community. But overall, when compared to the previous period, the Indian state and business actors 'have increasingly converged on such crucial issues as the approach to labour; the pace and pattern of external opening of the economy; and, most importantly, on how to enable Indian business to improve production and productivity'.[40] Such convergence can also be observed to a certain extent in the field of environmental governance, albeit on a different timeline. As the governance of environmental problems has become a major area where the state and other actors, including companies, address tensions between profit-making and competing collective values and interests, it deserves particular attention in the present study.

While the overall trend in state–business interactions since the early 1980s has been to ease the political regulation of business conduct, environmental governance has rather strengthened regulatory constraints. Following a global trend, the Indian central government started introducing policies and laws directed to environmental problems in the wake of the first United Nations Conference on the Human Environment, which took place in Stockholm in 1972.[41] The Wildlife Protection Act (1972), the Water Act (1974), the Forest Conservation Act (1980), and the Air Act (1981) were part of this constitutive moment of India's environmental governance framework. As the Bhopal gas leak of 1984 catalysed ecological themes in Indian politics and society, this framework was reinforced in 1986 with the adoption of the Environment (Protection) Act and the setting up of a central Ministry of Environment and Forests (MoEF). In the 1990s and 2000s, partly as an outcome of international agreements, a series of additional policies, laws, and notifications were issued to cover new problem areas such as biodiversity, coastal zones, marine life, hazardous waste, and climate change.

For the most part, this regulatory framework is based on a 'command and control' approach, whereby public authorities define legally binding environmental standards within which companies and other relevant actors are expected to operate. More specifically, this framework requires companies to obtain a 'consent to establish' and other clearances when they set up a new production facility; it defines parameters, such as air and water pollution norms,

---

[40] Kohli (2012, 7).

[41] (Post)colonial environmental laws and administrative bodies, in particular the Indian Forest Act of 1927 and the Indian Forest Service, were not about protecting the environment, but about the rational economic exploitation of natural resources. See, for instance, Williams and Mawdsley (2006).

which companies must follow to obtain or renew a 'consent to operate'; it allows the regulator to impose sanctions on non-compliant companies, such as fines and the temporary closure of production facilities; and it restricts economic activities in selected areas such as coastal zones, wildlife sanctuaries, and national parks. Administrative bodies under the MoEF, including the Pollution Control Boards and Forest Departments, monitor the implementation of these legal provisions at the national and regional levels.

This regulatory framework is formally rather stringent. But its constraining properties must be envisaged in relation to the actual enforcement of legal provisions. On the ground, environmental regulation is hampered by a number of factors. The environmental administration often lacks technical and human resources to conduct sufficient inspections as part of its monitoring function. Bureaucrats from the Pollution Control Boards and Forest Departments must also cope with pressures exerted by state governments and elected representatives, who sometimes ask them to turn a blind eye to certain cases. Complacent bureaucrats are generally rewarded with better career chances, while recalcitrant ones risk being transferred to unappealing positions. Such pressures can occur at the local and regional levels, but also in the commanding heights of the MoEF. In 2013, for instance, the central environmental minister Jayanthi Natarajan was asked by the Congress Party to resign. A public letter she wrote subsequently mentions pressures exerted by the vice-president of the Congress Party Rahul Gandhi to get the MoEF to deliver environmental clearances to given investment projects. Corruption is a further cause for deficient enforcement of environmental laws. Companies are often confronted with bureaucrats who expect bribes in exchange for the processing of files. Conversely, illicit transactions are a way for companies to avoid sanctions for non-compliance. Besides, it is not uncommon for companies that are unable or unwilling to comply with legal standards to provide truncated data to the regulator, with or without the latter's knowing. As a result, the gap between the legal framework and the ground reality of environmental regulation can be significant.[42]

Against the backdrop of a mounting environmental crisis, which triggers conflicts over resources (land, water, forest, and so on) and undermines the life chances of millions of people, this deficient enforcement of environmental law has prompted social movements and India's judiciary to challenge both companies and the government (see later). These mobilizations and judicial interventions question the basic consensus underlying the country's pro-

---

[42] See, for instance, OECD (2006), Panth and Shastri (2008), and Mejia (2009).

business development model. They view industrial and infrastructure projects not simply as contributions to economic growth cum 'development' but also as part of a self-undermining process that trades functioning ecosystems and the life chances of human beings against unequally distributed short-term economic wealth and political power.

India's policy-makers and business leaders have not remained insensitive to this challenging side of the conundrum between economic development and the environment. During the second term of the Congress-led United Progressive Alliance (2009–2014), in particular, the two environmental ministers Jairam Ramesh (2009–2011) and his successor Jayanthi Natarajan (2011–2013) have proven committed to environmental protection, including at the expense of investment projects. But this stance was heavily criticized by other ministries in the government, by business associations such as the CII and FICCI, and in the press.[43] More generally, the promotion of fast economic growth has clearly prevailed over environmental concerns in Indian politics. While policy-makers and business actors have joined hands to combine environmental and economic goals under the broad concept of 'sustainable development', they have also multiplied efforts to soften regulatory constraints that are perceived as bottlenecks for rapid industrial development.[44] This trend has gained momentum in recent years following the election of Narendra Modi in 2014. In addition to push for a business-friendly overhaul of key environmental laws, which was blocked in parliament in 2015, the central government has relaxed the distribution of environmental clearances and exempted several industries from selected regulatory constraints.[45] Attempts to weaken the independence and power of the judiciary (especially the National Green Tribunal) in environmental matters, and measures taken against environmental NGOs such as Greenpeace, which the government described as 'anti-people' and 'anti-development', are further indicators of a 'pro-business' trend in India's environmental governance.[46]

Taken together, these political and institutional changes have fostered the functional differentiation of India's economic system. Between the mid-eighteenth and the mid-twentieth centuries, monetization and the development

---

[43] The influential magazine *India Today*, for instance, wrote about how 'the Jairam–Jayanthi regime has jinxed development with an obstructionist approach in the environment ministry' (*India Today* 2012).

[44] See Bedajna (2012), Menon and Kohli (2014), and Kohli and Menon (2016).

[45] See, for instance, *India Today* (2015) and *Hindustan Times* (2015).

[46] See, for instance, *Business Standard* (2014) and *Hindustan Times* (2017) as well as *The Guardian* (2015) and *The Hindu* (2015).

of modern economic institutions (for example, markets, banks, business corporations) had contributed to a process of functional differentiation of the economy. But economic transactions, including the commercial activities of companies, had remained tied to a great extent to non-economic spheres of society. Functional differentiation of the economy continued to unfold during the interventionist period. But economic processes in the production sector were directed to a significant extent by political decision-making, for instance, through economic planning and the licence–permit system. Under the current 'pro-business' regime, profit-making based on economic efficiency (higher monetary gains, lower monetary costs) has been further institutionalized and strengthened as the primary guiding value in the organizational behaviour of companies from the organized sector – the size of which has expanded significantly in terms of value added.[47] Conversely, the political system has eased or scrapped many of the institutional constraints that were meant to subordinate economic processes to politically defined collective values and interests (for example, modernization through industrialization, national sovereignty, poverty alleviation, labour welfare).

The contentious interrelationships between profit-making and 'development'

By putting profit-driven companies at the centre of a development model based on private sector–led economic growth, the Indian state has made the country's development prospects more contingent on the profit-driven behaviour of companies. The underlying assumption is that such political–institutional arrangement increases the ability of the economic system to perform its basic functions: use resources efficiently to meet the needs of consumers by providing goods and services at the best possible quality–price ratio and accumulate monetary wealth in the process. The better the economy can perform these functions, so the assumption, the more it can contribute to the achievement of the country's development aspirations.

---

[47] The share of the organized sector in total manufacturing value added (at current prices) grew from about 52 per cent in 1980–1981 to 70 per cent in 2010–2011, and its share in service value added grew from 30 per cent to 41 per cent over the same period (Goldar 2014). Recent policies conducted by India's central government, in particular the sudden withdrawal of ₹500 and ₹1,000 value banknotes ('demonetization') in 2016 and the introduction of a national goods and services tax (GST) in 2017, are expected to reinforce the formalization of India's economy.

Economic growth rates are generally considered a good proxy indicator to assess the success of this strategy. And following this perspective, India's pro-business development policies have been rather successful.[48] The country's average GDP growth reached 5.7 per cent in the 1980s, and after a calamitous fall to 1.05 per cent in 1991, it recovered its average pace of 5.7 per cent between 1992 and 2002. Between 2003 and 2010 (with a short dive in 2008), the country experienced an economic boom with an average GDP growth of 8.3 per cent, which triggered a global wave of enthusiasm about the bright prospects of this new economic 'superpower'.[49] After a slowdown to 6.1 per cent between 2011 and 2014, India's fast growth recovered to 7.5 per cent between 2014 and 2016. However, notwithstanding this remarkable trend, India's 'pro-business' policies have placed private companies and the state at the heart of intense controversies regarding the developmental outcomes of profit-oriented corporate conduct.

During the 1980s and 1990s, while Indian politics was dominated by issues of caste reservations, Hindu nationalism, and the assertion of regional identities, gradual economic reforms remained mostly outside the ambit of electoral contention. Within the electorate, part of the upper class was firmly supporting the reform agenda, while other segments remained attached to Nehru's ideological legacy and/or they were opposed to reforms that threatened their rent. The middle and upper-middle classes, whose material condition had improved through the expansion of the interventionist state, had also mixed feelings vis-à-vis privatization and the downsizing of the public sector. Among the poor rural and urban masses, access to subsidies and other social welfare benefits were more important than the economic reforms per se. But the idea that reforms were serving the 'rich' while providing little benefits for the 'poor' was widespread.[50] Most political parties did not hesitate to use this sentiment against their opponents: as noted by K.C. Suri, '[invariably], the opposition parties lambast[ed] the ruling party for embarking on reckless and indiscriminate reform policies causing immense hardships to the poor and the disadvantaged, jeopardizing the economic sovereignty of the nation or leading to increasing economic disparities among different classes'.[51] But once elected, politicians from the former opposition would pursue the reform agenda of their predecessor, while incumbents would take over as the critics

---

[48] The following figures are based on data from the Word Bank: https://data.worldbank.org (accessed on 17 September 2017).

[49] See, for instance, *The Economist* (2006), *Time* (2006), and *Outlook Business* (2008).

[50] Suri (2004).

[51] Suri (2004, 5404).

of 'pro-rich' reforms. Only the left parties and most trade unions engaged in sustained opposition to economic reforms, with substantial effects on the (limited) extent of privatization of public enterprises.[52]

Since the mid-2000s, as both the 'pro-business' reforms and their socio-economic impacts have deepened, the mixed picture sketched above has evolved along a process of polarization. On the one hand, economic dynamics attributed to India's post-reform growth model have increased both the demographic size and the economic wealth of the country's middle and upper classes. A thorough analysis of consumption expenditures of various social groups in the years 1993–1994, 2004–2005, 2009–2010, and 2011–2012 points to 'an era of exclusionary growth', in which 'most benefits have flown to the country's most well-off members'.[53] Other economic studies converge on the fact that India has experienced a 'growing concentration of incomes at the top'.[54]

This upper layer comprises a very rich urban elite – for the most part successful entrepreneurs, business executives, high-skilled engineers, bankers, consultants, and other high-level professionals from the private sector, to which one should also add a significant part of the country's political class. Below this elite, India's post-reform economy has fuelled the development of a new upper-middle class which, as a trend, is characterized by social conservatism coupled with a strong consumerist culture oriented towards 'western' lifestyles.[55] Further below, India has experienced the rise of a broader 'aspiring' lower middle-class. The economic base of this class remains modest, but its members look at the new lifestyles of the upper strata as a model, which they seek to experience by adopting new consumption practices (for example, from traditional markets to shopping malls) and by investing in strategies of upward mobility (for example, sending children to English schools and colleges). Using daily consumption expenditures of US\$2–10 in purchasing power parity as a definitional criterion to circumscribe this lower and upper-middle classes, Sandhya Krishnan and Neeraj Hatekar find that their share in the total population decreased marginally between 1999–2000 and 2004–2005. However, between 2004–2005 and 2011–2012, their share jumped from 27.9 per cent to 50.3 per cent.[56]

---

[52] Candland (2007).

[53] Suryanarayana and Das (2014, 44). See also the Indian chapter of the *World Inequality Report* coordinated by Alvaredo, Chancel, Piketty, Saez, and Zucman (2018).

[54] Drèze and Sen (2013, 217).

[55] See, for instance, Fernandes and Heller (2006), Fuller and Narasimhan (2007), Jaffrelot and Van Der Veer (2008), Baviskar and Ray (2011), and Mathur (2010).

[56] Krishnan and Hatekar (2017).

This evolution of India's class structure has provided a growing political support base to economic reformers. As Aseema Sinha remarks, 'portions of [the] leading classes no longer rely on the central state for subsidies and patronage. Instead, they look to the private and globalized economy and to their local state governments rather than to New Delhi'.[57] The supportive disposition of India's new middle and upper classes vis-à-vis pro-business development policies also relates to the ability of these social groups to compensate deficient public services (for example, low quality education and healthcare) by buying alternative solutions on the market.[58] They associate ideas of 'development' with a dynamic market economy that should be supported by an effective managerial state, far from the perceived inefficiencies and corrupt excesses of India's parliamentary democracy.[59] During the campaign for the national elections of 2014, the BJP and its leader, Narendra Modi, skilfully built upon this sentiment. With the slogan 'minimum government, maximum governance', Modi pledged to put the country back on the track of fast economic growth by eliminating corruption and by launching a new wave of investor-friendly policies.[60]

While socio-political support for India's 'pro-business' development policies has gathered steam, so has discontent and overt opposition. Part of this opposition has been voiced by prominent intellectuals. For instance, the Nobel Prize–winning economist Amartya Sen and his colleague Jean Drèze expressed serious concerns in the public sphere about the outcomes of an economic model that caters primarily to material aspirations of the elite. As they put it, 'India has been climbing up the ladder of per capita income while slipping down the slope of social indicators'.[61] The renowned novelist and activist Arundhati Roy also pointed at the gap between the 300 million 'who belong to the new, post-International Monetary Fund (IMF) "reforms" middle class' and the 'ghosts' of India's contemporary capitalism – 'the poltergeists of dead rivers, dry wells, bald mountains, and denuded forests; the ghosts of 250,000 debt-ridden farmers who have killed themselves, and the 800 million who have been impoverished and dispossessed to make way for us [the middle

---

[57] Sinha (2007, 42).

[58] Drèze and Sen (2013).

[59] On this last point, see, for instance, Jaffrelot (2008), Sarangi (2016), and Vaishnav (2017).

[60] See Ruparelia (2015) and Jaffrelot (2015).

[61] Drèze and Sen (2013, 8). See also the authors' essay in *Outlook India* (2011) and Amartya Sen's essay in *The New York Review of Books* (2011).

class]'.[62] Many other intellectuals and scholars narrate a similar story, such as Swapna Banerjee-Guha, who writes:

> Areas with rich mineral deposits are leased out to global corporations leaving the poor tribal communities who usually live in such areas (fertile farmlands, common lands or even waste lands) homeless. These areas, which have long provided a means of livelihood to the poor, especially tribal and backward communities, are converted into Special Economic Zones (SEZs) or private cities; coastal areas with immense bio-diversity are handed over to corporations such as Dow Chemicals or Vedanta to build chemical hubs or private ports; water resources like rivers or estuaries with natural port facilities are given away to private corporations for industrial purposes; slums and squatter settlements in cities are demolished systematically to make way for upscale commerce and real estate; urban infrastructure is privatized thereby denying access to the majority and intensifying the gap between rich and poor. All this is causing unprecedented ecological damage that poses a serious threat to the environment and to the life of people, cutting across class, caste or community lines, and more than ever before making the future problematic.[63]

Criticism and opposition have also gained momentum in the form of social conflicts, protest movements, as well as public interest litigations (PILs) filed in High Courts and in India's powerful Supreme Court. By pointing at tensions and contradictions between the profit-oriented behaviour of companies and competing collective values and interests, this counter-movement[64] has questioned the founding assumption – and legitimizing claim – of India's 'pro-business' policies.

The country's lively culture of activism, which imbues a dense network of social activists and civil society organizations, has been a key driver of this counter-movement. This culture of activism has deep historical roots, which go back at least to the nineteenth-century peasant revolts against landlords and the owners of colonial plantations.[65] The struggle for independence

---

[62] Roy (2014, 8).

[63] Banerjee-Guha (2013, 166).

[64] This concept is borrowed from Karl Polanyi, who used it to describe labour and other social movements that emerged in the late nineteenth- and early twentieth-century western Europe, moved by a 'principle of social protection [from the commodification and marketization of society] aiming at the conservation of man and nature as well as productive organization' (1957 [1944], 132).

[65] For an overview of the history of social movements in India, see, for instance, Tandon and Mohanty (2002) and Ray and Katzenstein (2005).

strengthened Indian social movements, which were inspired in particular by the peaceful protest tactics developed by Gandhi as part of his doctrine of *satyagraha* (the 'embrace of truth'), including, for instance, *dharnas* (sit-ins) and hunger strikes. A further legacy of the freedom struggle was that after independence, most social movement leaders who pursued a redistributive agenda continued to operate from within the ambit of the Congress Party, which dominated Indian politics.[66] In the 1970s, which were marked by a difficult economic context, the failure of the Nehruvian developmental state to deliver on its promises of social justice and poverty alleviation spurred a new wave of social movements, whose discontent was directed towards the state. The suspension of fundamental rights and the brutal repression of dissent during the emergency rule of Indira Gandhi further widened the gap between the Congress and social movements. Former independence activists, such as Jayaprakash Narayan, and new activists, for instance, within the People's Union for Civil Liberties, organized the opposition to Indira Gandhi's autocratic temptation. A significant part of the social base underlying this new wave of protest was constituted by members of the country's educated upper-middle classes, which had adhered to Nehru's progressive ideology and felt betrayed by the Congress government.

New social movements of the 1970s and 1980s also experienced a thematic widening in terms of causes for mobilization, which echoes the rise of new social movements in other parts of the globe.[67] As part of this trend, mobilizations against the Sardar Sarovar Dam Project, which was expected to require the forceful displacement of 130,000 people, catalysed the emergence in India of a new kind of protest movement that combined social and environmental themes in a critique of modernist development.[68] Spearheaded by the Narmada Bachao Andolan (Movement to Save the Narmada), and supported by influential international NGOs such as Oxfam and the Environmental Defence Fund, this protest movement was also an occasion for Indian activists to strengthen their ties with the transnational anti-globalization movement.

The Bhopal gas leak in a factory of the American company Union Carbide in 1984, which killed around 15,000 people and injured hundreds of thousands,

---

[66] There were notable exceptions to this trend, however, such as the radical Naxalite movement, which developed in the late 1960s out of violent protests against the – not less violent – oppression of peasants by their high-caste landlords, and which was supported by the CPI-M.

[67] Tandon and Mohanty (2002).

[68] See, for instance, Dwivedi (1998), Bose (2004), and Baviskar (2005).

is a further milestone in the development of new social movements in India. As Ingrid Eckerman notes, this major industrial catastrophe became 'a symbol of transnational corporate negligence towards human beings' and acted as a 'wake-up call'.[69] While Indian social activists used to focus their energy and critiques on the post-colonial developmental state, they became increasingly vocal regarding private companies. As a CSR expert from the NGO Partners in Change recalled:

> If you look back at the early 1990s, when India was opening up its markets, or all the economic reforms of 91, most of the NGOs in India were rather neutral to business.... When NGOs had any complaints towards companies, they would complain to the government and tell the governmental regulators what had to be done. There was no direct engagement. In the early 1990s, we saw two things happening. At one extreme, NGOs saw companies as a source of funds, so they promoted corporate philanthropy. At the other extreme, NGOs started redefining their techniques on how they wanted to campaign against companies. This was the extreme of NGOs opposed to companies.[70]

Since this initial period of the 1990s, social movements that question companies' new role as the country's primary agents of development have gained momentum. These movements have also diversified in several respects.[71] In terms of ideological background, for instance, some of them follow a Gandhian alternative vision of development based mostly on rural community life, non-consumerist traditional lifestyles, and moral values such as probity and help towards the poor and vulnerable. The mass organization Ekta Parishad, which organizes peasants against the acquisition of agricultural land for industrial and infrastructure projects, is part of this trend. Other militant groups and organizations, such as the Corporate Accountability Desk or CMM, are closer to a neo-Marxist perspective. They envisage Indian and foreign companies mainly as predatory entities. In their view, acting in the name of 'development', these entities serve the interests of the dominant capitalist class by extracting natural

---

[69] Eckerman (2005).

[70] Interview conducted by the author, 21 December 2007.

[71] The following overview, which is illustrative, not comprehensive, is based on twenty-six interviews conducted in India with various activists who work on issues related to business–development interplays, as well as on the reading of various socially engaged magazines (*Tehelka*, *Frontline*, *Civil Society*, *Down to Earth*) and the following of discussions conducted between activists on Internet platforms such as Chhattisgarh. net (http://groups.yahoo.com/group/chhattisgarh-net/, accessed on 7 June 2009).

resources and exploiting a vulnerable workforce, with the complacent support of business-owned mass media and a corrupt 'pro-business' capitalist state.

Protest movements also vary in terms of their organizational form and *modi operandi*. While certain participants act as members of NGOs, such as the Centre for Science and Environment, Toxics Link, or the Business & Community Foundation, other social activists operate through loosely organized networks and collectives. In terms of *modi operandi*, these activist groups and organizations have used and combined a variety of means to exert direct or indirect influence on the behaviour of companies. Some of them conduct fact-finding research activities to gather evidence on questionable corporate conduct. This includes, for instance, the collection and analysis of air and water samples near production units to identify cases of non-compliance with legal pollution standards, or the gathering of testimonies from farmers or members of indigenous groups who were forcefully evicted to make room for industrial projects. Findings of such research can then be spread in reports, press articles, documentary films, and on the Internet to raise awareness, to scandalize, and to exert pressure on companies and public authorities. Another form of activism consists in working with companies to push for the adoption of business practices with better social and environmental outcomes. More confrontational tactics involve campaigning at the grassroots level to mobilize and support perceived victims of business activities (for example, expropriated farmers, displaced indigenous tribes, casual workers, working children, victims of pollution, consumers exposed to noxious products). Such grassroots campaigning is carried out through various means, such as the organization of protest actions, the filing of administrative complaints, and the filing of PILs in courts of law.

Among these various forms of collective action, PILs have had particularly far-reaching effects.[72] PILs were introduced in India's legal system in the 1980s by judges of the Supreme Court, in particular Justice P.N. Baghwati and Justice V.R. Krishna Iyer – two leading figures of judicial activism.[73] Through several decisions, these judges expanded the scope of Article 32 and Article 226 of the Constitution, which allow citizens to file litigations in High Courts and in the Supreme Court to defend their fundamental rights as defined in Articles 12–35 of the Constitution. Considering that many Indian citizens were unable to make concrete use of Article 32 and Article 226, for instance,

---

[72] For overviews, see, for instance, Verma (2004), Sen (2009), and Gill (2012).

[73] Judicial activism consists in legal courts going beyond adjudication of law by taking pro-active decisions that expand individual and collective rights beyond the supposed constitutional or legislative intent.

because of poverty, illiteracy, or oppression, the Supreme Court introduced the possibility for third parties to file PILs in the name of individuals and groups whose fundamental rights and other legal rights were harmed.

By allowing NGOs, social activists, and human rights lawyers to file PILs against the state and private parties, including against companies, the Supreme Court triggered a self-reinforcing mechanism that has increased the power both of protest movements and of the judiciary. On the one hand, the inflow of PILs has provided activist judges of the Supreme Court with an increasing number of opportunities to deliver socially progressive decisions, which expand the scope of social and environmental law by creating precedents in India's common law system. Conversely, the development of new social and environmental rights through decisions of the Supreme Court has widened the possibility for activists to file PILs against public authorities and companies. Some activists have used this mechanism purposefully by concentrating their resources on the development of cases which, once introduced in the Supreme Court through a PIL, had good chances to lead to a decision that would advance the regulatory framework in a certain direction.

As part of this self-reinforcing dynamic, a series of judgments formulated in the 1980s and 1990s had considerable impact by expanding the scope of Article 21 of the Constitution, which states: 'No person should be deprived of his life or personal liberty except according to procedure established by law.' The Supreme Court progressively turned this constitutional provision into a positive right to 'live with human dignity', understood as including inter alia a right to education, a right to clothing and shelter, a right to food, a right to drinking water, a right to livelihood, a right to medical assistance, a right to privacy, and a right to live in an unpolluted environment. In so doing, the Supreme Court constitutionalized rights, including labour rights and environmental rights, as well as general principles such as 'sustainable development'.[74]

Judicial activism also led the Supreme Court to reinforce the legal exposure of private companies. Its decision in the case *M.C. Metha* vs *Union of India*

---

[74] See the decision of the Supreme Court in the case *N.D. Jayal* vs *Union of India* (2003), which states:

> The adherence of sustainable development principle is a sine qua non for the maintenance of the symbiotic balance between the rights to environment and development. Right to environment is a fundamental right. On the other hand right to development is also one. Here the right to 'sustainable development' cannot be singled out. Therefore, the concept of 'sustainable development' is to be treated an integral part of 'life' under Article 21. (§23)

(1986), which introduces the principle of absolute liability, is a landmark in this regard. The decision requires hazardous industries to follow a precautionary principle, and it makes companies *and* their managers liable to fully compensate any harm incurred by persons and communities as a result of hazardous commercial activities. The justification provided by the Supreme Court in this judgement is typical of the spirit animating Indian judicial activism:

> This Court has throughout the last few years expanded the horizon of Art. 21 primarily to inject respect for human rights and social consciousness in corporate structure. The purpose of expansion has not been to destroy the raison d'être of creating corporations, but to advance the human rights jurisprudence. The apprehension that including within the ambit of Art. 21, and thus subjecting to the discipline of Art. 21, those private corporations whose activities have the potential of affecting the life and health of the people, would deal a death blow to the policy of encouraging and permitting private entrepreneurial activity, is not well founded. It is through creative interpretation and bold innovation that the human-rights jurisprudence has been developed in India to a remarkable extent and this forward march of the human rights movement cannot be allowed to be halted by unfounded apprehensions expressed by status quoists.[75]

In short, the dynamic described above has constituted the Supreme Court into a powerful law-making and law-implementing agency. As such, the Supreme Court can order the closure or the relocation of factories; it can stop investment projects or require them to fulfil specific requirements; it can expand the legal regulatory framework and set up new regulatory bodies (for example, the Central Empowered Committee); and it can order the central and state governments to adopt adequate public policies to put an end to the insufficient enforcement of fundamental rights.

Overall, while India's rising new middle and upper classes have provided growing support to the country's 'pro-business' development policies, which emphasize positive relationships between profit-driven business conduct and the achievement of collective developmental aspirations, protest movements and judicial activism have acted in the opposite direction. By producing narratives in the public sphere that emphasize tensions between the profit-driven behaviour of companies and competing collective values and interests, by advocating the

---

[75] Decision of the Supreme Court 1987 AIR 1086, §6.2 (https://indiankanoon.org/doc/1486949/) (accessed on 6 September 2017).

adoption of new regulatory measures to curb perceived harmful impacts of economic activities, by engaging with companies to influence their behaviour, by organizing protests, and by filing complaints in courts of law, new social movements and activist judges have pushed for a greater subordination of corporate conduct to non-profit collective values and interests.

Post-philanthropy and the development of CSR in India

For domestic and foreign companies operating in India, the combined development of inimical social movements and judicial constraints over the past two decades has been a source of serious concerns. The growing involvement of social activists and some political actors to mobilize rural communities against the forceful acquisition of agricultural land, in particular when such acquisition serves commercial purposes, created new hurdles for investments in production units and business-related infrastructure. Tata Motor's car factory project in Singur (West Bengal), which needed to be relocated to Gujarat in 2008 after violent protests by politicized local peasants, stands as a symbol for such costly land-related social conflicts. POSCO's large steel plant project in the Jagasinghpur district (Odisha), which the company abandoned in 2017 after years of harsh public resistance and legal challenges, is another famous case. But there are hundreds of others. As the economic boom of the 2000s stimulated new industrial investments across the subcontinent, conflicts over land became a common problem both for projects of individual companies and for the setting up of industrial development areas (for example, SEZs, industrial corridors).[76] According to a recent estimate, out of a total of US$3.1 trillion investments planned between 2000 and 2016, 16 per cent or almost US$500 billion were stalled because of land acquisition problems.[77]

As illustrated by the bauxite mine project of Vedanta at the foot of the Niyamgiri Hills in Odisha, which was cancelled by the Ministry of Environment, Forest and Climate Change in 2014 after protracted struggles and legal procedures, access to and exploitation of mineral resources has been another major source of conflicts – all the more so because a significant part

---

[76] Regarding the case of SEZ, which triggered a wave of protests because of large-scale land acquisition and displacement of rural populations to make room for corporate investments, see Jenkins, Kennedy, and Mukhopadhyay (2014).

[77] See http://rightsandresources.org/wp-content/uploads/2016/11/Land-Disputes-and-Stalled-Investments-in-India_November-2016.pdf.

of these resources are located under forest and/or tribal areas.[78] The efforts deployed by left-wing trade unions such as CITU, AITUC, CMM, or the New Trade Union Initiative to mobilize casual labour to demand similar wages and working conditions as those of permanent workers has also put some companies under pressure. Companies have been confronted with protest movements and mobilizations calling for new regulatory constraints in a number of other areas, such as consumer rights and public health (for example, scandal about the presence of toxic chemicals in bottled drinks commercialized by Coca-Cola and Pepsi Co.) or the commercialization of controversial agro-biotechnologies (for example, protests against Monsanto's BT cotton).

As companies either experienced direct opposition or observed in mass media and other fora how other companies got into trouble, they sensed a dynamic that seemed to endanger the investor-friendly climate created by India's 'pro-business' policies. Moreover, while being advertised and politically supported as key agents of the country's 'development' benefitted the companies' business prospects, it also exposed them to new uncertainties by putting the social and environmental impacts of their commercial activities under the spotlight. As a CSR expert from the CII explained:

> In the 1970s, when industries came to a village, people were very happy. They thought: 'In our remote village, we will also benefit from the development, be part of it'. In the 1980s, conflicts started to emerge. So the village people came to see the industries, who replied: 'Don't worry, we understand, we will do something and take care of it'. There was trust, people believed the industrialists. In the 1990s, people had lost this trust.... Stakeholders have evolved. Now, you have things like in Singur or in Nandigram. For Tata, it shows there is no trust outside Jamshedpur, the town they have built.[79]

In this context, previous forms of scattered philanthropic engagement seemed insufficient, if not outdated, as they could hardly address tensions and conflicts arising from the perceived harmful social and environmental consequences of core business activities. Conversely, while attempts to introduce CSR in India failed to pick up during the interventionist period (see Chapter 3), CSR has become increasingly successful since the late 1990s. In the words of a senior manager in charge of public relations in a large cement company:

---

[78] For a more comprehensive assessment, see the report on mining by the CSE (2008).

[79] Interview conducted by the author, 25 July 2007.

In the cement industry, you must spend on CSR. Otherwise, you will not survive. Previously, villagers were very innocent, very smooth. Nowadays, villagers know what is happening, and activists are very vigilant, very active.[80]

The Tata group, which has been considered one of India's most prominent corporate contributor to social (including labour) welfare since its inception in the late nineteenth century, was among the first to mobilize the CSR concept. The numerous community development projects that its companies and affiliated trusts (for example, Tata Steel Rural Development Society) used to carry out around production sites have been progressively integrated under this new category. In so doing, Tata – like other old business conglomerates – could build on its long-standing reputation and refer to previous forms of philanthropic engagement as evidence for its contemporary claims of social responsibility and sustainable development. In the words of an executive from the Tata Council for Community Initiatives:

> You come from a background where CSR has come quite recently. It is an add-on. But in Tata, it has always be there, inside.... You know, for us, sustainability, as the Group helped me to understand, is that it should always create lasting benefits. When you shift form short-term benefits to long-term benefits, you shift towards sustainability. Secondly, it should always serve a larger purpose, not a small group of interest.... Have you worked out what are employee's goals, what are customer's goals, what are other stakeholder's and village communities' goals? This can supplement financial goals and make the whole thing more sustainable. You need meaning. And for 100 years, Tata has done that, in its own way.[81]

While connecting with the past, the semantic shift to CSR and sustainable development also accompanied the adoption by Tata of new organizational structures and practices, which for the most part originate from the global CSR movement. In 1999, for instance, Tata adopted a code of ethical conduct. In 2002, it joined the UN Global Compact. One year later, it created a Tata Index for Sustainable Human Development, whose purpose is to generate data on the Group's various CSR-related activities, in order to improve coordination and reporting. Tata Motors was also the first Indian company in 2001 to release a CSR report according to the guidelines of the Global Reporting Initiative (GRI). Since this initial period, the organizational structures and activities

---

[80] Interview conducted by the author, 26 November 2008.

[81] Interview conducted by the author, 4 May 2008.

of the Tata Group and affiliated companies related to CSR and sustainability have grown manifold.

Over the past two decades, most of the large domestic and foreign companies operating in India have followed this lead, albeit to various degrees. The pursuance of community development projects such as the construction of local infrastructure (for example, ponds, wells, class rooms) and the organization of health camps for the benefit of villagers living near production sites has remained predominant. This absorption of philanthropy within the ambit of the CSR phenomenon is also reflected in the discourse of CSR managers and in the artefacts of corporate communication (for example, CSR reports, websites, brochures, PowerPoint presentations). CSR is commonly described as a way for the company to 'discharge its social responsibility' by 'giving back to society' and reduce the gap between corporate 'islands of prosperity' and India's 'sea of poverty'.[82] But the diffusion of CSR within India's large companies also comprises the adoption of new elements.

For instance, the number of companies with an environmental management system certified by the private norm ISO 14001 has grown from 111 in 1999 to 7,887 in 2017.[83] In recent years, reporting on CSR has followed a similar pattern. Among the 100 largest companies by gross revenue, 31 were reporting on CSR in 2011, of which 22 were following the guidelines of the GRI. According to the reports, 25 of the companies had 'established systems for managing, measuring and reporting on CR [corporate responsibility] issues'.[84] In 2013, the number of companies reporting on CSR had increased to 73, under which 46 were using the GRI guidelines. A content analysis of the CSR reports suggests that two-thirds of the reporting companies had 'a strategy in place to manage the CR [corporate responsibility] agenda of the company'.[85] The analysis also shows than an increasing number of companies had integrated environmental sustainability as a core area of CSR, which they associated with 'resource related risks and opportunities which have a direct linkage to business continuity, operational costs and increased revenues'.[86] In

---

[82] See, for instance, Sharma (2011), Sundar (2013), and Dhanesh (2015).

[83] Data compiled from http://www.iso.org/iso/home/standards/certification/iso-survey. htm?certificate=ISO%2014001&countrycode=IN#countrypick (accessed on 25 November 2016) and https://isotc.iso.org/livelink/livelink?func=ll&objId=1880877 2&objAction=browse&viewType=1 (accessed on 7 February 2019).

[84] KPMG (2011, 7).

[85] KPMG (2013, 19).

[86] KPMG (2013, 18).

2016, at least partly as a result of new regulatory structures (see later), all of the top 100 companies by market capital were reporting on CSR, and 97 of them had a more or less detailed CSR policy available in the public domain.[87]

The growing adoption of CSR-related organizational structures and practices by companies operating in India participates in a wider institutionalization process, which involves a variety of CSR-promoting actors and initiatives. Among them, India's three apex chambers of commerce and industry (FICCI, CII, and, to a lesser degree, ASSOCHAM) have been particularly active. In 1995, FICCI established the Socio-Economic Development Foundation 'to provide an institutional base to the social sector activities of the corporate sector and to promote corporate social responsibility'.[88] In 1999, it started organizing annual CSR awards to identify leading companies in CSR and encourage others to follow the lead. In 2010, in partnership with the Aditya Birla group, FICCI further strengthened its involvement by creating a CSR Centre for Excellence, whose formal goal is to 'incubate, nurture and accelerate a paradigm of sustainable and inclusive CSR in India and thereby raising the Human Development Index through poverty alleviation'.[89]

As for Tata's discourse, FICCI depicts CSR as a movement which is rooted in the country's philanthropic tradition, but which extends beyond that to encompass business-related contributions to development. For instance, its report entitled *Shaping India's Development Story: CSR Ideology and Investment* narrates how 'the tradition of charitable donations by Private Companies since generations is now coupled with companies like Tata Consultancy Services, Unilever and ITC Hotels, among many others, who have paved the way for strategic social investments (using core competencies) to solve social ills'.[90] Doing so allows FICCI to discursively blend societal progress and business goals, as CSR is also 'a strategic source of competitive advantage and to a lesser extent … a means to manage regulatory impacts and increase market visibility'.[91]

The involvement of FICCI is not an isolated case, as the CII has conducted similar activities. In 2006, the CII partnered with the Indian Tobacco Company (ITC) to create a Centre of Excellence for Sustainable Development.

---

[87] KPMG (2017b).

[88] See http://www.ficci-sedf.org/about-us.html (accessed on 19 May 2016).

[89] Inaugural address by the director, Rajashree Birla: http://www.ficci.com/events/20306/ISP/rajashree.pdf (accessed on 12 May 2011).

[90] FICCI (2014, 4).

[91] FICCI (2014, 5).

One goal of this centre is to help companies move forward from traditional philanthropic engagement to CSR and sustainability. As an executive of this centre explained:

> We try to convince industries that CSR is not philanthropy. It is rather about stakeholder management, integration of the stakeholders' concerns in their business. CSR is about creating inclusive growth, creating livelihood opportunities for the people on the long run, and not only small scaled actions on the short run.[92]

To concretize this agenda, the CII has carried out multiple activities such as the design of a sustainability framework, which is used in training sessions to guide companies in the adoption of CSR management and reporting systems, or the distribution of CSR awards meant to reward 'good companies' and inculcate 'good practices'. Publications and conferences where the promises of CSR are highlighted and illustrated with 'success stories' also contribute to promoting a shift from philanthropy to CSR, as well as to displaying the virtues of companies in front of invited high-level politicians and journalists. The title of a report published jointly by the CII and the World Wildlife Fund (WWF) in 2008 sums up the key message that the CII wants to spread: 'Indian Companies with Solutions that the World Needs: Sustainability as a Driver for Innovation and Profit'.[93]

In fact, as in the case of FICCI, the CII conceives of CSR as a useful resource to pursue its core mission, which is to promote the collective interests of its members and of India's business community at large. CSR is primarily meant to reduce the likelihood of conflicts where activists and political actors help village or tribal communities oppose large industrial investment projects, as such conflicts hurt both targeted companies and the overall social legitimacy of India's business community. As explained by an executive of the Centre of Excellence for Sustainability:

> The danger is that companies seek for one-shot solutions. They have one problem like in Nandigram, and they respond. Our purpose is to make them learn out of Nandigram so they integrate new parameters in their strategy.[94]

Besides business associations, non-profit organizations such as Partners in Change (PiC), Business & Community Foundation (BCF), the Centre for

---

[92] Interview conducted by the author, 25 July 2007.
[93] CII and WWF (2008).
[94] Interview conducted by the author, 25 July 2007.

Social Markets (CMS), or The Energy and Resources Institute (TERI) are also active promoters of CSR. Unlike other NGOs, which either 'partner' with companies to implement the latter's CSR programmes or which reject CSR altogether as 'window-dressing' and 'green washing', these non-profit promoters of CSR conceive of it as an opportunity to induce change in the behaviour of companies. BCF, for instance, was created in 1998 as a membership-based organization with the support of the British International Business Leaders Forum. Like other CSR promoters, BCF advocates for a vision of CSR that has absorbed philanthropy, but that also covers the introduction of development-related goals in the design of core business processes. For instance, besides numerous projects involving companies in the provision of services such as education and health to disadvantaged social groups (for example, the disabled, slum dwellers, indigenous communities), BCF supports business-related practices such as providing employment opportunities to disabled persons. BCF also cooperates with other protagonists of CSR, for instance, by assisting FICCI in the evaluation of candidates to its annual CSR awards or by providing expertise in public policy-making processes. While BCF mixes up 'philanthropic' redistributive practices and core business-related issues, its position on CSR draws a difference between the two. As a leader of BCF emphasized:

> We do not want money from Vedanta or from tobacco companies, for instance. We think that CSR should be about 'do no harm', not about charity. These companies violate human rights, environmental justice, and labour laws on a massive scale. Charity will not do much about that.[95]

The case of PiC, which was founded in 1995 with the support of the international NGO ActionAid, provides another example of how civil society organizations seize CSR to try to change the practices of companies. The manifold activities of PiC include, inter alia, the production and diffusion of CSR-related knowledge, participation in national and international expert meetings, and collaborations with companies to upgrade their CSR policies. These activities are based on a human rights–based approach of CSR. As the founding director and former chief executive of PiC explained:

> My point is to say 'How can CSR serve to create rights?' Because rights are a substantial thing, which people can lean on, and you have multiple Human

---

[95] Interview conducted by the author, 13 September 2014.

Rights which exist, which have been formulated. These are areas where interesting things can be done. Human Rights can be used to create a common language with an international scope between governments, companies and civil society organizations, a language which is clear and specific. Not these charity and philanthropy things, which are not bad as such, but beside the point.[96]

Since the mid-2000s, India's government has joined the bandwagon of CSR promoters by adopting several public policies (see Chapter 6).[97] The government's first intervention occurred in 2007 during the General Assembly of the CII. At this occasion, the then prime minister, Manmohan Singh, presented a 10-point Social Charter that urges companies 'to be a partner in making ours a more humane and just society'.[98] Soon after, the government launched another CSR policy initiative with the technical assistance of the German international cooperation agency Gesellschaft für Internationale Zusammenarbeit (GIZ). A main objective of this initiative was to develop national CSR guidelines that would strengthen and structure the CSR practices of companies operating in India. A multi-stakeholder committee was constituted in 2008 to elaborate the guidelines, and the central Ministry for Corporate Affairs issued the National Voluntary Guidelines for the Social, Environmental and Economic Responsibility of Business (NVGs) in 2011. In 2012, the financial market regulator Securities and Exchange Board of India (SEBI) issued a circular that builds on these guidelines to make CSR reporting mandatory for India's 100 largest listed companies by market capitalization. In 2013, the new Companies Act marked a further milestone in the state's efforts to promote CSR. According to the section 135 of this act, all companies above a certain financial size must spend 2 per cent of their net profit to fund non-business CSR activities.[99]

---

[96] Interview conducted by the author, 11 September 2014.

[97] The following presentation of India's CSR public policies focuses on those which target the private sector. The government has also introduced CSR and sustainability policies in 2010 for the Central Public Sector Enterprises, which were revised and integrated in 2013.

[98] A full transcript of the discourse of Manmohan Singh can be found here: http://archivepmo.nic.in/drmanmohansingh/speech-details.php?nodeid=529 (accessed on 11 September 2017).

[99] Section 135 of the Companies Act applies to companies having a net worth of ₹5 billion or more, a turnover of ₹10 billion or more, or a net profit of ₹50 million or more.

Finally, the past two decades have been marked by an increasing presence of international organizations in the field of CSR in India. The cases of BCF, PiC, and the NVGs mentioned here illustrate the role of foreign organizations in promoting CSR in India by supporting domestic NGOs and policy processes. In addition, a number of foreign CSR-related organizations have set up agencies in India. For instance, a Global Compact Network India (GCNI) was created in 2003, and the Global Reporting Initiative opened an Indian Focal Point in the offices of the Bureau of Indian Standards in 2010. Besides, a number of leading foreign companies specialized in business consultancy and auditing, such as Ernst & Young, KPMG, and PricewaterhouseCoopers, have actively promoted CSR as part of a commercial strategy to develop the Indian market for CSR-related business services.

Functional differentiation and the intermediary institution 'CSR': First results from the Indian case

A first series of findings can be formulated on the basis of the macro-sociological material presented so far. This analysis is guided by the hypotheses outlined in the first two chapters: the CSR phenomenon is envisaged as an intermediary institution, which has emerged historically in reaction to structural challenges arising from processes of functional differentiation, and which is set to change patterns of economic responsiveness – the observation and processing of social problems by the economy.

The gradual process of functional differentiation of India's economy, which can be traced back to the early nineteenth century, consists in three interrelated changes. First, while a variety of metallic and non-metallic currencies used to circulate in the subcontinent, the monetary policies of the colonial authorities and the development of a banking system encouraged the formation of *a unified monetary system*. By 1935, India was using the Indian rupee as a single currency, and the Reserve Bank of India was acting as a central bank that controlled monetary supply. The development of a unified monetary system facilitated a second structural change, which is the development and integration of *price-making markets*. While the multifunctional and ritualized *jajmani* system remained operative in a part of the economy, selling and buying commodities on the market became the new norm of economic life. Monetization and marketization are related to a third structural change, namely the development of *modern capitalist firms*. Caste-based division of labour did not stop entirely, and the social structures of the caste system extended their reach in the functioning of India's corporate capitalism. Nonetheless, the acquisition of production factors by registered companies to produce commodities and sell them on markets for a profit became the dominant mode of production, as measured by its share in the GDP.

As outlined in Chapter 2, profit-making has ambivalent effects on the responsiveness of such a functionally differentiated economic system towards social problems. Profit-making motivates capital owners to invest in companies whose business activities respond to social needs. But the self-referential character of profit-making also constrains economic responsiveness: profit-driven economic processes do not observe social problems located in non-economic meaning contexts but the monetary significance of such problems in terms of cost/benefit calculations.

As the Indian case exemplifies, the role of profit-making in the economy – in monetary transactions – is partly conditioned by the institutional and cultural setting in which business organizations operate.[100] In the early period of India's corporate capitalism, in the late nineteenth and early twentieth centuries, corporate conduct was guided by a blend of economic objectives (in particular returns on investment) and non-economic objectives such as improving the social position of business families and their ethnic community, or advancing the nationalist cause of independence. After independence, socialist development policies based on massive public investments and an extensive political-administrative regulation of the private sector created a new institutional setting, in which profit-making also played a limited role. The amount and sectoral distribution of investments, the geographical location of production units, wages and working conditions, and the price of a number of commodities were determined less by profit-driven calculations based on market prices than by political-administrative decisions.

Since the early 1980s, institutional changes introduced as part of 'pro-business' economic development policies have gradually strengthened the role of profit-making in India's economic system. On the one hand, the organizational behaviour of the corporate sector – in particular large private companies – has become more tightly coupled with objectives and calculations of financial performance. On the other hand, the removal or softening of regulatory

---

[100] Unlike what is claimed by the standard economic theory of firms, companies are not profit-maximizing economic unites, but complex organizations whose contingent structures and decision-making processes are conditioned, inter alia, by their institutional and cultural environment. See, for instance, March (1962), Simon (1991), Seidl and Becker (2005), Chassagnon (2014), and Kühl (2018).

constraints imposed by the state has increased companies' operational autonomy vis-à-vis politically defined objectives of 'development'.

This new institutional configuration rests on the assumption that profit-driven economic processes have positive outcomes for the country's developmental prospects. By raising the profitability of investments, business-friendly development policies encourage profit-seeking companies to generate more productive investments, more infrastructure, more employment opportunities, more useful goods and services, more research and development, more tax revenues for the state, and so on. The benefits of such a galvanized economy are considered to extend much beyond capital accumulation, as the added value it generates can be used for a wide range of other purposes that amount to improving the quality of life of Indian citizens. This assumption, which finds support in indicators such as higher economic growth rates and rising per capita income, has become a *doxa* – an orthodoxy that conceives of itself as an unquestionable objective truth – in large parts of India's public sphere, including in mass media,[101] among elite groups from the upper and upper-middle classes, and among the aspiring middle class.[102]

However, this positive vision of profit-driven companies as the new agents of 'development' has also been increasingly contested by pundits, scholars, new social movements, and judicial actors. This counter-movement denounces structural tensions and conflicts between profit-making and competing development-related collective values and interests. 'Displacement, dispossession and environmental degradation' are envisaged in this counter-movement 'as structural components of development, representing an irreversible socioeconomic structure that favours the rich.'[103]

As it questions the pro-business *doxa* by describing harmful consequences of profit-driven 'development' processes, this counter-movement actually contributes to bringing these tensions and conflicts into existence in society: the opposition between profit-making and competing collective values and interests exists in social communication by being described (observed) as such. This social construction of tensions and conflicts occurs in various spheres of society. It is voiced by authoritative sources in scientific publications, as well as in opinion pieces that receive domestic and international media coverage. It occurs in the political system, from the organization of collective protests

---

[101] See Mushtaq and Baig (2016).

[102] See Chopra (2003).

[103] Banerjee-Guha (2013, 166).

at the grassroots level up to statements being formulated at the highest levels of public policy-making. It unfolds in legal proceedings and court decisions that participate in the production and enforcement of legal norms. And it participates in moral communication, in which some profit-driven commercial practices are condemned for being socially unfair, corrupt, predatory, scandalous, or irresponsible.

Increased functional differentiation and the related development of new tensions and conflicts between the economy and other spheres of society have created a propitious context for CSR to take foot and expand on the Indian subcontinent. Empirical properties of this concrete phenomenon match the defining criteria of intermediary institutions:

1. The genesis of CSR in India cannot be attributed to a single social system, as it involves multiple organizations (for example, companies, business associations, NGOs) and function systems (for example, politics, law, the economy, mass media, morality), which all mobilize CSR in relation to problems arising from the aforementioned tensions and conflicts. In this respect, CSR is both a complement and an alternative to the intervention of the state as a societal problem-solver and a regulator of inter-systemic interplays.

2. The inter-systemic dimension of CSR also characterizes its concrete manifestations, as the growing use of the CSR concept in the Indian context (re)produces a complex set of discursive constructs, organizational structures, inter-organizational collaborations, formalized private and public norms, as well as economic transactions, whose reach transects systemic boundaries.

3. This inter-systemic dimension of CSR does not mean, however, that the boundaries between the various spheres of society become porous or blurred. CSR rather resembles a 'hinge' that provides new possibilities for the articulation and coordination of different systemic logics, without mixing these logics together.

This macro-sociological investigation leaves one main research question unaddressed: *how does the intermediary institution CSR change economic responsiveness vis-à-vis problems arising from tensions between profit-making and competing collective values and interests?* Addressing this question requires a more detailed investigation of the CSR phenomenon and the changes it introduces in interplays between business organizations, the economic system, and other social systems such as politics.

Chapter 5

✠

CSR at Work

Economic Responsiveness through Risk Management

To grasp how CSR, conceived of as an intermediary institution, has emerged from and retroacted on the way society responds to tensions and conflicts between profit-driven economic processes and other spheres of society, studying companies seems to be an obvious area of investigation. Indeed, companies operate at the crossroads between the economy and other function systems, and the introduction of CSR in their organizational structures and processes can be expected to change economic responsiveness vis-à-vis problems located in other spheres of society.

Business organizations and the interplays between the economy and other spheres of society

In the framework of SST, companies as organizations constitute a specific kind of social system that operates on the basis of decisions.[1] Of course, organizations involve human participants in the communicative production of decisions. But decisions are not intentional acts of individual human decision-makers. Decisions consist in the combination of two selections: the selection of a set of alternatives and the selection of one of these alternatives as the 'decision'. As such, decisions constitute the building blocks of organizations, and organizations reproduce themselves by maintaining the self-referential and autopoietic process of decision-making. More concretely, once an initial

---

[1] See, for instance, Luhmann (2000), Bakken and Hernes (2003), and Seidl and Becker (2005).

decision has been taken to create an organization, this decision creates the conditions for further decisions to be taken – about the legal status of the organization, its name, its internal structure of positions and the related division of tasks, the recruitment of members, and so on. Each of these decisions keeps the organization going and creates the conditions for further decision-making.

In this framework, unlike function systems, organizations do not operate along a binary code such as paying/not paying (the economy), powerful/powerless (politics), legal/illegal (law), true/false (science), and so on. Their decisions are guided by 'decision premises' that reduce uncertainty by structuring and stabilizing the organization's decision-making processes.[2] For instance, a company's strategy, its internal policies, or its annual budget are premises that structure and orient – without determining – a multitude of other decisions. Similarly, personnel decisions about recruitment and assignment of tasks structure a multitude of further decisions regarding the internal division of labour. And decisions on communication channels, such as hierarchical chains of command, define which decisions are expected to be considered as premises for which decision-making situation.

This operational autonomy of organizations vis-à-vis society's function systems allows organizations to participate in multiple spheres of society. Companies can participate in politics (for example, lobbying, public-private partnerships), in science (for example, research and development), in law (for example, production of international law through contracts with sovereign states), in mass media (for example, press releases, for-profit media groups), in education (for example, provision of training in corporate universities), and, of course, in the economy (for example, investments, purchasing, sales), among others. Organizations are structurally coupled with function systems in certain ways. For instance, the organizational structures of a company are structurally coupled with legal norms (for example, corporate law, labour law), as well as with structures of the economic system (for example, price-making markets). Tribunals and other organizations of constitutional states are structurally coupled with the legal system. Universities are structurally coupled with the function systems of education and science. And so on. Nevertheless, function systems are located in the environment of organizations, and vice-versa.

---

[2] An important theoretical point here is that decision premises by no means determine subsequent decision-making. They are premises in the sense that their status as decision is not being questioned. But their loose coupling with subsequent decision-making is neither a logical nor a causal relationship: 'Decisions cannot be deduced from their premises, nor are premises the causes of decisions in a way that setting premises would imply a causal closure of the system' (Luhmann 2000, 223).

Companies conceive of the economy as part of their environment, which they observe by processing information on prices and payment options in their decision-making processes. Conversely, the economy observes companies' decisions by way of the impact of these decisions on prices and monetary flows.

The operational autonomy of companies vis-à-vis the economic system means that corporate conduct is not necessarily and exclusively guided by the value of profit-maximization.[3] Companies' decision-making processes can also take non-profit considerations into account, including concerns for collective values and interests such as the social prestige of the business family, the social welfare of the family's caste community, or political objectives of national sovereignty. Whenever taking non-profit considerations into account impacts companies' monetary operations, these considerations are also observed by the economic system. For instance, a decision in a company to forgo the profitable retrenchment of employees, out of concerns for labour welfare, is an instance where labour welfare is observed both by the organization's decision-making process and by the monetized economic system – as the payment of wages to these employees will be maintained.

It follows that the selective observation of non-profit collective values and interests in companies' decision-making processes can directly change the way these collective values and interests are observed by the economy. The more the payment decisions of a company are directed towards profit-making, the more the economy is directed towards itself, so that its responsiveness to social problems is mediated and filtered by cost–benefit calculations. Conversely, the more the payment decisions of a company can take non-profit concerns into account, the more the economy can be responsive to non-profit collective values and interests.

---

[3] The idea that shareholders *own* the company, and that companies are *by definition* profit-maximizing, is a stubborn *doxa* to be found even in systems theory, such as in Darnell Hilliard's claim that '[the] organizational type of the corporation comes into existence if, and only if, an organization observes the unit of its operative distinction decision/non-decision, i.e. organization/environment, with regard to *exploitation of business chances*, i.e. *profit-maximization*' (2005, 334). In fact, the corporation owns itself as a legal person. Shareholders only own contractual claims on a share of profit, as per corporate law and profit-sharing agreements. The pre-eminence of profit-maximization as a corporate objective is not a necessity but the result of contingent cultural, institutional, and organizational arrangements. This point has also been emphasized in a number of contributions to the theory of firms, such as in Chassagnon (2014), Ciepley (2013), Robé (2011), Veldman and Parker (2012), Williams and Zumbansen (2011), and Kühl (2018).

Building on this conceptual framework, the present chapter analyses at a concrete level how companies mobilize CSR in reaction to tensions and conflicts between profit-making and other competing collective values and interests, and how this changes patterns of economic responsiveness. This empirical analysis proceeds along the three-step framework outlined in the second chapter. The *first step* investigates the conditions under which the CSR concept is introduced in the organizational structures and processes of companies. We find that companies mobilize CSR in reaction to dynamics of contention which are spurred by companies' increasing focus on profit-making, and which endanger companies' business prospects. In a *second step*, the study analyses how companies exploit the potential provided by CSR. We find that companies use it as a tool for 'second-order observation'[4] to identify threats on their business prospects, to translate these threats in manageable parameters of economic risks, and to address these risks primarily according to profit-driven cost–benefit calculations. The *third step* of the analysis examines consequences of this use of CSR with regard to the respective role of the economy and other spheres of society in the observation and processing of social problems.

A case-based approach: Lafarge India and the globalization of the Indian cement industry

This analysis is based on the in-depth qualitative study of the case of Lafarge India, which at the time when the fieldwork was conducted (2007–2011) was the Indian subsidiary of the French multinational company Lafarge S.A. To assess the relevance of this case for the study of broader social structures and processes, three of its characteristics can be considered.

First, *changes in India's cement industry reflect quite accurately the historical evolution of India's corporate capitalism*, and the development of Lafarge India in the Indian market since 1999 participates directly in political-economic changes that occurred after the 'pro-business tilt' of the early 1980s.[5] Prior to this period, the Indian cement industry was heavily influenced by the country's interventionist regime. A few private cement manufacturers had already emerged during the inter-war period, such as the Associated Cement Company

---

[4] Luhmann (2012).

[5] Data on the evolution of India's cement industry is based on Bagchi (1972), Chakravarty (1989), Sarathy and Chakravarty (1998), and statistics from the Cement Manufacturers Association.

Ltd. (ACC), which involved Tata and other conglomerates, or Dalmia Cement, which was founded by the family group Dalmia Jain in 1935. But the cement sector picked up only after independence, thanks in particular to significant public investments. Production capacities grew from 5.02 metric tonnes per annum (mtpa) in 1955–1956 to 22.58 mtpa in 1978–1979, and about 44 per cent of this growth was generated by the state-owned Cement Corporation of India Ltd. (CCI). Besides public investments, the interventionist state imposed extensive regulations on private cement manufacturers. It used the licence–permit system to determine the volume and geographical location of private investments in fixed capital, as well as the volume of cement production. With the Cement Control Order of 1956, which was renewed on a regular basis afterwards, the state could also control the price and distribution of cement. And national tripartite negotiations in the Cement Wage Board led to agreements on wages and working conditions that were favourable to employees – including contract workers – in a context of mutual support between trade union federations and the central Ministry of Labour and Planning.

The decision of the central government in 1977 to support private investments in the cement sector by guaranteeing 12 per cent return on investments is part of the beginning of the 'pro-business tilt'. In 1982, the cement industry was partially deregulated. Prices and distribution were fully deregulated in 1989, and the end of licences and permits in 1991 completed the deregulation process. While the state divested from the CCI, which closed seven of its ten cement plants between 1996 and 1999, massive private investments propelled the country's production capacities from 31.8 mtpa in 1982 to 107.5 mtpa in 1999. In the 2000s, India's cement industry experienced a globalization process, as the world's leading multinational cement manufacturers invested massively in the subcontinent in a context of economic boom and promising rates of return[6]: the French Lafarge (1999) was followed by the Italian Italcementi (2001), the German Heidelberg Zement (2006), the Swiss Holcim (2007), and the Mexican Cemex (2010). The past two decades have also experienced a further rapid increase in cement production capacities, which reached about 425 mtpa in 2017.

As an executive of Lafarge India pointed out, this period of growing integration of India's cement industry with the world economy was associated with growing competition and related pressures on industrial performance:

---

[6] In the mid-2000s, the profit–turnover ratio of most cement companies operating in India was situated between 17 per cent and 25 per cent (CSE 2005).

If we want to compete with the other companies, we will certainly have to improve the productivity. Otherwise, we will not remain in the market. The increase in productivity is a continual process. You are required to manage in a cost-effective manner, in order to remain in the market. If you are not competing with others, you will have to close your business. This is the major requirement of the day. This is the need of the time.[7]

For subsidiaries of multinational companies, economic expectations from the mother company added to the pressure arising from domestic market competition. In the case of Lafarge India, its mother company, Lafarge S.A., had to ensure sufficient financial returns to satisfy expectations of institutional investors, who in 2008 were providing 89.6 per cent of the company's capital.[8] To do so, Lafarge formulated a series of 'Excellence Plans' that were intended to promote a business culture centred on financial results in its 2,000 factories, which in 2008 employed about 84,000 people in 79 countries. For instance, the Excellence Plan 2006–2008 set the aim to reduce production costs by 400 million euros, to generate 1.5 billion euro additional cash flow, and to generate at least 10 per cent return on invested capital. As a company falling under the scope of these programmatic 'decision premises', Lafarge India is a prime case to study how the growing integration of India's post-reform economy in global markets and production networks strengthened the role of profit-making as a guiding value of economic processes.

A second characteristic that makes Lafarge India a relevant case for the present study is *the significance of social and environmental problems related to cement production*. With regard to labour, the cement industry is rather labour-intensive. In the mid-2000s, it employed about 135,000 workers in India, with an average of about 1,000 workers per cement plant. But the rapid increase in production capacities over the past decades has had limited impact in terms of employment generation, as the mechanization of production processes has limited the need for labour. Moreover, cement companies have increasingly resorted to contract workers, who are formally employed – with or without a valid employment contract – by subcontractors and intermediaries who provide workforce to the cement manufacturers. In the mid-2000s, contract workers

---

[7] Interview conducted by the author, 24 November 2008.

[8] For more details on the growing pressures exerted by institutional investors on the management of Lafarge S.A. since the 1990s, see in particular the testimony of Lafarge's former CEO Bertrand Collomb (Collomb and Soupre 2003), as well as Djelic and Zarlowski (2005).

represented half of the workers in India's cement industry, and 57 per cent of Lafarge India's workforce.[9] As a deputy secretary of the trade union federation AITUC explained:

> Cement industry, originally, was a labour-oriented industry. Handling, moving, packing ... people were very involved. On account of automation and mechanization, the production increased and the employment went down.... Lots of outsourcing and subcontracting of the work has been done. The number of contract and casual workers has increased, and they are employed in many places. The second arbitration of the Cement Wage Board says that contract workers employed in cement plants and their packing plants must get wages equal to the permanent workers. But this is invariably violated by the cement employers. Wherever possible, they have introduced contract labour system, offloading lots of work. So the percentage of permanent workers is much less in the cement industry compared to the contract workers. Trade unions are affected also. But unfortunately, trade unions were not strong enough to fight it efficiently.[10]

Cement manufacturing is also related to social problems experienced by village communities located near limestone mines and cement plants. Limestone quarries and the installation of cement plants usually involve the acquisition of large tracts of land. Given the industry's need for limestone, plants are usually located in rural areas, where limestone can be extracted. This often creates conflicts between cement producers and villagers, whose economy partly depends on agricultural land that is diverted for industrial production. Once the cement plants are operational, neighbouring village communities are often confronted with a variety of other problems. For instance, women can experience growing insecurity because of the presence of hundreds of workers and truck drivers who do not belong to the communities and who sometimes indulge in inappropriate behaviour.

Neighbouring communities also face problems related to the local environmental impacts of cement production.[11] The emission of cement dust and noxious gas (for example, NO_x and SO_x) leads to a high prevalence of chronic respiratory diseases among the local population. Cement dust is also perceived as a cause for productivity losses in the fields located near the production units. The use of explosives to extract limestone is a further cause

---

[9] CSE (2005).

[10] Interview conducted by the author, 17 March 2009.

[11] See CSE (2005).

for concerns. Apart from noise pollution, explosions can decrease access to water by damaging groundwater tables and generate vibrations that can create cracks in the walls of houses and other buildings located in the surrounding area. Besides local environmental impacts, cement production is a major contributor to greenhouse gas emissions. The transformation of limestone into clinker, which is an intermediary product in the manufacturing process, generates CO_2 both directly and through the use of energy to heat up the kilns to a temperature of 1500°C. According to estimates, the cement industry accounts for about 5 per cent of anthropogenic emissions of CO_2.

Finally, the case of Lafarge India is relevant because it allows us to *observe interplays between global trends and Indian dynamics in the field of CSR*. Before it merged with the Swiss company Holcim in 2015, Lafarge S.A. was a leading company not only in terms of size – it ranked 390 on the Fortune 500 list of the world's largest companies in 2010 – but also in terms of its engagement in the field of CSR. According to a former CEO of the group, this engagement is rooted in the catholic paternalistic culture of the company's founders, as well as in the public-spirited ethos of the French engineers who built the company:

> These two foundations of our culture led Lafarge to always consider that as a company, it was meant to make money, of course, to create wealth, but also to contribute to the common good, which is not 'I participate in the invisible hand of the market so I contribute to the common good', but 'I do very concrete things for the common good'.[12]

In the wake of the Rio Earth Summit of 1992, Lafarge moved beyond paternalistic practices by positioning itself at the vanguard of CSR and sustainable development. In 1995, a Department for Sustainable Development was created at the headquarters. The same year, Lafarge became a member of the Word Business Council for Sustainable Development, and it subsequently participated in the latter's Cement Sustainability Initiative and the Energy Efficiency in Buildings project. Lafarge also adhered to the United Nation's Global Compact in 2003, and it developed partnerships with major NGOs such as CARE (provision of HIV/AIDS treatment to Lafarge's workers in African countries), the WWF (reduction of CO_2 emissions and biodiversity protection), and Habitat for Humanity (affordable housing programmes). As

---

[12] Interview conducted and translated from French to English by the author, 18 November 2009. For a historic account of Lafarge's paternalistic ethos and practices, see Dubois (1988).

per the requirements of the French law Nouvelles Régulations Économiques (New Economic Regulations), Lafarge has produced annual CSR reports since 2001. Since 2003, these reports have been reviewed by an internal 'stakeholder committee', and since 2008, they have followed the reporting guidelines of the Global Reporting Initiative. The CSR performances of Lafarge have also been audited by specialized firms such as Ernst & Young and Vigeo, and the company's shares have been listed on 'socially responsible' indexes such as FTSE4Good and DJSI STOXX.

In spite of this track record, Lafarge's Indian subsidiary only picked up on CSR in 2007, mostly as a result of local dynamics, constraints, and opportunities. The possibility to conduct field research on Lafarge India at that time allowed us to study in real time how Lafarge India mobilized CSR, and how the introduction of related organizational structures and practices changed the way the company observed and addressed tensions between profit-making and competing collective values and interests.

In terms of empirical coverage, the detailed study of Lafarge India focuses on two large cement plants that the company acquired from Indian companies in 1999 and 2001 respectively, and one cement plant project that it launched in 2006 (see Map 5.1). The first plant, which is located in the village Sonadih in the state of Chhattisgarh, was commissioned by Tata Steel in 1993. The second plant, which is located in the village Arasmeta in the same state, about 65 kilometres away from Sonadih, was commissioned by Raymond Cement in 1981. The cement plant project is located in the village Alsindi, in the Himalayan state of Himachal Pradesh. The study of the cement plants of Sonadih and Arasmeta shows how the acquisition by Lafarge India galvanized tensions and conflicts between profit-driven economic processes and competing collective values and interests. The study of the plant project in Alsindi, which was used by Lafarge India as a pilot project for the development of a pan-Indian CSR strategy, shows how CSR changed economic responsiveness by improving the organizational capacities of the company to observe and process the aforementioned tensions and conflicts as parameters of economic risks.

Articulating business and social welfare: the production of cement under Tata Steel and Raymond Cement

Producing cement involves a complex bundle of local social relations that develop within and around the industrial investments and production processes. In cement plants like Sonadih and Arasmeta, these social relations usually

Map 5.1 Cement plants and plant projects of Lafarge India Pvt. Ltd (2010)

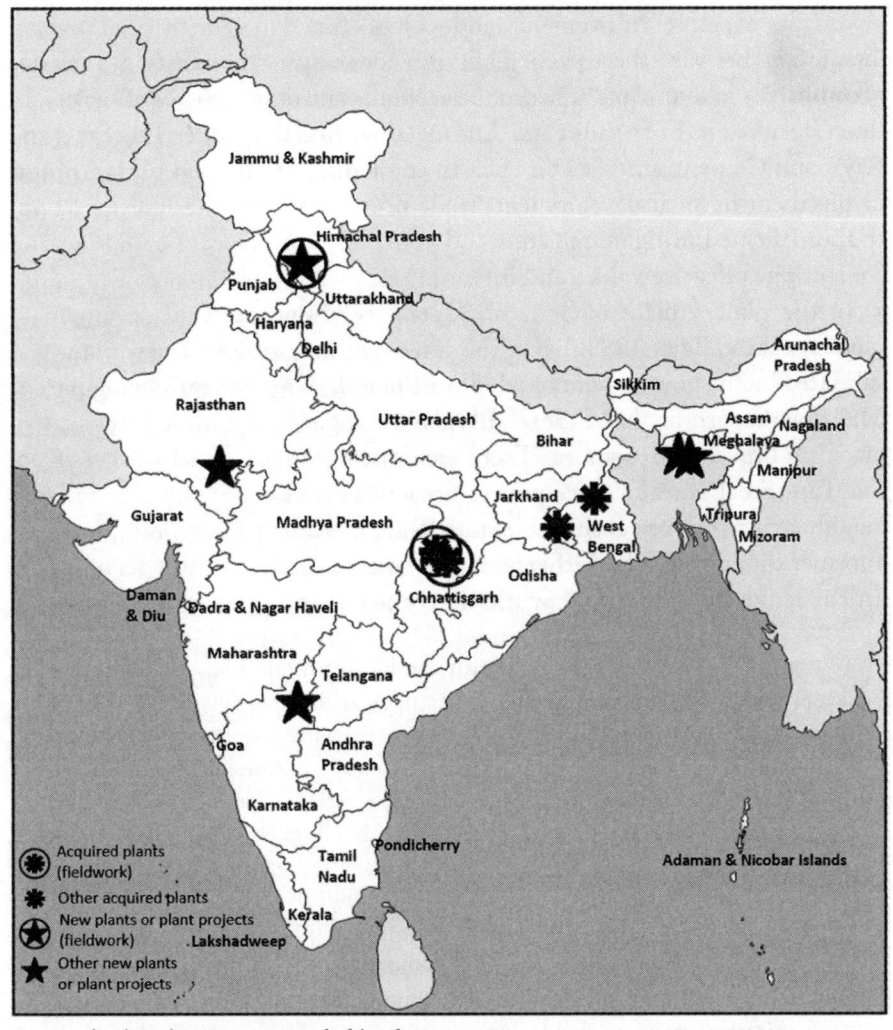

Source: Author, base map provided by d-maps.com.

Note: Map not to scale and does not represent authentic international boundaries.

involve the managers of the cement plants, permanent and contract workers, both internal and external trade union leaders, villagers residing near the limestone quarries and the plants, local bureaucrats and elected representatives, as well as politicians and bureaucrats from the regional state level. These persons are not just more or less rational autonomous actors. Their inclusion and participation are mediated by their roles in various groups and social systems such as families, caste communities, village communities, formal organizations, protest movements, and society's function systems. The study of interactions between these participants provides empirical insights into the role of companies in interplays between the economy and other spheres of society. In the cement plants of Sonadih and Arasmeta, we find that under Tata Steel and Raymond Cement, institutions such as companies' traditional philanthropic involvement in local development, trade unionism, and paternalistic labour relations helped mitigate tensions and conflicts between profit-making and competing collective values and interests.

In the cement plant of Sonadih, Tata Steel launched local development initiatives as early as 1988, when the project of investing in a new plant was validated by the government of Madhya Pradesh (Chhattisgarh being part of Madhya Pradesh at that time).[13] Besides geologists, who were in charge of mapping limestone resources, Tata Steel sent a team of social workers from the Tata Steel Rural Development Society (TSRDS) in the five villages neighbouring the project site – Sonadih, Raseda, Rasedi, Kafri, and Mead. As a former director of TSRDS explained, the core mission of this team was to articulate the industrial project with those who would be directly impacted by it:

> We were in charge of engaging with the local communities. Because, you know, just by announcing that a cement plant will come, you already have a social impact on those communities. So we were trying to understand the local people, to study the social and economic dynamics of those communities, to assess their situation and to identify their expectations. During the first year, we just talked with the villagers, explaining that Tata is coming, that it will be a different experience for them. We also took some villagers and village-heads to Jamshedpur and to other sites of Tata, so they could see what kind of things we were doing for rural communities.... Our approach was not to 'bribe' the local people, so as to get their land, like by providing some temples, some simple philanthropy which would have made them dependent upon us. Our objective was to create a long-term dialogue, to understand their needs.[14]

Relations between Tata Steel and local villagers were not always simple and cooperative, especially as far as land acquisition is concerned. According to the *sahr panch* – the elected head of the village council – of Raseda, Tata

---

[13] Chhattisgarh was carved out of Madhya Pradesh and constituted as a new regional state of India's federation in 2000. The city of Raipur was chosen as the capital of this new state.

[14] Interview conducted by the author, 17 December 2008.

Steel needed to acquire 809 hectares for the plant and the limestone mine. As part of the compensation package, Tata Steel promised one job for each land ownership account. But villagers recall that this promise was not always fulfilled, and that some of the promised positions were traded to people who had not lost any land.[15] Some villagers who did not get a job as compensation still regret that they sold – or were pushed to sell – their land to the company.[16]

After the cement plant started operating, neighbouring villagers also experienced adverse conditions created by local pollution and water shortage that they attribute to the presence of the plant:

> We have a lot of respiratory problems, everybody is coughing. Skin diseases also. Our clothes are dirty. The agriculture production is less. The water level of Rasedi is down.[17]

> All trees, all agriculture, all pounds are wasted. The water level is down. During the mining time, houses get cracked. Day to day the condition is bad.[18]

After the land was acquired, however, Tata Steel kept investing in the social welfare of the five neighbouring villages, which it formally 'adopted'. For instance, it constructed local infrastructure such as school buildings, dams,

---

[15] For instance, a villager from Rasedi recalled that

> there was cheating. I lost my land, but nobody from my household got any job. Some guy form Bihar or Bengal would come and claim it is his land, and he is now working in the plant. They were cheating inside the company. Tata Steel's officers and union leaders, and MLAs, all leaders were involved in this type of cheating.

Interview conducted by the author on 8 May 2008.

[16] The money that I got, it got eaten away very fast. When we were land owners, farmers, the life was much better. We were feeling proud. Now, we feel uneasy, and we don't have any proper place to eat and sit. We are uncomfortable, because we earn hardly 2,000 rupees a month, and it is not sufficient, even for our rice. We thought about a permanent position, with a payment of 8,000 to 10,000 rupees per month. This is what Tata promised to us. But now, all dreams have been washed away.

A broker came several times to me, again and again.... He said we should rather sell our land immediately, or we would not get anything. The villagers were afraid of losing everything. So they agreed with the broker.

Interviews conducted by the author with villagers in Rasedi, 5 April 2009.

[17] Interview conducted by the author with a villager of Rasedi, who is also a contract worker, 5 April 2009.

[18] Interview conducted by the author with the *sahr panch* of Kafri and Mead, which are two villages integrated into a single *panchayat* (the village-level administrative unit), 31 March 2009.

and ponds; it installed and maintained water pumps; it provided stitching classes for women; and it organized medical camps, local sport tournaments, and cultural events. Tata Steel also collaborated with public authorities in the local implementation of rural development programmes such as the Rajiv Gandhi Mission for Watershed Management, which was launched in 1994 by the government of Madhya Pradesh. To carry out these peripheral development activities, the local team of TSRDS had fourteen staff members, four vehicles, and significant funding sources. According to a former member of the team, 'there was no boundary to spend money.... It was like: "100 people will benefit from this programme? Ok. How much money do you need?" – "One lakh." – "Ok, but I want results"'.[19] Villagers also benefitted from informal arrangements such as the possibility to ride on the buses of the company. Combined with employment opportunities for a part of the local population, these various developmental benefits contributed to ensure rather peaceful relations between Tata Steel and local villagers.

Regarding labour relations, Tata Steel has long been considered one of India's most employee-friendly private companies. In spite of a progressive shift towards more efficient and flexible human resources management in the 1990s,[20] Tata Steel's paternalistic and socially progressive model also influenced labour relations in Sonadih, which at that time employed between 850 and 1,000 workers. According to a contract worker with long experience in the plant:

> During Tata, there was more freedom than now with Lafarge. There was little pressure while working in the company. Officers used to dialogue with us. They used to talk to us if there was any problem. In case of any necessity, they would fulfil our demand. Also, they were not talking about temporary or permanent. Everybody was permanent. I mean, temporary workers were made permanent progressively. At the time of Tata Steel, about 60 people were made permanent workers.[21]

In addition to wages and working conditions as per agreements with the Steel Wage Board, permanent workers received numerous benefits such as free healthcare for them and their family members, free education for their children, and subsidized housing and amenities. While contract workers had no access

---

[19] Interview conducted by the author, 28 November 2008.

[20] See, for instance, Singh (2008a).

[21] Interview conducted by the author, 7 May 2008.

to such benefits, they had certain rights such as medical treatments and access to the company's subsidized canteens. And an eight-day strike of contract workers in 1995 led Tata Steel to accept paying them a bonus of 8.33 per cent.

By and large, the case of Raymond Cement's plant in Arasmeta presents similar characteristics. After the plant project was launched in the late 1970s, Raymond Cement acquired large tracts of land in Arasmeta and the neighbouring villages of Sonsari, Parsada, and Amora. Some of the land was bought from wealthy and politically resourceful upper-caste landowners, who lived either in the villages or in nearby towns such as Bilaspur. Hundreds of socially weaker families, which owned and cultivated small parcels of land, were also affected. As for Tata Steel, Raymond Cement promised jobs as an alternative source of income for land losers, and it actually provided free training to hundreds of members of land-losing families at the Industrial Training Institute of Koni, about 35 kilometres away from Arasmeta. Most upper-caste landowners could secure good compensations, including permanent positions in the company. For instance, it is probably not by chance that the only inhabitant of Sonsari who got a position as manager in the plant belonged to a dominant land-owning family – the same person later became a *sahr panch* of Sonsari. But only some of the socially weaker families could get a job to make up for the loss of agricultural income. And in some cases, the positions they obtained were only as contract worker or as *badli* worker, that is, as replacement workers with an entitlement of a minimum of 13 days of work per month. As explained by a villager of Sonsari, whose family lost 3 acres of land without getting a job in return, those who lost their agricultural livelihood without getting a job had often little choice but to migrate or to send family members to work in faraway places.

As in the case of Sonadih, once production started, villagers living near the plant and quarries of Arasmeta were also exposed to environment-related problems. As a local doctor confirmed, cement dust has caused a high prevalence of respiratory diseases, and villagers complained that dust pollutes water bodies and reduces the volume and quality of yields. Regarding limestone mining, villagers complained about decreasing water levels in ponds, cracks in their houses, noise pollution that frightens grazing cattle, and cases of injuries caused by flying stones that the blasting of limestone throws outside the mining area.

In spite of these problems, villagers who were interviewed had a positive memory of Raymond Cement, in particular because it 'adopted' the villages nearby and conducted social welfare activities in the area. According to the *sahr panch* of Sonsari:

The relation was very good with Raymond. They would consider helping the villagers for many facilities. Raymond was providing help. We had regular meetings, weekly or twice a month. The rural development department of Raymond was also visiting the village regularly. Five-six people from this department were working with the villagers.... On 6th February 1982, they started the clinker production. After that, they started the development programmes. It was their own initiative. Raymond called the villagers and said: 'This is our budget, and this is our plan. Now, what do you want?'[22]

In 1993, after neighbouring villages provided support to a strike that lasted almost three months (see later), Raymond Cement reinforced its peripheral development activities. Apart from building local infrastructure (for example, school buildings, pathways, hand pumps, ponds), and providing health treatment through health camps and a weekly mobile dispensary, Raymond Cement distributed cattle to villagers and created a cooperative dairy farm. Other, less formalized arrangements existed as well. For instance, Raymond Cement would give villagers the wood it cut as part of the maintenance of trees in the plant and mining areas.

Regarding labour relations, the cement plant of Arasmeta employed between 1,500 and 2,000 workers. About 1,200 of them were permanent workers. These workers benefitted from the numerous labour rights introduced during the interventionist regime, as well as from additional benefits such as subsidized housing, free education for their children, healthcare for them and their families, and access to a subsidized cooperative food shop. Conversely, contract workers had lower wages and little benefits. As most contract workers were also villagers, who were thankful for the job and training provided by Raymond Cement, and who had little practice in matters of trade unionism, there was little open discontent in the 1980s. However, the situation changed towards the early 1990s, in a context of significant labour unrest in the Indian cement industry and in other sectors of the economy because of the economic reforms and related market fluctuations.

In the regional cement industry, contract workers from ACC's cement plant in Jamul, near the city of Bhilai, went on strike in 1989 under the leadership of the highly popular and powerful trade unionist and social activist Shankar Guha Niyogi from CMM, a left-wing political party and group of trade unions. In the early 1990s, CMM also organized strikes and hunger strikes for contract workers in the cement plant of Baloda Bazar, which at that time was

---

[22] Interview conducted by the author, 1 April 2009.

operated by Modi Cement. Tensions further built up following the murder of Shankar Guha Niyogi in September 1991,[23] the subsequent retrenchment of thousands of contract workers from various industries who had joined CMM, and the shooting of protesting workers by the police in 1992. Such a context was propitious for collective mobilization in Arasmeta. Under the leadership of Sambal Chakravarti, an external trade unionist from AITUC, permanent and contract workers started a strike of almost three months in 1993, which was supported logistically and economically by the surrounding villages. The key demand of the contract workers was the payment of bonuses and paid leaves. But according to a contract worker and plant-level trade union leader, this historic strike ended up benefitting only permanent workers, which at that time still constituted the majority of the workforce:

> After that, about 200 contract workers were kicked out of the factory. Also, permanent workers and contract workers got divided. The problem is that the trade union leaders, who had promised to speak for the contract workers, could not speak for the contract workers to the management. So the compromise had no benefits for them. The management said: 'Start the work again, and we will look after your problems'. So the work started again, but no benefits came.[24]

Lafarge India's focus on profit-making

When Lafarge India acquired the cement plants of Sonadih and Arasmeta, it inherited the social relations described earlier. However, in the years following the acquisition, the organizational focus of Lafarge India on short-term financial performance disrupted the prevailing local arrangements that Tata Steel and Raymond Cement had contributed to establish with their workers and the surrounding village communities. Profit-driven business expansion and all-round cost-cutting improved the economic efficiency of the two plants, and thereby the market position of the company in a context of growing

---

[23] It is suspected that several industrialists plotted and ordered the assassination of Shankar Guha Niyogi. But only the hired killer Paltan Mallah was sentenced first to death and then to life imprisonment, while the other incriminated persons – including two industrialists – were acquitted by the Supreme Court, mostly because of procedural matters.

[24] Interview conducted by the author, 3 April 2009.

competition.[25] Moreover, local plant managers were under strong pressure from their hierarchy to deliver good financial results as part of Lafarge's global Excellence Plan 2008.[26] But as it focused on its balance sheets, Lafarge India mostly overlooked the impact of its decisions both on the lives of local villagers and on the welfare of the workforce.

In Sonadih, after taking over the plant, Lafarge India invested in the modernization of the machinery as well as in the expansion of production capacities from 1.5 mtpa to 3 mtpa through the installation of a new production line. As part of the modernization of equipment, and in response to growing pressures of the State Pollution Control Board to bring cement dust emissions below 50 mg/m^3, Lafarge India also installed several pollution abatement devices – electrostatic precipitators and baghouse filters. But most of the interviewed villagers kept complaining about dust-related problems. As for the increase of production capacities and actual production levels, it increased the pressure on local natural resources, in particular land. For instance, to provide the plant with raw material, limestone mines needed to be expanded, and this created new tensions with villagers of Sonadih:

> Now, mines are 300 meters away from the village. Within 500 meters, it is illegal. Villagers were shouting their voice. But permanent employees came in the village, saying: 'Lafarge has manpower, it has money power also, and muscle power, so you don't do anything or it will not be good for you.'[27]

---

[25] In Chhattisgarh alone, between 2001 and 2009, extension of production capacities was carried out in five of the seven existing cement plants, and twenty-nine new cement plant projects were registered by the government of Chhattisgarh. As a regional executive of Lafarge India emphasized: 'Now, competition is more. Even in Chhattisgarh, for the last 3–4 years, competition has increased, because lots of new plants are coming. We are also doubling our capacities, other companies are expanding. So a lot of cement will flow in the market, and we have to be ready.' Interview conducted by the author, 26 November 2008.

[26] The shareholder care is very important in Lafarge. People who are investing their money, their interest is very much safeguarded. Because everything is conceived in terms of PVA [process value analysis – a strategic tool to identify and eliminate unnecessary expenses]. You must have heard about Excellence 2008. This is because people who have invested their money should also be given good returns.

Interview conducted by the author with an executive manager of the Sonadih cement plant, 24 November 2008.

[27] Interview conducted by the author with an elected member of the block-level council 'Janpad panchayat', 26 January 2011.

Moreover, to dispatch the growing volume of production in a more cost-effective way, Lafarge India decided to replace part of the transportation by truck with a 30-kilometre railway line that would connect the plant to the Nipania railway station. This railway line required the acquisition of 72 hectares across nine villages, including land owned by members of Scheduled Tribes, which can only be acquired for public purposes following strict procedures as per the Fifth Schedule of the Indian Constitution. In 2007, a group of affected villagers created an association to protest against the acquisition of their land by Lafarge India. This association filed a PIL in the High Court against Lafarge, which delayed the installation of the railway track by many years and increased the cost of land that Lafarge India still needed for its railway line project (see later).

While local villagers continued to be confronted with harmful consequences of the plant's operations after the acquisition by Lafarge India, they also experienced a significant decrease of resources allocated by the company for peripheral development. Out of the fourteen members of TSRDS posted by Tata Steel, only one was kept by Lafarge India, and the means at his disposal were reduced:

> Now, in Lafarge, only one CSR officer is recruited: myself. I will take care of civil construction jobs, I will take care of the accounts, I will take care of the supervising, I will take care of everything! I will be motivating the people, organizing the camps, everything.... Lafarge is saving a lot of money by not recruiting all those people. This is Lafarge's cost control. So when Lafarge asks me how I control the costs of CSR, I say I control it by having nobody working with me. This is one kind of cost control. Next, when we will go for a project or a programme, the community needs one lakh rupees. Lafarge knows that the actual beneficiaries will benefit from the entire one lakh, directly. But Lafarge says: 'No, don't go for one lakh. Please, make it 50,000 rupees'. The other 50,000 rupees are for cost control.[28]

As a result, the distribution of resources for local development became more selective, depending on the political power and overall attitude of the *sahr panch*. In the village of Raseda, for instance, the *sahr panch* organized a demonstration and a road block by villagers to ask for more benefits, and his political connections enabled him to mobilize support from the local Member of the Legislative Assembly (MLA). Other smaller protest actions

---

[28] Interview conducted by the author, 28 November 2008.

were organized subsequently, from time to time, as a way of maintaining the pressure. Simultaneously, the *sahr panch* developed good relations with the company, with which his brother was doing business as a supplier. This mix of political pressure and close ties helped Raseda secure the flow of resources granted by the company, which, for instance, provided a new school building, a boundary wall for the local primary school, a cow shed, and the deepening of ponds. Conversely, 'adopted' villages with less resourceful *sahr panch*s, such as Rasedi or Kafri and Mead, failed to avoid the shrinkage of developmental resources. As a villager from Rasedi complained:

> This is an adopted village, but there is no road, no electricity, no hand pumps, nothing. They gave hand pumps, but when one pump is broken, they do not repair it. Before Lafarge, we would have some chances for the repair by the company. But now, with Lafarge, there is no help and no chance. Now, with Lafarge, there are no benefits for villagers and local people.[29]

Similarly, the *sahr panch* of Kafri and Mead, which are mostly tribal villages, explained:

> There are some meetings with the company. Like two–three meetings took place since I became Sahr Panch [in 2004]. We asked for a cattle house, but they have never done it. Also a school building, but it was not fulfilled. We also asked for pathways construction and pond deepening, but they have never done it. We have meetings with the company, and they say 'Yes yes, we will do it'. But they never do it. Before, every Wednesday, a mobile dispensary was coming. But for the last seven years or so, it stopped coming.… The villagers here, they don't want to protest. I do not want to unite the villagers. If the villagers would get united, the company would shoot at sight. Villagers are afraid of the company. We are afraid of the company guards. You know, we are living in a very silent and peaceful way.… The company has a lot of guards. And they also have a lot of guards who are outsiders. Sometimes, outsiders are dominating the villagers. They are not answering in a proper way.[30]

Apart from reduced peripheral development activities, villagers were also confronted with a sharp decrease of employment opportunities in the plant. Part of this reduction is related to the modernization of equipment, which made the production process less labour-intensive, in particular with regard

---

[29] Interview conducted by the author, 5 April 2009.
[30] Interview conducted by the author, 31 March 2009.

to low-skilled labour. After the acquisition, Lafarge India also commissioned a study to optimize human resources. Following this study, more than 200 permanent and contract workers were terminated. As the *sahr panch* of Rasedi summed up:

> Under Tata Steel, we were more comfortable. The plant was small, and we could have some jobs. Now with Lafarge, they are expanding the plant more and more, but the manpower is less and less.[31]

In addition, villagers were frustrated by the decision of Lafarge India to avoid employing villagers for construction work related to the expansion of the plant. According to a villager of Rasedi, who is also an unrecognized trade union leader in the plant:

> Lafarge is constructing an extension of the cement plant, but the contractors are not taking any locals. There are many Bengali workers, who are preferred. This is because they work for 1,500 rupees per month. This is 60 to 70 rupees per day, plus meals. And they work 12 hours per day. They are so poor that they have no choice, they are working. Earlier on, 2 month ago, there were more than 3,000 people at work. Now, Bengalis have gone, and Biharis have come.[32]

Besides villagers, the acquisition of the Sonadih cement plant by Lafarge India also affected the conditions of permanent and contract workers. With regard to the reduction of the workforce mentioned above, Lafarge India used 'voluntary' retirement schemes that were not always voluntary.[33] As two interviews with contract workers suggest, the fact that about 150 contract workers lost their jobs also strengthened a sense of insecurity among at least a part of those who remained active:

> If I complain, I will be kicked out of the company. And it is the same for everyone. And if I raise my questions to the union, my name might come out. Then I will lose my job.

---

[31] Interview conducted by the author, 5 April 2009.

[32] Interview conducted by the author, 7 May 2008.

[33] As a contract worker explained, 'The management of Lafarge used to call those they want to retrench, and ask them to take VRS. They continuously called people like this. This happened only after Lafarge. In the process, 15 people were forced to take VRS.' Interview conducted by the author, 7 May 2008.

If I say anything, I will lose my job. So I don't say anything. I can lose my job without any prior notice. The company can kick us out very easily.[34]

A further consequence of Lafarge India's optimized human resources management has been heightened pressure on productivity. Thanks to the use of management tools based on individualized performance indicators, the plant managers tightened the control on those working in the plant:

> Relations with my employees are very good, very good…. This is a management style: how to extract the job from your worker. It doesn't mean you have to be always too polite. Be hard whenever things are not going well. But when things are going well, tap them on the shoulder: 'Hey, you are doing a very good job.' Punishments, awards, recognition, it should go parallel. If someone is not doing a good job, you should call him and say: 'Hey, don't you feel you should be penalized?' Your worker should say 'Yes', your trade union should say 'Yes'. If you don't punish this person for his wrong job, tomorrow he will become a rotten apple in your basket. The entire basket is going to be damaged, and you are going to close your plant. I always tell my workers: 'Look, you are not the only guy. You have family, you have children, you have parents. They are all dependent on you. So if you start becoming a rotten apple, you are going to damage the lives of all those who are dependent on you.'[35]

According to plant managers, the combination of this 'management style' with enhanced pressures on productivity have contributed to the good economic performances of the Sonadih cement plant, which exceeded productivity and profitability targets. But from the point of view of workers, this economic performance gain came at a cost:

> There is an overload of work. For example, at the conveyor belt, the work that was done by three to four persons is now done by one person. These three–four persons were looking at particular small areas. Suppose there is a length of 100 feet. Each worker had to look at 20 feet. Now, one person has to look at 100 feet. So it becomes difficult, and the worker has to run here and there. This is the problem.[36]

> Safety management is good in Lafarge, they do things for safety. There was not such a safety planning under Tata Steel. But, there were no accidents under

---

[34] Interviews conducted by the author, 7 May 2008.

[35] Interview conducted by the author, 24 November 2008.

[36] Interview conducted by the author, 8 May 2008.

Tata Steel either, because there was little work pressure. Under Lafarge, it is more working pressure, more accidents, and more safety management.... The management says: 'I want 10 tons production'. During Tata Steel, they would say: 'I want 10 tons production', but if we would do only eight tons, there was no problem. Now, if you do not deliver, you take a VRS and go out, back to your home, and you sit there. Also, the workforce was very high under Tata Steel, so the production was high but the workload was low. Now, the workforce is low, the production is high, so the workload is high.[37]

While permanent workers have experienced more pressure but also more reward, in particular in terms of wage hikes for semi-skilled and high-skilled employees, contract workers seem to have experienced mostly a plain degradation of their situation. In fact, unlike its predecessor, Lafarge India reinforced differences between permanent and contract workers. For instance, while under Tata Steel, both permanent and contract workers would get overtime with a double wage rate, Lafarge India transferred most overtime work to contract workers, without paying them more than the normal rate. In its deals with contractors, Lafarge India also reduced costs by excluding most contract workers from access to facilities such as canteens. As a trade union leader of contract workers explained:

When Tata Steel was there, it was good. Canteen was allowed to everybody. It was a canteen with reasonable rates: 3 rupees for breakfast, 5 rupees for a meal. There were no restrictions. After, when Lafarge refused to grant access to the canteen to contract workers, we filed a case against Lafarge. Only permanent workers and those chosen by the company could access the canteen.... Another issue is that there is a difference in the quality of food and the items served between permanent employees and contract workers. There is a difference. Permanent employees have the right to sit within the canteen, and they get all items: rotis, samosas.... For the contract workers, there is a limitation. They are only given selected items. Moreover, they pay the meals and have to sit outside the room.[38]

While collective action and complaints filed at the Labour Court by the trade union CITU have pushed Lafarge India to make concessions (see later), overall, the company refused to address most requests of contract workers on the ground that intermediary contractors are responsible for this, since

---

[37] Interview conducted by the author, 5 April 2009.
[38] Interview conducted by the author, 8 May 2008.

they are the contract workers' employers. As a consequence of this position, Lafarge India refused to include the union of contract workers at the table of negotiations between the management and labour representatives. And while the work of many contract workers was actually monitored by Lafarge India, contract workers had little chances of getting requests across:

> Here, with Lafarge, they don't want to listen to anything. If we go and talk to them, they say that whatever job they gave, we have to do it or get out. This is why I hate them.[39]

By and large, the study of the Arasmeta cement plant confirmed what was observed in the case of Sonadih. In spite of investments in new equipment, including pollution abatement devices, villagers continued to report problems related to cement dust. While the use of a more efficient controlled blasting technology in the mines reduced noise pollution and vibrations, and put an end to the problem of flying stones, resource extraction and more selective mining to optimize the quality–cost ratio of limestone created new conflicts with villagers. For instance, according to the *sahr panch* of Arasmeta, the mining area kept being expanded towards the village under Lafarge India, to reach 150 metres from the village. As part of this expansion process, around 2006, Lafarge India claimed three parcels of land amounting to 46 hectares, on which Raymond Cement had obtained a mining right that it never used. As one of the parcels was home to sixteen households, and the other parcels were used by villagers for cultivation, villagers protested vehemently and blocked bulldozers that had been sent to destroy the crop. In an interview, one affected villager also mentioned threats formulated by middle-men, according to whom the company would send bulldozers and destroy the houses at night, whatever and whoever was in them. While the Revenue Court gave a judgment in favour of the villagers, in 2008, the High Court of Chhattisgarh overturned the judgment in favour of Lafarge India.

With regard to peripheral development in adopted villages, as in Sonadih, Lafarge India mostly discontinued the involvement of its predecessor in this domain. In the words of the *sahr panch* of Sonsari:

> Raymond used to talk with the people, to try to solve the people's problems. Raymond constructed a school building, for example. An approach road was

---

[39] Interview conducted by the author, 7 May 2008.

constructed, a village pond was constructed, a village temple also. But nothing was done by Lafarge.... Lafarge stopped all the programmes.[40]

Local bureaucrats such as the sub-divisional magistrate and the *tehsildar*,[41] as well as the *sahr panch*s and villagers of the three other adopted villages, gave similar statements, emphasizing, for instance, that Raymond Cement was doing '99 per cent' while Lafarge India was doing just '1 per cent' for villagers. In fact, Lafarge India conducted a few activities in the villages. In particular, while it stopped the mobile dispensary that was much appreciated by villagers, it constructed two small dispensaries in Arasmeta and in Parsada, and paid a doctor to provide free consultations there two hours once a week. But further investigations revealed that the doctor preferred to send a medical student rather than to come himself. This student would not come on a regular basis. When we met him in one of the shabby dispensaries, which had broken chairs and many cobwebs but no medical equipment, the medical student complained that he had only a canister of cough syrup to treat villagers, who also suffer from other illnesses than the widespread respiratory diseases caused by local industrial pollution.

Villagers also experienced a significant reduction in employment opportunities, as Lafarge India reduced the manpower in the plant. After the acquisition, the company made extensive use of VRS and reduced the number of permanent workers from about 1,200 to about 400. According to many villagers, at least part of these VRS were 'forceful'. Some contract workers also lost their jobs. But most contract-based jobs were maintained, as the plant management externalized non-core activities to lower production costs:

> Lots of work has been uploaded to contractors – mostly the non-core activities. The core activities are operational and some maintenance activities. Those we would not like to outsource, because it would obviously impact the quality of the product.... What we have offloaded are mostly the non-core activities, like housekeeping, canteen services, basically mostly the service parts. All those things have been offloaded, also because it is a demand of the time. Every other company is doing the same, and you can't survive without that. You can't have so much liability with you, which you cannot take care of.

---

[40] Interview conducted by the author, 1 April 2009.

[41] The *tehsildar* and the sub-divisional magistrate are local civil servants who are attached to the Revenue Department, which also manages land-related affairs. They combine executive and judicial functions, and are the main representatives of the state at the *tehsil* and the sub-divisional levels.

… Contractors can better control the people. So we need only to control the contractors, in terms of timing, productivity. We set contracts defining the means and limits of the work that should be executed by a contractor. We negotiate with the contractor for the cost, for the manpower, for the timeline. He has to complete a certain amount of tasks within a particular timeline, and if he doesn't do that, we can penalize him. There are clauses in the work order, saying that we can deduct this amount. We can also stop awarding him other contracts if he is not efficient or proficient. So we have that sort of flexibility with us. We can obviously keep on changing contractors, and if we don't like one, we can take another one. In case of a permanent liability, or a permanent employment, you cannot do so.[42]

With regard to the 135 *badli* workers who got this position as compensation for the loss of land, while Raymond Cement used to give them more than fourteen days of work per month, Lafarge India only provided eight to ten days of work. The resulting loss of income incited about twenty *badli* workers to stop coming every day at the factory gate to check if their services were required. But as a consequence, Lafarge India terminated their employment on the ground of 'absenteeism'.

The reduction of the workforce not only affected villagers and other individuals who lost their source of income but also impacted those who continued to work for Lafarge India and its contractors. While some categories of permanent workers benefitted from increased salaries, and while overall working conditions improved, pressures on productivity increased significantly:

Since Lafarge has taken over the plant, over 1,000 people have been retrenched. And the production has increased. Before, a staff of 10 people had to carry out a certain work. Now, the work is more, but the staff has been reduced to three.

There is a measure taken by the company, which is called KPI [key performance indicators]. The full meaning of KPI I don't know. It is linked to productivity. It came three–four years ago. They ask to increase the KPI level. It means the company wants more production and better quality for less costs. The productivity will increase only by workers, on the worker's expense. But the company's management doesn't recognize the extra efforts put by the workers.[43]

---

[42] Interview conducted by the author with a human resources manager at the Arasmeta cement plant, 3 December 2008.

[43] Interviews conducted by the author with permanent workers, 6 May 2008.

While such pressure generated palpable dissatisfaction among the workforce, the threat of forced VRS and the insecure position of contract workers led most workers to comply. In the packing unit, for instance, a contractor asked the workers to forgo a fifteen-minute breakfast break. Three workers refused, and they were retrenched on this ground. After filing a case at the Labour Court, two of them were taken back on the condition that they accept in written not to take a break. According to a plant-level trade union leader, a further condition was that they leave the contract workers' union – which is affiliated to AITUC. Similar pressures were allegedly exerted on other workers, and in the end, 250 of the 600 contract workers employed in Arasmeta left the union for fear of being dismissed in the future.

Taken together, the changes that occurred after the acquisition of the Sonadih and Arasmeta cement plants by Lafarge India indicate a stronger focus of the company on the self-referential economic objective of profit-making. This does not mean that the entire organization was solely and flawlessly directed towards this objective. However, when compared with its predecessors, Lafarge India operated through decision-making processes that were guided more predominantly by profit-driven cost–benefit calculations. While this increased the sensitivity of the organization to opportunities of improving capital accumulation, it blunted the organization's ability to observe and process how its decisions were being observed and experienced by others. For the company, reducing expenses related to the peripheral development of village communities seemed a logical decision to improve its financial bottom line, as peripheral development has little to do with the core business of producing and selling cement for a profit. The meaning of this decision for most villagers, who felt that Lafarge India was impacting their living conditions and life chances negatively, seemed irrelevant for the company. Similarly, rationalizing the workforce was a logical decision to take so as to improve productivity ratios. But what this meant for workers seemed to have little relevance in terms of profit-driven decision-making.

Politics of contention and Lafarge India's growing exposure to discontent

In their direct relationship with the company, most villagers and workers were not in a position to force the company to take their concerns into account. However, the collective frustration and discontent generated by Lafarge India's focus on profit-making created a situation that more resourceful actors – in particular political actors and left-wing trade unions – could leverage in *their* respective relationship with the company. While most local and regional political actors had a supportive stance towards Lafarge India, which provided them with various economic benefits, collective discontent created opportunities for them to exert pressure on the company in a way that threatened the latter's business prospects.

At the regional state level, since its creation in 2000, the government of Chhattisgarh has pursued an aggressive industrial policy meant to attract and retain investors on its territory. Boosting the extractive industry in mineral-rich – and conflict-laden – areas of the state was an official priority in the 2000s.[44] More generally, the government was keen on boosting economic growth, tax incomes, and employment generation by acting as an 'investor friendly administration'.[45] However, notwithstanding this pro-business political orientation, the supportive behaviour of the regional state did not always come for free, as some bureaucrats traded their support for money. In the words of an executive of Lafarge India:

> Other companies, they pay money to them [civil servants]. Indian culture is there. If you have a work, if a paper needs to be signed … you pay some money. But they know that Tata people, and Lafarge people, they never pay. Those companies are working transparently. But this is a problem also.… The senior officer, of course, he always prefers the other companies, because they are giving some money. So their work will be done quickly, and my work will be delayed.… Somewhere, you have to compromise. At the lower level, the people know me. So when I come, the file is prepared, it is there. But after, at the senior level, they will say: 'Yes, the file is there, don't worry, I will do it.' They will fool me. But the work of other companies is finished, they have

---

[44] Parts of Chhattisgarh where the most valuable mineral resources are located are also in the 'red corridor', where the government-supported mining industry relates in complex ways with the Naxalite guerrilla and counter-insurgency para-military operations, expropriation and forceful displacements of indigenous groups, and the infamous government-sponsored 'self-defence' movement Salwa Judum ('purification hunt'), as part of which multiple human rights abuses were committed allegedly to serve the interests of the mining industry. This context provides ample indications of the extent of the regional government's support to certain industrial interest groups. But as Lafarge India's cement plants were located outside these areas, the present argument does not need further elaborations on this element of context. For more information, see, for instance, Chakravarti (2008) and Miklian (2009, 2012).

[45] See, for instance, the Industrial Policy 2004–2009 of Chhattisgarh.

gone. Here, everybody is corrupted. Particularly the government, it is very corrupted. So for me, who is sitting there, it is very, very, very critical.[46]

According to a regional political actor – but such unsubstantiated allegation must be taken carefully – Lafarge India might not be completely insulated from such practices, which are not only a constraint for companies, but also a means to secure business-friendly political and administrative decisions:

> What Lafarge is doing, there are several types of corruption. What Indian companies do, they bribe the people from down till up. What Lafarge is doing is to bribe only people at the top. And they are bribing the government machinery, meaning local police stations, local government officers, the District Commissioner, the Sub-Divisional Magistrate, the Member of Legislative Assembly, be it Ganesh Shankar Vajpayee – the Congress MLA in Sonadih – or Chakran Dewangan – the BJP MLA in Arasmeta.... One rupee per bag is the money that the Chief Minister gets from Lafarge. Say they produce 50,000 bags in a day, 50,000 rupees is what the Chief Minister gets. I will tell you how it works. They cannot give it directly, so they use their own dealers. Cement is manufactured and distributed to the local dealers. Once they give it to the dealer, they give a margin to him, 2 or 3 rupees. But less is given to the dealer. The bill is 174 rupees to the dealer, but actually, what he gets is 172 or 171 rupees. And this extra margin of 2 or 3 rupees is being passed to the dealer, and from the dealer, it is passed to someone else. Corruption money is routed through the dealer.[47]

Besides bribes, public authorities also expected companies such as Lafarge India to contribute resources to the provision of public goods. This includes general expectations, such as employing at least 50 per cent people from Chhattisgarh, who also constitute the relevant electorate for local and regional politicians, or conducting peripheral development activities in villages surrounding production units. These expectations were expressed in interviews at every level of the administration, from Chhattisgarh's minister of commerce and industry down to the *tehsildar*. But expectations of public authorities also include one-time contributions such as providing relief to victims of a catastrophe or planting and maintaining trees along defined sections of roads as part of the chief minister's 'Green Chhattisgarh' initiative.

---

[46] Interview conducted by the author, undisclosed date due to sensitive material.
[47] Interview conducted by the author, undisclosed date due to sensitive material.

Political parties – in particular the Congress and the BJP – were also rather supportive to companies. But political support also came at a cost. During election campaigns, for instance, candidates and their parties asked companies such as Lafarge India for material support in the form of funding or the provision of cars to move around in the constituency. Once in power, elected representatives kept asking companies for resources that they could distribute to voters as part of their clientelistic politics. In the words of an executive of Lafarge India:

> Plenty of demands are coming. MLAs, they are the most problematic people. They belong to different parties. Congress, BJP .... So who will win the election, we don't know. Accordingly, they will create problems. So many parties are there. And they are asking so many things: they want a vehicle, support for their election campaign ... so many things.... Also, when land acquisition takes place, a lot of political interference is there. Political parties will come; they want to take advantage of it.... The political parties, we cannot entertain them, because they are headache people. They are problem creators. So always, I try to keep those parties away. They always demand. They want a vehicle, they want money, etc. So we cannot give all this. I have a good rapport with the people, so I make them understand: 'You see, the company is not supporting any political party. We never entertain any political party. So why are you losing your time, and my time?'[48]

In such a context, the discontent created among villagers and workers by Lafarge India's focus on profit-making was a useful resource that various political actors nurtured and leveraged, both to extract personal benefits and/ or to access, to maintain, or to exert political power. In Sonadih, for instance, an MLA who also worked as a contractor to transport cement by trucks from the plant to the Nipania railway station saw her business threatened by Lafarge India's railway line project. In 2007, she bought some of the land required for the project, and to increase her bargaining position, she encouraged tribal landowners to challenge land acquisition by filing a PIL in the High Court. This move, which meant higher land prices and costly delays of several years for Lafarge India, pushed the company to seek the support of the regional government, which it obtained – maybe not for free. In 2010, the High Court decided in favour of Lafarge India. In an interview, a lawyer involved in the case suggested off the record that political pressures from the government were likely to have played a role in this judgment. In any case, Lafarge India and

---

[48] Interview conducted by the author, 26 November 2008.

the MLA came to an agreement, as suggested by the written endorsement of Lafarge India's CSR activities in Sonadih by the same MLA one year later.

In the case of Arasmeta, local discontent started being politicized by the *sahr panch*s of the four adopted villages towards 2005. In reaction to the sharp decrease in employment opportunities and peripheral development activities, the *sahr panch*s joined hands and wrote several letters of complaints to various public authorities, including the regional Ministry of Health, which asked the district collector to look into the matter. A series of letter exchanges and unfulfilled promises by Lafarge India followed. Between 2006 and 2008, several demonstrations and road blocks were organized by the *sahr panch*s to increase pressure on the company. But these protests yielded little results. Recalling a protest action conducted in January 2008, which followed a letter sent by the villagers to Lafarge's CEO, the *sahr panch* of Arasmeta explained:

> We blocked the trucks on the main road. But the upper management level does not do anything for us. I guess they don't know what Lafarge is doing in Chhattisgarh. The District Collector was not there. There was only the police, the *tehsildar* and the SDM [Sub-Divisional Magistrate].

> The *tehsildar* told us to come with him, he told we would go together to the company and he would sort out this problem. But Lafarge just gave some empty promises. The SDM told me to leave the strike. He told me 'Leave the strike. I will talk to Lafarge, pressurize them, so they will do something.' But the SDM didn't do anything, and Lafarge didn't do anything either. The police officer was shouting: 'You have some complaints, but I have orders from the upper level to register a FIR [First Information Report] against you, so you leave it!' I replied: 'You do your job, and I will do my job.' At the end, the police did not register any FIR.[49]

While local mobilizations failed to induce immediate change, they did not go unnoticed. In 2006–2007, they were identified by an activist from the NGO Tribal Welfare Society (TWS), who had started gathering information on social and environmental issues related to the cement industry in Chhattisgarh. In collaboration with other regional, national, and international civil society actors, including the CMM, the work of this activist focused on another conflict-ridden cement plant of the region, which led to a critical report on the Swiss company Holcim and the company being selected for the famous

---

[49] Interview conducted by the author, 1 April 2009.

Public Eye Swiss Award 2008 for its 'irresponsible' behaviour in India.[50] But the activist of TWS also intervened in support of the villagers and workers of the Arasmeta cement plant, for instance, by writing a letter to the governor of Chhattisgarh and the district collector to list perceived misdeeds of the company and ask for political intervention.

This growing local mobilization against Lafarge India was also identified by the son of a former MLA of Bilaspur – a powerful upper-caste landowner. As part of a project to run for the regional legislative elections of November 2008, this son and future candidate of the Bahujan Samaj Party (BSP) saw local discontent about Lafarge as an opportunity to garner electoral support. He joined hands with the activist of TWS and a human rights activist from CMM to strengthen and politicize the mobilization of villagers and workers against the company. In September 2007, for instance, a large public meeting was held in Arasmeta, with hundreds of participants, during which villagers were called to 'raise their voice' and 'put this plant on fire' to oppose Lafarge India's 'dictatorial' and 'anti-human' attitude based on the 'destruction' of villages and the 'exploitation' of workers and villagers.[51] During the election campaign, the candidate visited the area several times to showcase that he was 'with the villagers', 'protecting them against the corporate houses'.[52] In November 2008, the son of the former MLA won the elections and became the new MLA of the constituency where Arasmeta is located.

The discontent of villagers and workers was also noticed by left-wing trade unions, in particular by AITUC, by CITU, and by the cement workers' union of CMM. In Sonadih, while contract workers were not unionized during Tata Steel (apart from a group of coal workers), CITU started organizing contract workers in 2003. In 2008, more than 400 of the contract workers were registered. This unionization allowed CITU to inform workers about their rights. In 2004, CITU also addressed written demands to Lafarge India and sent a copy of the letter to the Labour Commissioner of the government's Labour Department. A demonstration was organized in support of this demand. First, Lafarge India refused to endorse any responsibility as 'employer' vis-à-vis the contract workers. And both local civil servants (the SDM and the *tehsildar*) and elected representatives, some of them being also contractors

---

[50] For more information on the Public Eye Awards, see https://www.publiceye.ch/en/ (accessed on 14 October 2017).

[51] These expressions were used either in the leaflet announcing the meeting and/or by the activist of TWS when he narrated the event in an interview.

[52] Interview conducted by the author, 2 December 2008.

for Lafarge India or having relatives working as contractors for the company, intervened and broke the movement by convincing a sufficient number of workers to stop the protest. But in the following years, CITU filed several cases at the Labour Court, which pushed Lafarge India to make concessions in settlements, such as providing contract workers with an access to the factory's canteens.

In Arasmeta, the acquisition was also followed by a growing unionization of contract workers, this time under the leadership of AITUC. Six hundred contract workers joined the union, and a series of cases were filed in the Labour Court to demand an equal treatment between permanent and contract workers – 'same work, same wage, same bonus'. The contract workers also organized a strike in 2004 in support of this demand. The dispute went from the Labour Court to the Industrial Relations Court and finally to the High Court of Chhattisgarh. While Lafarge India consistently refused to endorse any responsibility as employer of the contract workers, it conceded in a settlement to give contract workers a bonus of 8.33 per cent.

Yet another contribution to the organization of contract workers came from CMM. In 2007–2008, building on its experience and position as a contract workers' union in other cement plants of the region,[53] CMM's Pragatisheel Cement Shramik Sangh (Progressive Cement Workers Union) started deploying efforts to enter Lafarge India's two Chhattisgarh plants. Its collaboration with TWS and the candidate to the Legislative Assembly for organizing the public meeting in Arasmeta in 2007 was part of this strategy. CMM also developed contacts with internal trade union leaders of contract workers. Building on these ties, it succeeded in bringing trade union leaders of various unions together for a joint demonstration of cement workers that was held in 2011 in the state's capital, Raipur. In parallel, CMM communicated increasingly on national and transnational activist platforms to denounce perceived misdeeds of Holcim and Lafarge in India – for example, flouting agreements of the Cement Wage Board and exploiting contract workers, grabbing the land of villagers, extracting limestone without paying the due royalties to the government, and fabricating false cases to get local activists and trade union leaders in jail.[54] Such issues were also raised by CMM in a pamphlet

---

[53] ACC's Jamul cement plant in Bhilai and Ambuja's plant in Baloda Bazar, which both came under the control of the Swiss company Holcim in 2005, and UltraTech Cement's plant in Hirmi, which belongs to the Indian conglomerate Aditya Birla Group.

[54] See, for instance, the letters posted by CMM on South Asian Citizens Web (http://www.sacw.net/article1957.html, accessed on 15 October 2017), India Resist (http://

entitled 'Gravest Displacement, Bravest Resistance: The Struggle of Adivasis in Bastar, Chhattisgarh Against Imperialist Corporate Landgrab', in which Lafarge is explicitly mentioned. While CMM failed to take over as a union of contract workers in the plants of Lafarge India, its engagement in two plants of the region owned by Lafarge's competitor Holcim were fruitful. After filing a complaint at the Swiss National Focal Point of the OECD (Organisation for Economic Co-operation and Development) in 2012, with the support of the global trade union IndustriALL, it negotiated an agreement with Holcim which, inter alia, allowed 500 contract workers to get permanent positions.

The attractive promises of CSR as a means to address threatening contention

For Lafarge India, swelling discontent and the use of such discontent by political actors, activists, and combative trade unions to extract collective and/or personal benefits from the company was identified as a growing threat to the company's business prospects. In a context where Lafarge India was experiencing costly discontent elsewhere, where investments in India worth hundreds of millions of euros needed to be protected, and where a growing number of other companies seemed to experience similar problems, the promise of CSR to help companies manage their stakeholders and pacify business–society interplays seemed to be worth considering.

For several years, the managers of Lafarge India in Chhattisgarh had relied on arrangements with regional and local authorities and power brokers to maintain expectations of villagers and contract workers at bay. MLAs or close allies of them were provided with contracts as suppliers. At the local level, influential *sahr panch*s or relatives were also offered contracts or positions as permanent workers, while powerful villagers who had demonstrated their ability to mobilize villagers against the company were granted privileges such as having the possibility to use a car from the company. *Sahr panch*s were also invited by the company to discuss peripheral development, and according to one of them, they would receive a lump sum for this purpose, without having

---

www.indiaresists.com/labor-day-release-lakhan-sahu-and-6-other-trade-unionists-chhattisgarh/, accessed on 15 October 2017), and MultiWatch (http://www.multiwatch.ch/cm_data/HolcimIndien_undatiert.pdf, accessed on 15 October 2017), as well as the petition launched on Change.org to free the activist Bhagwati Sahu (https://www.change.org/p/release-trade-union-leader-bhagwati-sahu, accessed on 15 October 2017).

to give any account on the use of this gift. Part of the company's budget line earmarked for peripheral development was also used by Lafarge India for purposes that have little to do with peripheral development, such as sponsoring the construction of a new building for a police station in the nearby town of Janjgir, or constructing a welcome arch over the National Highway 200 – an arch that, according to a *sahr panch*, was billed for 5 million rupees and may have been used to channel benefits to local political or administrative actors. Furthermore, while Lafarge's Code of Business Conduct requires its employees to avoid any form of bribery, according to one of its Indian managers, the company sometimes used consultants as intermediaries to transfer money so as to facilitate transactions, for instance, in relation to land acquisition.

In spite of these local arrangements, in the second half of the 2000s, Lafarge India perceived signs of increasing hostility and business-relevant uncertainties. The decision of the MLA in Sonadih to turn against the company, the mobilization of villagers against Lafarge by the candidate who ran for elections in 2008 in the area of Arasmeta, the written complaints addressed by some *sahr panchs* to public authorities and their connections with activist organizations such as TWS, as well as the growing pressure exerted by left-wing trade unions who had succeeded in organizing the contractual workforce in the two plants were dangerous dynamics of contention that seemed to outgrow the problem-solving capacities of the pre-existing local arrangements. While market competition and the financial expectations of the Parisian headquarters pushed Lafarge India to focus on economic efficiency and profitability, competing expectations were becoming increasingly disturbing.

Moreover, the company could relate signs of increasing hostility with information on similar dynamics occurring elsewhere. For instance, major investments of Lafarge India in a large-scale limestone mine project and a cement plant project in the tribal state of Meghalaya were facing costly opposition, including through a PIL filed at the Supreme Court by activists and indigenous communities from the Shella Action Committee. Information also circulated within professional networks and in mass media regarding protest movements affecting other cement manufacturers across the country. And in 2007, highly mediatized conflicts that blocked major industrial projects, such as the car factory project of Tata Motors in West Bengal or Vedanta's bauxite mine project and POSCO's integrated Steel Plant in Odisha, were perceived by Lafarge India as a clear indication of a growing threat. In the words of a plant-level CSR manager:

> Now we are taking various types of permissions from the government, like for starting a factory. The same thing is that we have to take the social license

from society, because now, people are aware. Before, they were not so educated, they did not know if you were extracting their resources.... Now the Nano project [of Tata Motors in West Bengal] was there. Now, they have to move the project from West Bengal to Gujarat. Many companies had problems, like POSCO also. Those problems are happening more frequently. If you don't do any community work, they can do such type of protest. This way they can punish [companies].[55]

While Lafarge India was starting to recognize the deficiencies of the way it had managed its non-market environment so far, CSR was gaining traction both globally and in the Indian context. Companies, business associations, CSR experts and consultants, management scholars, NGOs, international organizations, state actors, as well as international and domestic mass media, to quote only the key protagonists, were advertising CSR en masse as a relevant resource for companies to better manage their socio-political environment (see Chapter 4). Lafarge India was not insulated from this expansion of the CSR phenomenon, whose promises seemed to match the problems the company was experiencing in its acquired plants and ongoing industrial investment projects.

With regard to its thematic relevance, CSR was providing interesting perspectives for the company to address any actual or potential problem arising from tensions between its profit-driven business operations and competing collective values and interests. Indeed, the indication of 'social' responsibility makes the CSR concept relevant for a broad and open-ended range of issues, as it covers anything that can be referred to the company's social environment. Child labour, gender discrimination, exploitative labour conditions, rising economic inequalities, dispossession of indigenous communities, corruption, non-democratic forms of lobbying, industrial pollution, biodiversity, and climate change are some of the many thematic issues that companies can address through CSR. This wide and open-ended thematic scope also makes CSR particularly flexible, as it allows companies to select issues that are particularly relevant for them in terms of their business prospects.

The pragmatic relevance of CSR for Lafarge India was further strengthened by the concept's reference to 'corporate' responsibility. By putting companies forward as responsible entities, CSR allows them to transform more or less scattered 'evidences' of 'socially responsible' behaviour into claims of moral quality. From local peripheral development projects to global partnerships with NGOs and international organizations, any activity that seems to mitigate

---

[55] Interview conducted with the author, 5 December 2008.

adverse impacts of a company's business operations, or to strengthen the latter's positive outcomes for society, can be integrated into discursive constructions that depict the company as a 'socially responsible' organization – or any other equivalent descriptor such as 'good corporate citizen'. This transformation of CSR activities into moral claims enables companies to put synergies between profit-making and social problem-solving forward, while overshadowing tensions and conflicts between the two. Doing so also enables companies to argue for more supportive politics and less regulatory constraints, as policymakers would be ill-advised to hamper the development of 'responsible companies', whose business activities are depicted as contributions to the solution of societal problems.

Finally, CSR seemed relevant for Lafarge India because of the concept's forward-looking dimension. In fact, building on the underlying distinction between socially 'responsible' and socially 'irresponsible' corporate conduct, CSR has been commonly depicted both in scholarly work and in popular discourse as a progress-oriented 'movement' that can gradually align profit-making with collective goals such as social justice, democracy, and environmental sustainability (see Chapter 1). This forward-looking dimension of CSR supports 'aspirational talk': CSR allows companies to overcome present problems such as growing discontent by garnering support through the promise of a better future.[56] Moreover, by endowing companies with a future-oriented role in societal problem-solving, CSR 'gives corporations the political power to define what our public problems are and how they should be fixed'.[57] By joining the 'CSR movement', individual companies such as Lafarge India get identified with the movement's progressive aura – they become part of the club of corporate problem-solvers, on the right side of the distinction of socially responsible/irresponsible.

While CSR entails a promising horizon of opportunities for companies such as Lafarge India, whose business prospects are threatened by discontent, making use of these opportunities requires companies to explore this horizon and to make choices – to reduce complexity. What does the contested concept of CSR exactly mean for the company? Which issue-areas should be selected from the wide range of possible themes and problems? How should CSR be integrated within the company's organization, and what activities should the company carry out in this particular field of management? How can the

---

[56] See Christensen, Morsing, and Thyssen (2013).

[57] Marchildon (2016, 60).

instrumental resources of CSR as a business-oriented managerial device be articulated with CSR's claim of being directed towards moral values and societal problem-solving? How to maximize the potential of CSR for public relations without exposing the company to damaging accusations of 'window dressing'?

In the case of Lafarge India, the process of exploring opportunities provided by CSR was initiated by the board in 2007 and entrusted to a newly appointed senior vice-president for corporate affairs. A first step taken by the senior VP for corporate affairs was to assess the pre-existing CSR activities of Lafarge India. An internal review was conducted by a new CSR manager, who had been appointed in the cement plant project of Lafarge India located in Alsindi, in the Himalayan state of Himachal Pradesh. The findings of this internal review pointed at the mismanagement and inefficiency of the peripheral development activities conducted around the acquired plants of Lafarge India, including the plants of Sonadih and Arasmeta. The diagnostic was clear: Lafarge India had no functioning CSR policy in place, and the scattered peripheral development activities conducted in the name of CSR under the pressure of political actors had limited value both for the company and for the villagers residing near the plants.

Departing from this diagnostic, the senior VP for corporate affairs organized a series of meetings with different CSR experts such as the CSR office of FICCI, the Business Council for Sustainable Development of the NGO TERI, and the NGO PiC. For these CSR experts, these meetings were an occasion to exercise their formal mandate, which is to promote CSR among companies. Moreover, some of these CSR experts depend on collaborations with companies to gain access to the financial and reputational resources they need in order to operate and grow. As a consequence, when the new CSR team of Lafarge India first met the team of PiC, the latter strived to convince the company of the strategic virtues of CSR. Echoing the *doxa* of the managerial CSR literature, the team of PiC emphasized that CSR can facilitate the acquisition of useful certifications such as the private environmental norm ISO 14001, that it can protect and nurture the reputational value of the company, that it can reinforce the commitment of employees to their employer, that it can help the company preserve its 'social license to operate' by improving relationships with its 'stakeholders', and so on.

Convinced by these arguments, Lafarge India decided to collaborate with PiC to design a comprehensive national CSR policy for the company. The cement plant project in Alsindi, which had been launched in 2006 and was in the implementation phase, was selected as a pilot project to design and test the local features of the new CSR policy before scaling it up to the national level. While the Parisian headquarters of Lafarge – in particular the Department for Sustainable Development and the Department for Communication – were informed of the development of a new CSR policy in the Indian subsidiary, they played almost no role in the process beyond providing support such as booklets on how to communicate on sensitive topics (for example, air pollution) with stakeholders.

CSR and the translation of socio-political dangers into economic risks

A detailed study of the elaboration process and initial implementation of Lafarge India's new CSR policy provides insights into how CSR can change the observation and processing of tensions and conflicts opposing profit-making and competing collective values and interests.

While being part of the elaboration of a national CSR policy, the introduction of CSR in Lafarge India's industrial project in Alsindi was also oriented towards project-level objectives. As popular discontent and political opposition in other production units and project sites were putting a strain on Lafarge India's business prospects, the integration of CSR at an early stage of the project in Alsindi was expected to enhance the company's ability to prevent and/or manage such dynamics of contention. This would help secure the economic benefits of an investment initially estimated at about 145 million euros, but which internal estimates of Lafarge India in 2008 were putting at about 300 million euros. In addition, a smooth implementation of the Alsindi plant project would provide a useful success story for Lafarge India to convince the group's headquarters and its investors to invest more in the subcontinent.

Lafarge India's strong motivation to ensure the success of the project was shared by the regional government of Himachal Pradesh. Overall, the regional government was keen on taking advantage of the country's economic dynamism to increase its fiscal revenues, to provide employment opportunities to its electorate, and to open up the region's mountainous valleys through the development of new infrastructure and economic activity. As stated in its Industrial Policy of 2004, the state government's strategy to fulfil these objectives consisted primarily in providing extensive support to industrial investors and in minimizing business-unfriendly regulatory constraints:

The Liberalisation era that the Country is now witnessing has spurred an intense, inter-state competition to attract industrial investments. This calls for the State Government to play an increasingly proactive role as facilitator of industrial development. This necessarily requires benchmarking of our policies and approach to industrialization with not only the best in the country but with world class standards, particularly if we are to target at attracting both domestic and foreign direct investments.

Government intends to provide maximum freedom to operate to the entrepreneurs so as tap the full potential of industry.[58]

In addition to facilitated administrative procedures through the creation of a single window clearance system, substantial tax incentives as part of a Special Industrial Package, and the promise that '[adequate] emphasis will be laid on attitudinal changes of the delivery institutions so as to minimise harassment of the entrepreneurs',[59] this pro-business orientation of the state government materialized in a supportive attitude of civil servants towards Lafarge India. In the words of the project's liaison officer, who was in charge of managing interactions with state authorities:

> It is easy to deal with the government. Bureaucracy is good. There is a lot of political will also. Red-tapism is not prevalent. Generally, industrialists complain about red-tapism, because files do not move. Here, bureaucracy is very good, and red-tapism is not prevalent at all. They provide all kinds of help, in every field. Like getting all the approvals required for the establishment of a plant. Procedures are simple.[60]

While expectations of personal enrichment seem to have played little role in the supportive stance of the state government towards industrial investors, the government was eager to ensure positive developmental outcomes that would also benefit its electoral chances. To do so, when negotiating the Memorandum of Understanding with Lafarge India, it introduced a clause that requires Lafarge India to employ at least 70 per cent of Himachalis in the Alsindi cement plant and its limestone mine. Moreover, Lafarge India was to pay 1.5 per cent of the project's capital expenditure to the Local Area Development

---

[58] Government of Himachal Pradesh (2004, 1 and 10).

[59] A commitment formulated with particular reference to labour-related issues (Government of Himachal Pradesh 2004, 12).

[60] Interview conducted by the author, 5 January 2009.

Authority (LADA) – an administrative body that identifies and implements development projects at the district level.

Regional public authorities were aware of the harmful environmental consequences of industrialization in a mountainous region known for its beautiful landscapes and fragile ecosystems. But it considered that the socio-economic development benefits to be expected from Lafarge India's project outweighed environment-related problems. For instance, during interviews, both a senior bureaucrat from the State Pollution Control Board and the District Forest Officer from the Forest Department cast doubts over the prevalent discourse that cement plants with modern technology generate no significant pollution. But both also evoked people's need of economic development as being a political priority. Similarly, the SDM from the project area emphasized that industrialization did not only mean better incomes, more job opportunities, and overall socio-economic development:

> My personal view is that it may also have some bad environmental impacts: soil will be damaged, erosion will take place, and temperatures will rise, also because of global warming. Where Ambuja set up its plant, it was very green, very nice. Now it is polluted, clearly. Air is polluted, noise has increased, roads are overloaded with trucks. Possibly, there is also water pollution and reduction in water tables. So these repercussions are there.[61]

But these thoughts were explicitly presented as a personal opinion, and the SDM underlined that he had to implement the government's policies and help Lafarge India 'in all possible ways'.

Unlike the state government, local villagers, elected representatives, and politicized associations had mixed feelings regarding Lafarge India's industrial project.[62] In the area where the cement plant would be built, below the small thermal town Tattapani in the valley of the Sutlej river, many villagers and most *panchayat pradhans*[63] were rather in favour of the project. Local pollution and the development of new problems such as criminality were serious concerns. But many people expected the cement plant to provide precious direct and indirect employment opportunities, in a context where government jobs and

---

[61] Interview conducted by the author, 13 February 2008.

[62] The following findings on the position of affected village communities towards the Alsindi plant project are partly based on two unpublished surveys conducted by PiC for Lafarge India.

[63] *Panchayat pradhan* is the name given in Himachal Pradesh to the elected head of a village (*sahr panch*).

employment provided by thermal tourism were declining, while an increasing share of the youth was educated and wanted a life outside agriculture.

In and around the mining concession, which covered 800 hectares in a remote mountainous area located 8 kilometres above the plant site, public opinion and the position of *panchayat pradhan*s were more negative. Most villagers depended on agricultural and horticultural (apple orchards) activity, which yielded good incomes to landowners. This rural economy would be badly affected by the limestone mine, and many villagers did not believe that Lafarge India would provide them with an alternative income source. Moreover, many villagers were emotionally attached to their traditional way of life, which they did not want to trade for a life near a huge limestone mine. The mining concession also implied the relocation of forty-eight households, the relocation of the Deo Badeyogi temple, and the fencing of large areas that villagers used to occupy. In short, many villagers from the mining area expected more harm than good from Lafarge India's industrial project. In 2007, ten of the *panchayat*s from the area constituted the Paryavaran Bachao Sangharsh Samiti (PBSS, or Struggle Association to Save the Environment). Soon after, an oracle from the Deo Badeyogi temple declared that Lafarge India should not be allowed to come to the area. And several local associations with ties to local politics (for example, youth clubs, women associations) joined PBSS to form a Joint Action Committee against the Alsindi plant project.

For Lafarge India, this nascent opposition constituted a source of threatening uncertainties. The hesitant oscillation of a majority of the affected population between a minority of clear project supporters and a minority of clear opponents created a challenge, as this hesitant majority needed to be pushed towards the supportive pole. Moreover, politicized opposition could trigger a snowball effect that would hurt the project:

> The Panchayats, they are supported by political parties. These parties provide funds and development work. In our plant, the Panchayat is supported by the BJP. If we don't support their development work, they will put pressure by press releases, blockades at the construction site, etc. They can also go to court, since the PIL makes it very easy. And they have their own powers. They can ask you to come and justify yourself on anything. Actually, they are the lowest government body, but also the most powerful ... especially here, where politics is very sensitive: people have no jobs, so they do party politics.... Mahila mandals are women groups. Like the Panchayat, they are politically motivated. If one of those groups is agitating, all local groups will come together. So you need their support, very clearly. And it's the same for

youth clubs, farmer's clubs, all these local associations.... If Lafarge is strong in CSR, I can manage them. If not, I will have to pay them.[64]

The scenario of a growing socio-political opposition to the project was all the more threatening given that Lafarge India's investment project required a number of clearances that involved *panchayats*. In particular, the affected *panchayats* had to deliver a No Objection Certificate for Lafarge India to get the forest clearance it needed to divert forest land for non-forest purposes. In 2007–2008, Lafarge India was also busy obtaining the environmental clearance from the central Ministry of Environment and Forests in New Delhi. This environmental clearance would be based not only on the environment impact assessment provided by Lafarge India to the authorities but also on the records of a public hearing that would take place in December 2008, during which citizens would be allowed to raise concerns and voice opposition to the project.

Besides creating hurdles in the clearance processes, popular opposition to the project could also undermine the propitious bargaining position of Lafarge India vis-à-vis the state government. As mentioned earlier, the government was very supportive to companies in general, and to Lafarge India in particular – all the more so because it was the first foreign MNC to invest in Himachal Pradesh. In the case of popular opposition to the project, Lafarge India could count on such support:

> If there is any agitation, the government has a procedure to follow. We send some inspectors, we make an enquiry. But to be open, ultimately, we will support the industry. The government is a big facilitator to help companies set up plants. This is important, also for companies. Without companies, you cannot do anything. They provide employment, they provide tax revenues. And Himachal Pradesh is a fairly small state, so a lot of help is provided directly to companies.[65]

Notwithstanding this supportive stance, as Lafarge India and the state were involved in multiple bargains, popular discontent would increase the government's leverage to obtain more resources from the company to fund public goods:

---

[64] Interview conducted by the author with a project-level manager in charge of land acquisition, 5 February 2008.

[65] Interview conducted by the author with a senior bureaucrat of the Department of Industries from the Government of Himachal Pradesh, 5 February 2008.

The power of the government is that if people start some agitation, the government will not help you. It will wait until the conflict is high, and then they will say: 'You have to give this and that.'[66]

Finally, local opposition to the project could attract regional and national activists with sufficient resources to activate mass media, the judiciary, and the political system against Lafarge. In fact, the Alsindi plant project was already on the radar of organizations such as the Centre for Science and Environment in New Delhi, which considered this industrial investment 'irresponsible' as 'Himachal Pradesh is one of the most eco-sensitive area of the country'.[67] Moreover, other existing and forthcoming cement plants in the region were scrutinized and criticized by the Environment Research & Action Group – a regional network of environmental activists. Given the ideological positioning of this campaigning and advocacy group, local discontent would make Lafarge India a perfect prey:

The current model of neo-liberal development that has been thrust upon the people of the country and states like Himachal Pradesh mainly aims at rapid exploitation of natural and human resources for unbridled consumption by the globalized economy. This development is at an enormous cost to the local, natural resource based communities, their economy and ecology. Even thriving rural economies are considered dispensable by governments whose only considerations are the projected revenues to the state. Himalayas too have not been spared despite being vulnerable due to their fragile topography and unique ecosystems. The scale and attitude with which new projects are being implemented have left little scope for reviewing their impacts on local people, local economy and ecology, and possible alternatives. The governments in Himachal Pradesh, in the past decade, have promoted cement plants, hydropower projects, SEZs [Special Economic Zones] and urbanization plans at a fast pace resulting in displacement and wide-spread destruction and privatisation of natural resources. There is an ever increasing shift in the control of resources from communities and state to private companies for profit motive.[68]

---

[66] Interview conducted by the author with a project-level manager in charge of land acquisition, 5 February 2008.

[67] Interview conducted by the author, 18 September 2007.

[68] Excerpt from a text published online by the Himalaya Bachao Rally and the Him Niti Abhiyan at the occasion of a meeting of activists organized in 2009 on the issue of industrialization in the Himalayan regions. Grasim's project is explicitly mentioned under the name of Grasim's subsidiary Harish Cement: http://delhisolidaritygroup. wordpress.com/2009/04/06/himalya-bachao-rally/ (accessed on 6 April 2011).

While these threatening uncertainties were out there in the environment of Lafarge India's organization, they were not obvious to Lafarge India. The director leading the Alsindi plant project was aware of such uncertainties in the broad lines, and he believed that CSR could help manage this aspect of the project. But at a lower hierarchical level, most managers were focused on their own function, such as accounting and finance, industrial engineering, or human resources management. These project managers considered CSR-related areas such as interactions with local political actors and villagers as a distant and somewhat irrelevant reality. Given the supportive position of public authorities at the government level, the liaison officer also viewed CSR as a non-essential part of the project. Only the team working in the field for land acquisition was concerned with interdependencies between the project and local politics, as their work and achievements depended directly on the quality of interactions with these actors.[69]

Against this backdrop, the first change induced by the introduction of CSR into the project was to enhance the organizational ability of Lafarge India to observe the threatening uncertainties outlined earlier. Following the company's decision to reinforce CSR, and to use the project of Alsindi as a pilot project to elaborate a national CSR policy, the position and role of the project-level CSR manager was strengthened. Previous CSR-related activities, such as a donation of ₹30,000 to the district capital Karsog to fund new waste bins, were dropped. Instead, the senior VP for corporate affairs asked the CSR manager to adopt a systematic, effective, and efficient approach based on the careful analysis of situations, objectives, means, strategies, and outcomes. In this perspective, Lafarge India decided to start with a detailed study of the conditions, needs, and mindsets of affected villagers and their elected representatives. The company commissioned PiC and its sister-organization Praxis to carry out a comprehensive socio-economic need assessment survey in project-affected villages. In addition, PiC and Praxis conducted focus groups with villagers to

---

[69] When such a project comes to place, people wait and watch what will happen. And when the construction is starting, they will agitate. But because the company has some timelines, some objectives, the result is that the company will not have to pay 80,000 rupees or one lakh per acre of land, but two or three lakhs. For this project, if we go to the people, if our compensations and CSR are generalized to everybody, things will be easy.... For me, a good CSR program will reduce apprehensions from the people, and I'll be able to get lower land acquisition rates.

Interview conducted by the author with a project-level manager in charge of land acquisition, 5 February 2008.

identify their vision of a future with the cement plant. And PiC made a detailed mapping and analysis of the 'stakeholders' related to the project, including key local political actors such as *panchayat pradhan*s and MLAs.

These surveys provided Lafarge India with valuable information to identify actual and potential allies and opponents, as well as to analyse the parameters that conditioned the dynamic positioning of their 'stakeholders' vis-à-vis the project. Moreover, the extensive presence of CSR experts in Lafarge India's local offices and on the project sites during the data collection phase, as well as the meeting that was organized with the entire team of the Alsindi project and senior-level managers to present the survey's findings, raised the profile of CSR in the eyes of other project managers. After the meeting, the CSR manager could further strengthen the position of CSR in the project by referring to the survey's findings when asking his colleagues to share information, or to take interdependencies with villagers and politicians into account. About a year after the CSR surveys were conducted, the CSR manager of the project noted with satisfaction:

> I am seeing that [my colleagues] have now started to realize that we are dealing with core, core, hardcore issues, which cannot be looked at lightly, and which have to be put into the system, into the core strategy. There are so many things that we can showcase through CSR to all the stakeholders. Their knowledge base on CSR has, I think, improved a lot. When I conducted health camps, organized the summer education campaign, and the community gave this response that it had proved beneficial for them … it also increased our reputation in the eyes of the government, that our company is doing something for the communities … then the other team members realized that it is very important that CSR stays in the project.
>
> I also always share my activities with them. We [CSR managers] form an important link between the local people in the area and the project team. Because sometimes, it happens that the community has a different perception, which is not able to reach the company. Because we are the fieldworkers, we see things, we gather information, we meet people, we know their views, and then we pass these issues to the company so they can use it.[70]

A second impact of the initial CSR surveys and the subsequent emphasis on a systematic approach to CSR was that Lafarge India could regain autonomy vis-à-vis political actors in the management of social welfare activities. With

---

[70] Interview conducted by the author, 5 January 2009.

regard to formal political expectations, Lafarge India used its systematic approach to CSR as an argument to ask the state government to free the company from the obligation of transferring 1.5 per cent of the project's capital expenditure to the LADA. However, while presenting its CSR activities as an equivalent of a contribution to the LADA, the company did not view these two forms of social welfare spending as equivalent. CSR activities could be designed and implemented by the company according to its own concerns and requirements, which were focused on the plant project's success chances. And the company could take credit for these activities and use them to showcase its 'social responsibility'. Conversely, the LADA would use Lafarge's monetary contribution according to unrelated political-administrative logics, and attribute the credit of local development projects to the government.

Lafarge India's systematic approach to CSR also helped the CSR manager keep informal political pressures at bay:

> You know there are different kinds of pressure groups within a community. The community does not always think about its development only. There are certain pressure groups like Panchayat Pradhans, political parties, local leaders, who have their own ideology. They don't understand CSR. The biggest challenge is that we have to make them understand that: 'Look, we are not doing CSR to please, or to appease pressure groups. We are doing it for the overall development of the community, as a contribution.'[71]

In short, while companies' peripheral development activities in India are often driven by the bargaining power of political actors, the formalization of a CSR strategy based on 'scientific' data supported a growing autonomy of the company vis-à-vis politics in this area of operations.

Overall, the organizational strengthening of CSR in Lafarge India's plant project and the pulling out of CSR-related activities from the grip of external political pressures allowed the company to use CSR as a risk management device. More specifically, CSR developed the organizational ability of the company not only to generate information on external political dangers but also to translate these dangers into parameters of economic risks that can be managed according to a profit-driven logic of cost–benefit calculations. Unlike dangers, which are possibilities of damages arising from external circumstances, risks are a combination of possible gains and possible losses attached to one's own behaviour. Prosaically, one is exposed to dangers that are

---

[71] Interview conducted by the author, 5 January 2009.

more or less dreadful, whereas one decides to take risks that are more or less manageable. Depending on situations, probabilities of gains and probabilities of losses attached to alternative courses of action can be manipulated, at least to a certain extent, so as to improve chances of gains and minimize chances of losses.[72]

In the case of the Alsindi plant project, risk management through CSR focused on economic risks related to the perception of the investment project by external actors. What was at stake was the company's business prospects, that is, the chances of implementing this industrial project at the lowest possible cost (for example, price of land, delays to obtain environmental clearances), without triggering protest movements that could generate monetary losses. As described earlier, the presence of CSR in the project's organization increased the company's ability to observe external uncertainties that could impact this economic equation. For instance, the CSR surveys and the information gathered by the CSR manager during field visits in villages provided information on people's moral sentiment regarding the company: To what extent were they considering Lafarge India as an egoistic and predatory company that only cares about profit, or as a responsible and benevolent company that cares for 'development' beyond its financial bottom line? Similarly, the CSR wing of the project provided information on people's perception of likely impacts on their socio-economic condition: To what extent was the project welcomed as a new source of employment, or rejected on the ground that it might destroy income sources (for example, horticulture in the mining area) and damage public health through industrial pollution?

Once business-relevant uncertainties were identified, CSR provided resources to manage these uncertainties – with more or less success.[73] For instance, in coordination with the land acquisition team, a series of health

---

[72] On the conceptual distinction between dangers and risks, see in particular Luhmann (1993).

[73] As it eventually turned out, the use of CSR as a risk management device by Lafarge India did not prevent opposition to the Alsindi plant project by the Joint Action Committee from gaining momentum. In 2009, activists intervened in support of the Joint Action Committee and helped it challenge the environmental clearance that had been granted the same year by the Ministry of Environment and Forests. Following lengthy judicial procedures, the clearance was cancelled by the High Court in 2011. In a context of global economic downturn, which was followed by the merger of Lafarge S.A. with its Swiss competitor Holcim and subsequent changes in LafargeHolcim's business development strategy in India, the plant project of Alsindi was abandoned.

camps were organized in villages where land was still to be acquired for the project. Similarly, the CSR manager organized a seminar on women empowerment with local women's associations (*mahila mandals*), as part of a strategy to secure allies among affected village communities. In the words of the CSR manager:

> To build the relationship [with communities], we need to carry out activities that can produce immediate good results, and that can create good will for the company.[74]

For a later phase, the CSR manager envisaged the development of CSR programmes and activities that would focus more thoroughly on the development-related needs of village communities affected by the plant project. Besides favouring supportive behaviours among local 'stakeholders', who can influence Lafarge India's business prospects in Himachal Pradesh, such CSR programmes and activities were conceived of as contribution to improving the company's business prospects all over India and beyond:

> If you do nice CSR, centred on the welfare of the people, you will reap the benefits on the long run. Look at Tata, they clearly benefit today from the CSR they did several decades ago. It would be the same for Lafarge. On platforms, at seminars, in business schools, CSR would improve the brand image of Lafarge, because Lafarge would be regularly quoted as a good example, for its good practices. Now, with the media, with Internet, things have become more transparent. So if a good practice is found in another site, the people impacted by a plant project can get this information, or the land officer and CSR managers can use this information to calm the apprehensions of people. If I was a villager, and I would know that Tata is coming, I would be happy about it, because of its reputation.[75]

Over the course of 2008 and 2009, the new approach to CSR that had been developed in the Alsindi plant project was scaled up and integrated into a countrywide CSR structure. The CSR managers of existing plants and ongoing plant projects were gathered several times to create a team dynamic and facilitate coordination and learning across production units. Each CSR manager was asked to conduct a stakeholder analysis and a need-assessment survey along the model that had been used in Himachal Pradesh. Moreover,

---

[74] Interview conducted by the author, 5 January 2009.
[75] Interview conducted by the author, 5 January 2009.

CSR managers were required to abandon CSR activities driven by local political pressures, which were deemed inefficient both in terms of developmental impact for targeted beneficiaries and in terms of benefits for the company. Instead, CSR managers were to follow a cost-effective and impact-driven approach, with tangible positive outcomes both for surrounding village communities and for the company. On the latter point, as a senior executive emphasized in front of the CSR managers: 'We have to look after the economic costs of CSR for Lafarge, and the social performance and benefits of our activities for Lafarge'.[76] Notwithstanding expectations of cost-effectiveness, the CSR budgets allocated to each plant were raised from about ₹2 million in 2009 to about ₹4 million rupees in 2011. CSR was further strengthened by the setting up of a foundation called NIDHEE, which in Hindi means 'community wealth' and which stands for National Initiative for Dwellings, Health and Safety, Education and Employability.

Besides fiscal advantages related to its status, NIDHEE provided a key organizational structure to develop common CSR programmes that would be implemented in each cement plant and plant project. For instance, in 2010, NIDHEE launched a CSR programme on employability to provide vocational training to young villagers living near the company's cement plants. Conversely, CSR activities that were designed and conducted at the plant or project-level could now be integrated into NIDHEE's broad framework, which comprised dwellings (local infrastructure projects), health and safety, education, and employability. This overarching framework facilitated the use of both national- and local-level CSR activities as pieces of evidence in the discursive construction of Lafarge India as a 'socially responsible' company. As one can read in the annual CSR report of NIDHEE 2010:

> Lafarge India through its foundation NIDHEE has been able to give back to the communities in which we operate. Quoting from Lafarge's Principles of Action: 'Wherever present we operate with the utmost respect for the common interest of present and future generations; we act as responsible members of our communities by contributing to the development of people, their health, rights and well-being by generating economic growth and supporting social, educational and cultural advancement'.[77]

---

[76] Excerpt from discussions during an internal meeting of Lafarge India on CSR.

[77] Lafarge India (2010, 4).

CSR, second-order observation, and economic responsiveness

As the macro-sociological part of the present study showed, the CSR phenomenon has gained momentum in India in a context marked by heightened functional differentiation – the growing significance of profit-making as a guiding value in economic processes. The gradual 'pro-business' shift in the country's development strategy induced political and institutional changes that, as a trend, have increased the operational autonomy of companies vis-à-vis external regulatory constraints, while strengthening the role of profit-making in organizational decision-making.

This political-economic setting has fostered the contributions of private companies to economic growth. The Indian state has remained a powerful economic actor, in particular via its large public sector enterprises. But private companies have taken over as the primary engines of economic development, with positive outcomes in terms of production efficiency and monetary wealth creation. At the same time, India's new political-economic setting has been prone to growing tensions and conflicts between profit-driven economic processes and competing collective values and interests. Concretely, companies' production processes and investment projects have been increasingly exposed to public criticism, protest movements, and legal complaints, as part of a 'counter-movement' that emphasizes perceived harmful consequences of corporate conduct. Business actors, public policy-makers, and some NGOs have used and institutionalized CSR mostly as a response to these tensions and conflicts. While the resulting CSR phenomenon covers a great variety of norms and practices, it has institutionalized the claim that CSR can realign business practices with society's 'well-being', beyond the basic economic function of companies which consists in responding to actual or potential needs by producing goods and services that are sold on the market for a profit.

The study of the case of Lafarge, whose investments in the subcontinent since the late 1990s have participated in the aforementioned political-economic changes, provides more detailed insights into the relationships between increased functional differentiation, disruptions in economy–society interplays, and the expansion of CSR as an intermediary institution.

First, the case of Lafarge India displays the ambivalent consequences of heightened functional differentiation with regard to economic responsiveness. On the one hand, Lafarge's acquisition of the two cement plants in Chhattisgarh improved economic responsiveness towards society's need for quality and cheap cement. Concretely, thanks to investments in new machinery, a more thorough extraction of limestone in the plant's quarries, human resources management practices that boost productivity, as well as an overall focus on cost-cutting, Lafarge India could produce more and better cement for a lower cost than its predecessors. Lafarge's cement plant project in Himachal Pradesh is a further case of economic responsiveness: this investment was triggered by the perception of unaddressed need for cement by the country's booming construction sector, which itself responds to the need for infrastructure and housing facilities for India's expanding population.

On the other hand, Lafarge's organizational focus on profit-driven economic efficiency constrained economic responsiveness towards competing collective values and interests, which are not captured by market-based economic responsiveness. In the acquired plants, many of the company's productive operations either maintained or worsened harmful outcomes for other actors, in particular among neighbouring village communities (for example, respiratory diseases induced by cement dust; shortage of land due to the expansion of mines). In addition, the stark reduction of the workforce, sub-contracting, and higher pressures on productivity were decided and implemented by the company at the cost of labour welfare and employment opportunities for low-skilled labourers. Lafarge's cost-cutting spree also undermined 'philanthropic' contributions to local development, which villagers used to obtain from the plants, and which correspond to institutionalized (expected) practices in India's cultural and social-structural context.

What is more, Lafarge's organizational focus on profit-making reduced its ability to observe and anticipate the likely consequences of its own behaviour for others. This organizational myopia is apparent in the two acquired plants in Chhattisgarh, but also in greenfield investments such as the mining and cement plant projects in Meghalaya, where Lafarge India underestimated potential contention. Overall, to use the terminology of SST, Lafarge India's focus on financial performance favoured a mono-contextual first-order mode of observation: a 'narcissistic perspective from within which the organization applies distinctions blindly, and from where the organization takes its own worldview for given, takes what it sees to be the one reality, the only truth – and consequently conflicts blindly with different worldviews'.[78]

Conversely, Lafarge's behaviour and the resulting discontent among villagers and workers was observed carefully by political actors, including local and regional elected representatives, trade union leaders from the left political spectrum, as well as local and regional activists connected with transnational

---

[78] Holmström (2010, 137–38).

activist networks. Driven by various motivations, but claiming to speak in the name of affected village communities and workers, some of these political actors leveraged local discontent to denounce the company's 'greedy' and 'socially irresponsible' behaviour. The result was swelling political, legal, moral, and mass media communication that pitted Lafarge's profit-making operations against competing collective values and interests (for example, social justice, lawfulness, labour welfare, welfare of local communities, environmental protection). At some point, the actual and potential economic costs induced by this growing dynamic of contention, combined with the observation of similar troubles affecting other large companies on the subcontinent, became significant enough to alert the company to the presence of a new danger located outside market transactions, which threatened its business prospects.

As it faced threatening dynamics in its non-market environment, Lafarge India became sensitive to the promises of CSR. Unlike the concept of 'philanthropy', which refers to the distribution of added value for purposes that seem distant with core business operations, the concept of CSR seemed to open up relevant opportunities to address the challenges outlined earlier. The broad and open-ended thematic scope of CSR could cover any actual or potential issue pertaining to tensions and conflicts between Lafarge's commercial operations and competing collective values and interests. Putting the company's responsibility forward could facilitate the use of selected CSR-related activities to construct general claims of moral righteousness and commitment to the public good. Moreover, joining the CSR bandwagon could make Lafarge India appear as a valuable contributor to the progress-oriented 'CSR movement', which claims to turn companies from societal problem-makers into societal problem-solvers.

Once Lafarge India had recognized CSR as a relevant managerial field of opportunities, it started exploring and exploiting this field. The explorative moment was all the more crucial since the meaning horizon opened up by the CSR concept is broad and contested. Relying on resources such as practice-oriented academic literature,[79] expertise (for example, FICCI, PiC), documentation from Lafarge's group-level CSR policies, CSR policies and practices of other Indian cement manufacturers, and the professional knowledge

---

[79] For instance, at the occasion of participatory observation in an internal meeting of Lafarge India, we witnessed the senior VP for corporate affairs carrying with him John Elkington's classical book *Cannibals with Forks* (1998), which advertises the concept of the triple bottom line (people, planet, profit).

of the members of the CSR team, Lafarge India initiated the elaboration of a CSR policy that covered both the national level of Lafarge India and the local level of plants and plant projects.

This managerial process led to the development of new organizational structures within Lafarge India. Step by step, 'decision premises' were taken, which set the conditions for the subsequent CSR-related operations of the company. With regard to personnel, managers of peripheral development in acquired plants and new CSR managers appointed in plant projects were put together in a 'CSR team'. Their missions and tasks were explicitly redefined, with an emphasis on change. From now on, their role was not to respond to local political pressures with scattered contributions to 'peripheral development'. Their role was to regain control over CSR-related activities, which were to be designed on a systematic and cost-effective basis so as to maximize benefits both for external 'stakeholders' and for Lafarge's business development. In addition, CSR managers were to scrutinize the mindset and behaviour of relevant 'stakeholders', to build networks of allies, and to identify sources of actual or potential trouble.

To prevent or minimize opposition to Lafarge India's business, the CSR team was asked to deploy targeted CSR activities – including but not limited to public relations tactics. Local CSR managers were also to implement company-level CSR programmes and projects, and to provide information for Lafarge's reporting on its CSR activities. With regard to these CSR programmes, new priority areas were defined, budgets were allocated, and the NIDHEE foundation was created as a central CSR unit to coordinate and integrate plant-level CSR activities within a pan-Indian framework. Decision premises were also set with regard to communication channels. While CSR managers were formally under the command of plant or project directors, it was decided that they would report directly to the senior VP for corporate affairs. At the local level, coordination structures were introduced between the CSR managers and the heads of other relevant departments, such as liaison officers, land acquisition officers, and human resources directors.

An analysis of these CSR-related organizational structures and their effects on subsequent decision-making provides insights into how the CSR phenomenon can change economic responsiveness vis-à-vis societal problems in general, and problems arising from tensions between profit-making and competing collective values and interests in particular.

First, CSR-related organizational structures enhanced the ability of Lafarge India to observe and make sense of its environment. More specifically, CSR-related organizational structures provided Lafarge India with capacities of second-order observation – the observation of observation. Unlike first-order observation, which is mono-contextual and considers what is observed as a given, second-order observation allows an observing system (here the company) to realize that other social systems (for example, politics, law, mass media, morality) have different perspectives and that its own viewpoint is contingent. Consequently, second-order observation increases the ability of an organization to decipher how its own operations are observed by other social systems:

> The organizational system sees itself as if from outside and re-enters the distinction between system and environment within the system.… [It] enables the organization to understand itself in a larger interdependent societal context and to develop self-restrictions out of consideration for its environment in order to secure its own independence and self-referential development (autopoiesis) in the long term.[80]

A second impact of CSR is that by strengthening the capacities of second-order observation, CSR improved the ability of the company to address the threatening dynamics of contention outlined earlier. More specifically, while Lafarge India maintained a primarily profit-driven operative logic, which focuses on distinctions about monetary costs and gains, its CSR structures helped the organization address actual or potential reactions of other social systems to its behaviour, *insofar as these actual or potential reactions seemed relevant for profit-making*. For instance, thanks to the work of its CSR staff, Lafarge India could better discern which of the problems faced by villagers and workers needed to be addressed, and how to prevent politicians, trade unions, and activists to leverage such problems in a way that could generate costs or even destroy profitable business opportunities. Activities that could be labelled as 'CSR', such as more targeted peripheral development projects (for example, health camps in areas where land was to be acquired), or CSR programmes on employability, were one way to manage these parameters of economic risks. The advantage of such CSR activities is that, in addition to their local impact, they can be integrated into CSR reports and other communication artefacts to support moral claims of social responsibility. But Lafarge India could also use other means to control non-market economic risks, such as securing the cooperative behaviour of elected representatives by providing material resources to them and/or to their family members.

---

[80] Holmström (2010, 138).

A third impact of CSR that can be observed in the case of Lafarge India is that CSR strengthens the role of the economy in the way society processes tensions and conflicts between profit-making and competing collective values and interests. As outlined earlier, CSR-related organizational structures did not strengthen non-economic logics and guiding values in the operations of Lafarge. What CSR strengthened was the observation of probable adverse economic consequences arising from reactions of social systems to the company's profit-driven operations. In other words, thanks to second-order observation, the economic operations of Lafarge India could better take actual or probable consequences of non-market but profit-relevant interplays between the economy and other spheres of society into account. Moreover, as CSR is conceived of and implemented by companies to undermine the processing of business-related societal problems by politics, law, mass media reports, and morality, it is set to weaken the role of these social systems in societal problem-solving. In the case of Lafarge India, for instance, CSR was used purposefully to undermine the influence of external actors, such as elected representatives and activists, in the formulation of problems related to the company's operations, as well as in the formulation of expectations vis-à-vis Lafarge India and public authorities to address these problems.

That being said, the CSR phenomenon is not solely an outcome of profit-driven corporate conduct. Companies are central actors in this field, and the structures and activities they develop in relation to CSR is an outcome of internal decision-making processes that are operationally autonomous. Even political decisions of sovereign states cannot decide *in* a company – they can only define norms and exert power on corporate conduct from the outside. But as an intermediary institution, the CSR phenomenon extends beyond the organizational boundaries of companies. More specifically, the CSR concept is used and institutionalized in the communication processes of other social systems, such as politics and law, with potential consequences on their own behaviour. While a comprehensive study of social systems involved in and affected by CSR is beyond the scope of the present study, the next chapter complements the analysis of the case of Lafarge India with an analysis of the development of CSR within India's political system.

Chapter 6

India's CSR Public Policies and the Politics of Economic Responsiveness

Ambiguities in CSR public policies

Since the early 2000s, political systems have gained increasing significance in terms of their role in the (re)production of the intermediary institution of CSR. Concretely, a growing number of national states and intergovernmental bodies from around the globe have formulated public policies that formally aim to promote and shape the CSR behaviour of companies.[1] European countries such as the United Kingdom and France have been forerunners in this emerging policy field, for instance, with the setting up of a British Ministry for CSR in 2000, and the law Nouvelles Régulations Économiques of 2001 which requires companies listed on the CAC40 index to issue a yearly CSR report. Most other members of the European Union have followed this lead, encouraged by a series of European CSR policies and strategy documents, including the Green Paper 'Promoting a European Framework for Corporate Social Responsibility' of 2001, the document 'A Renewed EU Strategy 2011–2014 for Corporate Social Responsibility' that was released ten years later, and the Directive 2014/95/EU on non-financial reporting. Outside Europe, CSR policies have also spread in most OECD countries, as well as in numerous emerging and developing countries (for example, India, China, Brazil, South Africa, Vietnam, Mexico, Egypt, Mozambique).

---

[1] See, for instance, Fox, Ward, and Howard (2002), European Commission (2007), Albareda, Lozano, Tencati, Midttun, and Perrini (2008), Steurer (2011), Gond, Kang, and Moon (2011), Kinderman (2013), and Knudsen and Moon (2017).

As part of a broader trend towards collaborative forms of governance, which rely on issue-centred and efficiency-driven partnerships between public and private actors, these various CSR policies formally aim to engage companies in societal problem-solving. By promoting and structuring CSR among targeted companies, for instance, through norms (for example, laws, guidelines, standards) and the provision of dedicated resources (for example, knowledge platforms, toolkits), governments seek to increase economic responsiveness beyond the level that would be reached if CSR was left to the work of market forces and managerial risk-management.

The driving forces and the impact of this growing 'government of self-regulation'[2] are not straightforward, as the position of states vis-à-vis CSR is deeply ambiguous. As emphasized in the first chapter, historically, CSR has been closely associated with voluntarism as an *alternative* to state intervention. Business ethics was to a large extent about minimizing legally binding regulation of economic activity by putting the virtues of self-regulation forward. Following this lead, the American pioneers of CSR used it as a means to contain state intervention: business corporations, rather than state authorities, were to decide how commercial operations should mind the public interest.[3] Up to now, the idea that CSR is voluntary, in the sense that it takes place beyond legal obligations, has been considered a central attribute of CSR.[4] Against this backdrop, growing state intervention in this field could indicate a change through the reassertion of state regulation and political goals in an intermediary institution designed initially to weaken the state. But CSR policies could also amount to states undermining their own regulatory power over the economy by sharing or even transferring key regulatory and redistributive functions to private business actors.

This ambiguity of CSR public policies is reflected in the diversity of their institutional characteristics. First, CSR policies can give various – more or less accurate – meanings to CSR, either in explicit definitions of this essentially contested concept, or implicitly, as they expect different behaviours from 'socially responsible' companies.[5] Second, as emphasized in a number of typologies and empirical studies, CSR policies can occupy various positions on a continuum that ranges from rather business-constraining to rather

---

[2] Gond, Kang, and Moon (2011).

[3] Abend (2014), Kaplan (2015).

[4] See, for instance, Dentchev, van Balen, and Haezendonck (2015).

[5] See Bernhard and Christian (2010), Archel, Husillos, and Spence (2011), and Vallentin (2015).

business-supporting measures.[6] Business-constraining measures, such as extra-financial reporting obligations, are softer than traditional 'command and control' regulations. Their requirements are generally broadly defined, and their enforcement mechanisms are flexible. Nevertheless, these measures provide the state with subtle regulatory resources to get companies to contribute to political objectives, including objectives that diverge from corporate interests. CSR policies that rely on public–private partnerships, which companies can join on a voluntary basis, provide opportunities for state and business actors to tackle societal problems on the basis of a win–win formula. At the other end of the spectrum, business-supporting policies generally endorse and facilitate CSR practices that are based on purely voluntary and profit-driven *modi operandi*. Depending on the meaning they give to CSR, and on their position on the continuum, CSR public policies can be expected to have quite different impacts on this intermediary institution, and hence on the way CSR changes the respective roles of the economy and other social systems in the observation and processing of societal problems.

In India, the interest of public policy-makers for CSR can be traced back to the mid-2000s, at a time when CSR itself was gaining traction in the subcontinent. In 2007, the government made the first intervention at the occasion of the annual General Assembly of the CII. Prime ministers are usually invited to this event, and Manmohan Singh used this opportunity to urge India's business community to act in a socially more responsible manner. In his speech, the prime minister outlined a 'Partnership for Inclusive Growth' based on a CSR Charter that entailed ten guiding principles, which ranged from fair labour conditions and ethical business practices to socially responsible advertising and the use of environment-friendly technologies. In 2011, the government carried on with the release of National Voluntary Guidelines for Social, Environmental and Economic Responsibilities of Business (NVGs). A year later, the financial market regulator SEBI issued a circular on Business Responsibility Reports. This circular requires the hundred largest listed companies by market capitalization to report annually on their social responsibility along the lines indicated in the NVGs. In August 2013, yet another step was taken with the adoption of the new Companies Act. Its section 135 requires all companies above a certain size to spend at least 2

---

[6] See, for instance, Fox, Ward, and Howard (2002), Gond, Kang, and Moon (2011), Knudsen, Moon, and Slager (2015), and Kinderman (2016). For a literature review, see Krichewsky (2017).

per cent of their net profit in the pursuance of a CSR policy approved by the board of directors.

To analyse this growing involvement of India's central government in the field of CSR, the present study focuses on its two main policy measures, the NVGs of 2011 and the CSR clause of the Companies Act of 2013. These two measures are all the more interesting as they feature contradictory definitions of CSR, and as their structures are located at opposite sides of the business-constraining/business-supporting continuum. Following the three-step analytical framework outlined in Chapter 2, the detailed comparative study of the NVGs and the Companies Act starts by examining how and in reaction to which problems was the CSR concept selected by India's political system, and what kind of policy options it introduced in India's regulatory politics. The second step investigates how the political system and its participating actors exploited this horizon of policy options over the course of the policy-making processes underlying the NVGs and the Companies Act. Finally, the third step analyses how the resulting institutional features of these two CSR public policies contribute to changing the respective role of the economy, politics, and other social systems in the observation and processing of societal problems in general, and problems arising from tensions between profit-making and competing collective values and interests in particular.

The rise of CSR as a policy option in India's pro-business setting

In spite of its 'essentially contested' character, the CSR concept opens up a meaning horizon that is given. The three words it combines can be meaningfully connected in various ways with a broad variety of other words and underlying distinctions, such as 'sustainable', 'profitable', 'fair', or 'window-dressing'. But this meaning horizon is not infinite. The boundaries of this horizon circumscribe the opportunities of meaning construction that CSR provides to social systems. While in the case of companies such as Lafarge, these potentials of meaning construction are envisaged primarily as managerial options attached to economic concerns, for political systems, they appear primarily as policy options attached to political concerns.

In the Indian context of the mid-2000s, the political relevance of CSR as a policy option was identified in relation to the growing tensions between profit-driven economic processes and competing collective values and interests. In general terms, the development of protest movements and litigations that challenged major investment projects, including projects involving resourceful foreign investors, were perceived by central and regional state governments as a threat to the investor-friendly setting they were trying to establish.

Governments were also concerned with how voters perceived their political position. In 2004, the Congress-led United Progressive Alliance had been elected on the basis of a social democratic programme that promised to improve 'the welfare of farmers, agricultural labour, weavers, workers and weaker sections of society' and emphasized an irrevocable commitment 'to the daily well-being of the common man across the country'.[7] In the words of Zoya Hasan, 'reconciling the welfare of the people at large with economic liberalization alongside political pressures for distribution was the greatest challenge confronted by the Congress after it returned to power in 2004'.[8] Against this backdrop, social conflicts surrounding companies were politically dangerous for incumbents. They exposed governments to public accusations of siding with powerful companies and the country's elite against the 'people' and, in particular, the weakest sections of society that the government had promised to serve. Such accusations were voiced beyond social activist circles. Political opponents and some parties of the central government's coalition also used such critics to exert pressure on the Congress Party. The political use of peasant protests against Tata Motor's plant project in West Bengal by the All India Trinamool Congress party in 2007, which helped propel its leader Mamata Banerjee to the post of chief minister in 2011, is a case in point.

From the point of view of the central government, CSR offered promising political perspectives to address this threatening dynamic. As already noted previously, with regard to the factual dimension of meaning, 'social responsibility' covers a broad and flexible horizon of problem-areas. Public policy-makers could, therefore, use CSR to address at once multiple problem-areas related to business–development interplays: child labour, poor working conditions, gender as well as caste and religious discrimination, consumer safety, public health, rights of expropriated farmers and indigenous communities, corruption, industrial pollution, industrial hazards, nature conservation, climate change, and so on. More generally, promoting CSR could be used to legitimize contentious pro-business development policies by depicting companies as resourceful partners for 'development'. As explained by a senior bureaucrat of the Ministry of Corporate Affairs:

---

[7] *The Hindu* (2004).
[8] Hasan (2012, 123).

We realize that the government alone is not equipped to solve the social problems like education, health, local infrastructure, etc., on its own. We need the business sector to work with us, so as to make sure that the benefits of development reach the bottom of the pyramid.[9]

The broad and flexible thematic scope of CSR also made it seem like a relevant means to palliate the deficiencies of the existing regulatory framework:

In India, we have a large number of laws, rules, regulations, that companies have to follow. On environment, pollution, labour. But the compliance of so many laws is an issue. Our laws in India are good laws, and there is a law for everything. But you know, as for other countries, we have a problem in implementation and enforcement. The corporate sector raises the issue of compliance cost very strongly.[10]

With regard to the social dimension of meaning, the concept of CSR shifts the focus away from *government* responsibility by emphasizing *corporate* responsibility or by mixing the two. This semantic property opens up opportunities to redefine the respective roles of state authorities and private business actors in the regulation of corporate conduct and the solution of societal problems. As Susanne Holmström writes, with CSR, 'the political system relieves the pressure on own risky decision-making and increasingly sends on the responsibility, in particular to the economic system, by means of political initiatives aiming at internalizing the societal horizon within the business community'.[11] For Indian policy-makers, this could mean expecting companies to weaken the wave of protest movements and popular discontent in a way that reduces the government's responsibility for this daunting task. As explained by an executive of the National Thermal Power Corporation (NTPC), who was closely involved in the design of India's CSR policies:

At that time, the perception of the people regarding companies was getting negative, and the government wanted CSR to become something which companies would do systematically, not just according to the good will of the CEO.[12]

---

[9] A senior bureaucrat of the MCA, December 2008.

[10] A senior bureaucrat of the MCA, December 2008.

[11] Holmström (2010, 150). See also Kaplan (2015).

[12] An executive of the National Thermal Power Corporation, September 2014.

This objective was also shared by MPs who participated in the making of CSR public policies:

> The first purpose is that it will decrease and appease the discontent of localities where people have to part on a permanent basis with their land, their forests and their livelihood. And the second purpose is that it will commit the local people to the company. They will come to the company to discuss about these CSR projects, and it will create an interface. It will help minimize the turmoil.[13]

As for the temporal dimension of meaning, the concept of CSR opens up a forward-looking horizon of progressive opportunities by suggesting that companies can move away from the negative side of the distinction (socially 'irresponsible') towards its positive side (socially 'responsible'). Pointing at and encouraging this promising *movement* seemed politically advantageous for India's pro-business policy-makers, as they could claim to help companies mutate from being societal problem-makers to becoming societal problem-solvers. Projecting the possibility of such desirable convergence between 'business' and 'development' could be expected to strengthen support within public opinion. It could also help counter those who accused the government of neglecting the life chances of the masses by focusing on the interests of the country's elite.

While CSR was supplying India's political system with promising opportunities of intervention, exploiting these opportunities required policy-makers to define what CSR actually means as a policy instrument. The following section compares how this meaning-generating process unfolded in the making of India's two major CSR public policies, the NVGs and the section 135 of the Companies Act.

The National Voluntary Guidelines (NVGs): CSR as a business case

The policy initiative which led to the formulation of the NVGs by the Indian Ministry of Corporate Affairs (MCA) in 2011 is a direct follow-up of the Partnership for Inclusive Growth presented by Manmohan Singh at the CII in 2007. The same year, as the proposed partnership seemed to have little effects, the Union Cabinet mandated the MCA to explore further CSR policy options.

---

[13] A member of the Lok Sabha, September 2014.

Previous exchanges between the MCA and the German international cooperation agency Gesellschaft für Internationale Zusammenarbeit (GIZ) had already revealed an opportunity for collaboration: GIZ was running a programme designed to promote CSR in developing countries as an instrument to boost 'business success' and 'competitiveness' by involving companies as partners for 'economically feasible, socially fair and ecologically stable development'.[14] Building on this programme, the MCA and GIZ launched an Indo-German Corporate Social Responsibility Initiative in 2008, which resulted in the development of the NVGs.[15] Three characteristics of the policy-making process shaped the way it gave meaning to CSR by relating the concept of CSR with certain distinctions and not others.

First, at least partly as a result of the involvement of GIZ, the initial policy goals of this initiative were informed by the global mainstream CSR discourse of the 2000s. In particular, the MCA and GIZ adopted the dominant view of that time that CSR can most effectively enhance the contribution of companies to socially inclusive and environmentally sustainable 'development' when it is inscribed in the core business activities of firms.[16] Following this perspective, the predominant conception of CSR among Indian companies, according to which being 'socially responsible' primarily means carrying out philanthropic activities such as community development projects in the vicinity of production units, appeared as outdated. To leverage the opportunities provided by CSR, the state needed to get companies to envisage CSR as being about inventing 'socially responsible' ways of doing business.

In addition, both the MCA and GIZ adopted the dominant view that CSR is a discretionary domain of corporate management.[17] This premise meant that public authorities could intervene as a facilitator, but not dictate what companies should do with regard to CSR. In the words of a senior bureaucrat from the MCA:

---

[14] GTZ (2011, 3).

[15] This Indo-German cooperation is a good illustration of the transnational dimension of CSR, which also characterizes the promotion of CSR by national public authorities. While the present study focuses on CSR policy-making processes that are internal to India's political system, the claim is obviously not that these processes were insulated from transnational communication flows, in which they were embedded.

[16] See, for instance, Porter and Kramer (2006).

[17] See, for instance, McWilliams and Siegel (2001).

Since CSR should be voluntary, since only the management of a company can decide if the company should adopt CSR or not, the government can only incite companies, encourage them, upskill them.[18]

A further consequence of this premise was that to change the CSR practices of companies through voluntary means, public authorities would need to motivate them by sticking to forms of CSR that can benefit the financial bottom line of companies (see later).

Against this backdrop, the MCA and GIZ decided to organize a multi-stakeholder deliberation, whose role would be to adapt this global CSR approach to the Indian context, as well as to specify its content with a set of voluntary CSR guidelines. In July 2008, a multi-stakeholder Guidelines Drafting Committee (GDC) was constituted. Formally, members of the GDC were selected so as to involve representatives of all relevant institutional stakeholders. But in practice, the MCA and GIZ handpicked the GDC's members from within a small epistemic community based primarily in New Delhi.[19] To ensure that the guidelines would fit with the initial policy goal, these members were chosen not only for their expertise but also for their commitment to the vision of CSR outlined earlier.[20] Trade union leaders and activists who were more critical towards CSR were not invited.

This particular setting led to a second characteristic of the policy-making process, which is the strong cohesion among the members of the GDC, which a former member described as 'something of a club'.[21] As the GDC deliberated on the principles that should structure the CSR guidelines, in sub-groups and during plenary sessions, this common ground facilitated collaboration while allowing dissent:

---

[18] A senior bureaucrat from the MCA, December 2008.

[19] An epistemic community is 'a network of professionals with recognized expertise and competence in a particular domain and an authoritative claim to policy-relevant knowledge within that domain or issue-area' (Haas 1992, 3).

[20] The GDC comprised the project coordinators from the MCA and GIZ, representatives from Indian and foreign companies (Tata, NTPC, Microsoft), representatives of apex business associations (CII, FICCI, Federation of Indian Micro and Small & Medium Enterprises), CSR experts from civil society organizations (TERI, PiC) and from consultancy service providers (SustainAbility), as well as a representative from the apex grouping of NGOs Voluntary Action Network India.

[21] Interview conducted by the author, September 2014.

One could propose a text on his or her field of expertise, and the other members would react. Because we had a good knowledge of the subject, we could counter each other, discuss each and every point.

We could have bitter fights sometime. But there was trust, and you knew you could disagree without threatening the relationship. [22]

For instance, one member tried to convince the committee that the entire NVGs should be based on human rights, because 'rights are a substantial thing, which people can lean on, and you have multiple human rights which exist, which have been formulated'.[23] To reinforce this proposal, he collected letters of support from about 100 civil society organizations. After discussions, the idea was rejected for being too at odds with the economic interests of companies, which also needed to be taken into consideration. However, owing to the importance of the topic of business and human rights in the field of CSR, the committee agreed to dedicate one of the guidelines' principles to this theme.

In another case of contention, some members of the GDC proposed to tackle the topic of legitimate/illegitimate business lobbying and political influence in the guidelines. Members of the GDC who were affiliated to the business associations CII and FICCI objected that their superiors would not allow them to support this idea, as this topic was too sensitive. Other members opposed the idea on the ground that the NVGs should not legitimize any form of lobbying, which they perceived as a threat to democracy. But a series of scandals involving collusion between large companies and high-level politicians and bureaucrats (for example, 2G spectrum allocation scam, coal block allocation scam, illegal mining scam in Karnataka), which triggered large-scale social and political mobilizations, created favourable conditions for a compromise. A principle was included in the guidelines which recognizes the right of businesses to influence government and public opinion, but which emphasizes that 'policy advocacy must expand public good rather than diminish it or make it available to a selected few'.[24]

The third characteristic of the policy-making process underlying the NVGs was the ability of the GDC to avoid direct external interferences from political actors and business interest groups. While arguments within the GDC were mostly based on 'the current literature and knowledge',[25] members of the

---

[22] Interviews conducted by the author with two members of the GDC, September 2014.

[23] Interview conducted by the author, September 2014.

[24] Government of India (2011, 21).

[25] Interview conducted by the author with a member of the GDC, September 2014.

GDC mobilized other resources against external interferences to secure the approach to CSR which they were committed to, and for which they had been initially selected.

Soon after the beginning of the drafting work of the GDC, a new minister took office at the MCA, whom former members of the GDC describe as being close to business interest groups. In November 2009, the MCA suddenly announced that the minister would release the CSR guidelines in December on the occasion of the India Corporate Week. The GDC presented a first draft, which had been put together on short notice. But the MCA put the committee aside and solicited an alternative document from experts close to the CII and FICCI. The resulting CSR Voluntary Guidelines 2009 translate the policy preferences of the MCA. A single 'fundamental principle' states that 'each business entity should formulate a CSR policy ... which should be an integral part of overall business policy and aligned with its business goals'. Moreover, the social responsibility of 'Indian entrepreneurs' is presented not as a normative expectation, but as an existing reality rooted in 'India's ancient wisdom'.[26] This political move took most members of the GDC by surprise.[27] However, in early 2010, negotiations with the MCA enabled the GDC to be reconstituted, and to resume its work under the Indo-German CSR Initiative.

After this first victory of the GDC, the MCA insisted it should design a flexible document, which should be easy for companies to follow. In spring 2010, the MCA strongly opposed the intention of the GDC to submit its first draft of the guidelines to a consultation open to a variety of civil society actors in Delhi, Mumbai, Bangalore, and Kolkata. The ministry suggested that the consultation be narrowed down to exchanges with business actors. But again, the GDC succeeded in imposing its preferences: the government retreated when the GDC threatened to disclose the MCA's position in a public letter that would be communicated to the press.

Yet another conflict arose when members of the GDC tried to get the MCA to introduce a mandatory CSR reporting framework for large companies, which would be based on the guidelines. The ministry refused and released the NVGs in July 2011 without such a mandatory component. But some members of the GDC turned to SEBI, which is the Indian financial market

---

[26] Government of India (2009, 9–11).

[27] 'The document was shoddy, and we were really aghast, taken by surprise with what had come out. On the other hand, we were also happy that our name did not appear on this document' (a member of the GDC, September 2014).

regulator. Interested in an opportunity to upgrade Indian rules to international accounting standards, SEBI issued a circular in August 2012 on Business Responsibility Reports, which requires the 100 largest listed companies by market capitalization to report annually on their social responsibility along the lines indicated in the NVGs.

As a result of this policy-making process, in the NVGs, CSR is defined as a field of opportunities for companies to conduct business operations that 'harmonize' their financial performance with 'the expectations of society, the environment and the many stakeholders [they] interface with in a sustainable manner'.[28] A series of concrete expectations are outlined in the document, which comprises nine principles. For instance, businesses should 'inform all relevant stakeholders of the operating risks and address and redress the issues raised' (excerpt from Principle 1), 'provide and maintain equal opportunities at the time of recruitment as well as during the course of employment irrespective of caste, creed, gender, race, religion, disability or sexual orientation' (excerpt from Principle 3), and 'take measures to check and prevent pollution' as well as 'assess the environmental damage and bear the cost of pollution abatement with due regard to public interest' (excerpt from Principle 6). But the NVGs also explicitly suggest that companies should consider these expectations depending on their own strategic priorities and the economic benefits they can expect from CSR – the 'business case' for CSR.

The NVGs were welcomed both by reformist CSR experts, that is, experts who believe CSR can enhance the contributions of business to the well-being of society at large, and by most of the Indian business community. Business associations, in particular, considered the NVGs to be a useful contribution to their agenda that promotes self-regulation and frames business as a driver of social welfare and environmental sustainability (see Chapter 4). Core institutions of India's political system, however, were already engaged in a different process of CSR policy-making, which ended up overshadowing the NVGs.

Section 135: CSR as material contributions to 'development'

The introduction of a CSR clause in India's new Companies Act constitutes the second main CSR policy adopted by the central government. The conditions of production of this policy and the conception of CSR which it institutionalized depart from the NVGs on a number of points.

---

[28] Government of India (2011, 6).

First, unlike the initial premises underlying the NVGs, which emphasize the superiority of global business-related CSR over Indian philanthropic CSR, section 135 originated from actors whose views on CSR were deeply embedded in this Indian philanthropic approach. More precisely, the origin of section 135 goes back to the mid-2000s, when major programmes of rehabilitation and resettlement conducted by the public enterprise NTPC were coming to an end. These programmes comprised mainly local development initiatives implemented among village communities neighbouring NTPC's power plants. To avoid conflicts with these communities, NTPC decided to continue providing peripheral development in the name of its social responsibility. This decision was picked up by the central government, which envisaged extending CSR to all central public sector enterprises (CPSEs). In the late 2000s, CPSEs knew that the government would soon require them to spend part of their profit on such kinds of CSR activities, and they asked the government to impose a similar constraint on their private competitors.

In a context where CSR was increasingly considered by the government as a relevant policy option, this idea resonated favourably among the Union Cabinet and within the leadership of the Congress Party. In 2009, it was caught on by MPs, who were reviewing a Companies Bill that the MCA had introduced earlier in the law-making process in order to modernize corporate governance law in India. As the Standing Committee on Finance (SCF), a permanent parliamentary committee, was examining the bill, the idea emerged to recommend that the government adds a CSR clause in the legal text. Such clause would require companies to spend a share of their net profit for CSR activities. This idea was welcomed by most members of the SCF, irrespective of their party affiliation.

A second difference between the two policy-making processes is that unlike the NVGs, section 135 was crafted in the midst of India's parliamentary institutions through a process driven primarily by political calculations. Such political calculations motivated a large majority of the thirty-one members of the SCF to support the idea of mandating private companies to spend more for CSR. This strong support might reflect a certain conception of public interests. As explained by a parliamentary member of the SCF:

> I have seen the amount of exploitation [of people and natural resources] going on, and the discontent of the people. Other MPs too. This is from where the initiative comes.... The country needs industry, and the local people need to be satisfied. Both have to function together. The balance has to be maintained.[29]

---

[29] Interview conducted by the author with a member of the SCF, September 2014.

Mandating private companies to increase CSR spending was also opening promising perspectives in terms of power politics. Indeed, CSR in India is not only a national issue but also a regional and local one. Concretely, getting more companies to spend more money for local development projects would increase resources that MPs and their local affiliates could use for patronage. Patronage refers to candidates who obtain votes by promising to reward supporters if they are elected, through the channelling of public resources extracted, for instance, from social welfare programmes. The ability of candidates to convince voters in their respective constituencies that they can be resourceful patrons is a strategic asset in Indian elections.[30] As the case of Lafarge India illustrates, peripheral development initiatives implemented by companies as part of their CSR programmes are usually part of this patronage system: companies secure the support of elected representatives by letting them influence the allocation of CSR resources in their constituency, while elected representatives improve their popularity by displaying this influence in public, for instance, during speeches in inauguration ceremonies of CSR-funded projects.

Political calculations also favoured the positive reaction of the central government towards the proposal of the SCF. Policy-makers in favour of this measure argued that a greater involvement of the private sector in development initiatives would help India achieve the Millennium Development Goals. In a context of rising socio-economic inequalities, higher CSR spending would also help improve the perception of companies among the general public:

> We have seen a big division in this country, the divide between the rich and the poor is getting bigger and bigger. It is about time that we do a *perception correction*. That can only be done if the companies themselves move forward and show that they are responsible, sensitive and they want to give back to the society.[31]

In a context where protest movements such as those against Tata Motor's car factory in West Bengal and Vedanta's bauxite mines in Odisha were 'on the minds of policy-makers',[32] upscaling CSR was also expected to minimize such

---

[30] For an overview of patronage in India's democracy, see Corbridge, Harriss, and Jeffrey (2013, ch. 8). On the role of clientelism and patronage in Indian politics, see also Sarangi (2016).

[31] Minister of Corporate Affairs, minutes of the plenary session of the Lok Sabha on December 18, 2012. Emphasis added.

[32] Interview conducted by the author with a senior bureaucrat of the MCA, September 2014.

conflicts, which were hurting the investment climate of the country and the popularity of the government's pro-business development policies. The request of CPSEs were a further 'deciding factor' in exchanges between the SCF and the MCA, as 'the argument became: if the public sector has to do it, so the private sector should do it as well'.[33]

This constellation of political interests led the SCF and the MCA to officially agree in the summer of 2010 that section 135 of the Companies Bill may now require every company above a certain financial size to formulate a CSR policy and to ensure that every year at least 2 per cent of its average net profit during the three preceding financial years are spent on CSR activities.[34] A 'comply or explain' mechanism of implementation was chosen, according to which companies that failed to comply with this requirement would need to provide 'suitable reasons' in the report of the board of directors, which is attached to the yearly financial statement of companies.

A third difference between the NVGs and section 135 is that while experts of the GDC limited interference from political and business actors in the making of the NVGs, in section 135 it was politics that limited the interference of business actors and experts in the policy-making process. The project of introducing a mandatory CSR clause in the Companies Bill triggered strong opposition from Indian business interest groups. During consultations organized by the SCF as part of its examination of the Companies Bill (2009), both the CII and FICCI argued that only voluntary CSR was appropriate, and that companies operating in India were already spending significant amounts in this domain. However, while business interest groups usually exert significant influence over the Indian law-making process, for instance, by colluding with MPs,[35] in this case, most members of the SCF and the parties they were affiliated with were too interested in the political resources provided by the CSR clause to change their position. In the words of a member of the SCF:

> To be very frank, some members of the Committee were in favour of voluntarism, and these members were those who have a direct or an indirect

---

[33] Interview conducted by the author with a member of the SCF, September 2014.

[34] Standing Committee on Finance (2010). The clause applies to companies having a net worth of ₹5 billion or more, a turnover of ₹10 billion or more, or a net profit of ₹50 million or more.

[35] Hazra (2011).

interest in the business of private companies. But they were a minority, maybe seven or eight members.[36]

The MCA also refused to withdraw the proposed CSR clause from the bill. When business interest groups asked the government to make a tax instead of mandating large companies to spend 2 per cent of their profit for CSR, the MCA replied:

> We look for corporate social responsibility, not for government social responsibility.... We do not want to make a new tax, we want you to do your projects, to give back to society, to take your responsibility.[37]

However, the MCA was more receptive than most MPs to the pleas of business actors. While revising the Companies Bill (2009), which became the Companies Bill (2011), it tried to soften the terms of the CSR clause that had been agreed upon by the ministry and the SCF: the requirement that companies shall 'ensure' to spend at least 2 per cent of their average net profit on CSR became 'shall make every endeavour to ensure'.

Besides the MCA's reputation of being rather receptive to concerns of private sector companies, its partial responsiveness towards the demands of business interest groups also reflects the central government's political interest in this matter. While the MPs were interested mostly in the material resources that a CSR spending requirement would provide for patronage, the central government was primarily interested in the symbolic resources such a policy could provide. By appearing to 'mandate' large companies to invest more in the country's development, the government could display itself as a political authority that withstands the opposition of business interest groups for the benefit of the Indian people. The ambiguous formula 'shall make every endeavour to ensure' could secure this symbolic resource, while giving companies leeway to determine how much they would actually spend for CSR.

The mandatory CSR policy also met with criticism and resistance from members of the GDC, who were working in parallel on the NVGs. They perceived the mandatory CSR clause as defeating the very purpose and potential of CSR, as they understood it: 'We were against the 2 per cent, because what

---

[36] Interview conducted by the author, September 2014.

[37] Interview conducted by the author with a senior bureaucrat from the MCA, September 2014.

matters is how you make your profit, not how you distribute your profit.'[38] Concerns were also raised about practical effects of the mandatory CSR clause. For instance, within large companies, CSR departments would be incentivized to focus on the spending of CSR budgets rather than on inducing changes in the core operations of their company, such as improving working conditions or designing eco-friendly products. Moreover, the management of small and medium enterprises might deduce from such a law that CSR is only relevant to large companies.

Members of the GDC tried to defend these positions within the MCA, but the ministry was now following another path, in which the NVGs had become a secondary concern. Evoking attempts to convince a senior bureaucrat of the MCA in charge of section 135, a member of the GDC explained:

> He has been avoiding me for the past five years. Anyway, the government has not discussed this CSR policy. They have elaborated it behind closed doors, with just a handful of experts to advise them.[39]

The GDC also asked the MCA to consider referring to the NVGs in section 135. But the ministry refused to do so. Conversely, promoters of the CSR clause within the MCA saw the NVGs with a critical eye:

> These other people from the former guidelines drafting committee, they come from a previous era. What they will tell you is that CSR and the NVGs were a broader framework than the CSR of the Companies Act, that CSR is now restricted to the 2 per cent. But bringing CSR into the legislation, it is something very different. Here we talk about companies investing their money for the development of the country. Not principles, but actual money, rupees that you can count.[40]

In short, opposition from business actors and CSR experts failed to derail or substantially alter the policy-making process, which moved forward as per the law-making procedures. The final version of section 135 was negotiated in a plenary session of the Lok Sabha, the lower house of Parliament, before the Companies Bill was put to a vote. Most MPs who intervened on CSR in the debate suggested that the law be strengthened. Propositions were made to increase the required CSR spending above 2 per cent of net profit, to provide

---

[38] Interview conducted by the author with a member of the GDC, September 2014.
[39] A member of the GDC, September 2014.
[40] A senior bureaucrat of the MCA, September 2014.

for the monitoring or even the steering of CSR spending by a dedicated administrative structure, and to replace the 'comply or explain' mechanism with a clear binding mandate. But the minister of corporate affairs argued in favour of the flexible comply or explain mechanism, while rejecting the idea of a direct oversight of companies' CSR spending by the government:

> There were some suggestions made to us saying that this bill should be more stringent, corporates will try and get out of CSR.... My response to them was that the citizens in this country are as much Indians and want to improve this country. So, we must make the law in good faith hoping and assuming that their objective and the Government's objective is the same.... We believe that this is your country also. It is the corporates' and the companies' country also, and they, I think, are more than willing. So, they should be allowed to do the work that they want to do.[41]

In the end, the Companies Bill was passed with an amended section 135. The formulation 'shall make every endeavour to ensure' introduced earlier by the MCA was replaced by 'shall ensure', and a sentence was added which expects the CSR policy of each company to 'give preference to the local area and areas around it where it operates'. Section 135 was debated when the bill was put to a vote in the Rajya Sabha (the upper house of the Indian Parliament). But its formulation remained untouched, and on 29 August 2013, it became law as part of the new Companies Act.

The common voluntaristic core of the NVGs and section 135

A systematic comparative analysis of the NVGs and section 135 reveals significant variations as to how India's political system exploited the meaning horizon opened up by the CSR concept in these two policy initiatives. Depending on the conditions of production of these two policies, and the underlying constellations of interests and power relationships, CSR was selectively associated with different distinctions such as about profitability, the thematic scope of CSR activities, or the degree of autonomy or constraint with which companies can design their CSR programmes. These meaning-generating processes resulted in the production of different regulatory structures. However, the comparative analysis also reveals a series of commonalities, which have consequences in terms of how these CSR policies

---

[41] Minister of Corporate Affairs, minutes of the plenary session of the Lok Sabha on 18 December 2012.

are set to change the observation and processing of tensions between profit-making and competing collective values and interests.

With regard to the factual dimension of meaning, the NVGs associate CSR with *profit-generating* business operations, which would be 'socially responsible' inasmuch as companies 'integrate' and 'embed' the guideline's principles in their 'core business processes'.[42] Conversely, section 135 associates CSR with the *redistribution of profit* through the funding of development-related activities. The CSR Rules (2014), which provide legally binding indications regarding the implementation of section 135, stipulate that CSR is 'excluding activities undertaken in pursuance of [a company's] normal course of business', and that 'the surplus arising out of the CSR projects or programs or activities shall not form part of the business profit of a company'.[43]

However, this does not preclude indirect economic benefits, which are put forward in both public policies. The NVGs claim that implementing the guidelines will 'improve the ability of businesses to enhance their competitive strengths, improve their reputations, increase their ability to attract and retain talent and manage their relations with investors and society at large'.[44] Moreover, the NVGs provide management tools to help companies identify how they can derive economic value out of CSR, and shape their CSR strategy accordingly. Similarly, while addressing business executives in a filmed debate that followed the adoption of the Companies Act, the minister of corporate affairs emphasized that section 135 will 'make sure that people in India believe that corporates are not just there looking at bottom lines and quarterly profits, but that they are also concerned with the situation in which these people are living', and that this 'good will' would pay back, also in economic terms.[45]

A further point of comparison in the factual dimension of meaning is the thematic scope of issue-areas related to CSR. In the NVGs, the issue-areas distinguished in the list of nine principles are rather connected to business operations. They comprise themes such as ethics, transparency and accountability, the environmental quality of goods and services, the well-being of employees, human rights, inclusive and equitable development, and environmental protection. For section 135, the Schedule VII of the Companies

---

[42] Government of India (2011, 27)

[43] Government of India (2014).

[44] Government of India (2011, 6).

[45] The minister, Sachin Pilot, speaking at the occasion of a Google Hangout organized in August 2013 by NextGen and CNBC TV18: https://www.youtube.com/watch?v=i-boKITJ-7U (accessed on 22 August 2014).

Act indicates development-related areas in which companies are expected to implement CSR activities, such as poverty alleviation, the promotion of education, gender equality, rural development, the promotion of heritage, and environmental sustainability. However, in both cases, the thematic scope of CSR is defined in such broad and open terms that companies can use CSR to address most societal problems that are of strategic relevance for the development of their business performances and prospects.

With regard to the social dimension of meaning, both policies differ in terms of *who* between the public regulator and companies is to control what companies do in terms of their 'social responsibility'. The NVGs contend that 'if a business endeavours to function responsibly, it would have to adopt each of the nine (9) principles in their entirety rather than picking and choosing what might suit them'.[46] But the *voluntary* guidelines remain 'not prescriptive in nature', and they only 'urge' companies to take the guidelines into consideration.[47] Moreover, the management tools that are provided explicitly intend to help each company identify which of the guideline's components are relevant for it in terms of CSR's 'business case'. On the contrary, section 135 is presented as a 'mandatory' CSR policy, which is an integral part of India's positive law.

However, section 135 also gives significant discretions to companies. First, the 'comply or explain' mechanism provides companies with the possibility to choose the extent to which they want to comply, as long as they provide some sort of justification: only the absence of any justification exposes a company to sanctions. Second, section 135 lets companies choose what CSR projects and programmes they want to conduct. While it indicates a preference for projects located near the production units of companies, companies can deviate from this preference. Moreover, while Schedule VII indicates issue-areas that companies should consider, the CSR Rules state that 'CSR means and includes but is not limited to' the Schedule VII and companies' official CSR policies. As emphasized by the minister for corporate affairs:

> It is not up to me to say this is CSR or this is not CSR. It is up to the Board of the company, how they want to use the fund....] It is not a tax, a cess that companies have to pay to the government. We are only urging companies to spend their own money in the areas they feel most comfortable with through the agencies they are familiar with.[48]

---

[46] Government of India (2011, 5).

[47] Government of India (2011, 6).

[48] Government of India (2011, 6).

Both CSR policies also present differences with regard to the temporal dimension of meaning. The NVGs conceive of CSR as a forward-looking movement that both generates and realizes opportunities of synergies between successful business development, social welfare, and environmental sustainability. In this perspective, the guidelines encourage and support companies to 'self-steer and regulate their journey towards becoming sustainable and responsible businesses'.[49] Section 135 is more oriented towards the present. The Companies Act set a date when section 135 entered into force, and section 135 aims to get companies to spend on CSR projects and programmes that should make immediate contributions to the country's development. However, from the point of view of the public policy-maker, requiring such contributions by law was primarily a means to attain the same forward-looking objective as for the NVGs: enhance the popularity of pro-business development policies by steering public opinion towards a more positive perception of business-development relationships.

The political management of economic responsiveness: institutional change and its implications

Overall, India's CSR public policies can be understood as a reaction of the political system to the growing tensions and conflicts that have arisen from the restrictions imposed by profit-driven economic processes on economic responsiveness. While these tensions and conflicts have been perceived by companies in terms of a danger for their business prospects, a number of incumbent politicians have experienced the same tensions and conflicts as a threat to their political – electoral – prospects. For them, adopting policies that foster economic responsiveness by promoting and institutionalizing CSR seemed like a promising strategy to address this political threat. Framing companies as socially responsible 'partners', whose contributions to development can be substantially enhanced without harming their competitiveness and profitability, was likely to strengthen the popularity of the government's contentious pro-business policies. In addition, promoting CSR was expected to have positive effects on economic growth, as the legitimation of profit-making and the attenuation of protest movements against companies would participate in creating an investor-friendly context.

---

[49] Government of India (2011, 6).

To analyse how the resulting CSR public policies have changed the observation and processing of tensions between profit-making and 'development' in India so far, a first aspect to be considered is institutional change. In this regard, India's CSR public policies have induced several changes. By inscribing specific definitions of CSR in regulatory norms, the state has contributed to shaping formation of the intermediary institution of CSR in the Indian context. Concretely, the adoption of section 135 of the Companies Act, which overshadowed the NVGs, made the association of CSR with 'philanthropic' redistributive practices official. Other definitions of this essentially contested concept, including the definition formulated in the NVGs, but also more critical definitions of the term, were consequently discarded as irrelevant or deviant. This political and legal institutionalization of a selected definition of CSR circumscribed the 'social responsibilities' that the state, acting in the name of the Indian nation, attributes to companies, that is, the behaviour companies need to follow to be deemed socially responsible. Since the adoption of the Companies Act, large companies that spend 2 per cent of their net profit on CSR projects can claim to have discharged their social responsibility. They need to do that, but not necessarily more than that.

A more detailed examination of the NVGs and section 135 of the Companies Act provides further insights into their institutional features and outcomes. First, while the formulation of CSR policies allowed Indian policy-makers to address in one stroke a large number of multifaceted societal problems, this also meant sticking to regulatory expectations that are general and flexible – if not vague. This characteristic can be found both in the NVGs and in section 135: these norms define broad and blurry issue-areas, in which companies can choose strategically between problems they want to address and problems they want to leave untouched. CSR also offered opportunities for Indian policy-makers to relieve political pressure by sharing responsibilities for societal problem-solving with companies. But this meant foregoing the use of constraints based on command and control, as such constraints require enforcement mechanisms that increase rather than lower the burden of the state. As a result, both the NVGs and section 135 emphasize the responsibility of *companies* in areas where the state describes itself as insufficient and/or deficient, and both policies avoid bureaucratic enforcement mechanisms based on monitoring and sanctions. Finally, CSR allowed policy-makers to suggest possibilities of convergence between profit-making and development. But this required policies that outshine contradictions between profit-making and societal problem-solving: the NVGs emphasize synergies between profit-making, social welfare, and environmental sustainability, and section 135 defines profit-making as a source of corporate contributions to the country's development.

These institutional characteristics have consequences with regard to the respective roles of politics and the economy in the selective observation and processing of societal problems in general, and of tensions between profit-making and competing collective values and interests in particular. The NVGs involve companies mostly in the performance of regulatory functions. Formally, the guidelines '*assume* that compliance with the laws of the land is necessary for a business to operate, and this is non-negotiable'.[50] Nevertheless, the NVGs are not a voluntary supplement to well-functioning legally-binding regulations. They were conceived by the government as a response to the deficient enforcement of legally binding regulations (see earlier). The voluntary guidelines even entail a table of correspondence between its nine principles and India's legally binding regulatory framework. Section 135 rather attributes redistributive functions to profit-driven companies. Public authorities emphasized the supplementary character of such transfer: according to the minister for corporate affairs, 'not for a second should anyone believe that the government is abdicating its responsibility, that it will not make roads, schools and electricity'.[51] Nevertheless, the Companies Act institutionalized CSR as an alternative to taxation for the partial transfer of wealth generated by companies to beneficiaries of social projects and programmes.

While the two policies attribute regulatory and redistributive functions to companies, they provide significant discretion to companies regarding the exercise of these functions. The NVGs encourage companies to become full-fledged 'responsible businesses', but companies are also encouraged to conceive of CSR as a 'business case', that is, to consider societal issues such as labour welfare, human rights, and environmental sustainability primarily as a function of profit-making. While section 135 is more restrictive in terms of organizational and financial means companies are expected to mobilize, it also leaves companies free to determine the extent of their involvement and the societal problems they want to address on the basis of their own strategic priorities. As a result of these institutional characteristics, both the NVGs and

---

[50] Government of India (2011, 28), emphasis added.

[51] The minister, Sachin Pilot, speaking at the occasion of a Google Hangout organized in August 2013 by NextGen and CNBC TV18: https://www.youtube.com/watch?v=i-boKlTJ-7U (accessed on 22 August 2014).

section 135 are conducive to an increasing role of profit-making as a guiding value in the selective observation and processing of societal problems, including in particular problems that are attributed to tensions between profit-making and competing collective values and interests.

A second aspect to be considered in the analysis is the concrete impact of the institutional arrangements described earlier on the actual behaviour of companies and their relationship with their social surrounding. How and to what extent have India's CSR policies changed corporate conduct and related patterns of economic responsiveness? Unfortunately, available reports and scientific studies provide insufficient information to tackle this difficult question in an empirically rich and methodologically thorough way, as they rely primarily on data provided by companies in their CSR reports. Interviews conducted with CSR managers of four large Indian companies (Tata, Vedanta, Jindal Steel, Cairn India) as part of the present study provide useful complementary indications. But these interviews were conducted in September 2014, so they do not capture the impact of India's CSR policies that occurred afterwards. Moreover, as the complexity of the case of Lafarge India exemplifies, a single interview with a CSR executive is not sufficient to grasp the complex effects of CSR public policies on a company's policies and practices in this field – not to mention outcomes of these organizational changes in terms of economic responsiveness. These caveats notwithstanding, a few observations can be formulated.

Regarding the NVGs, their impact seems to have been limited. An executive from Jindal Steel explained that as a result of the guidelines, a three-day seminar was organized at the Global Jindal University in collaboration with FICCI to sensitize students and the faculty on human rights issues, 'to explain to them how Human Rights are in fact a business case'.[52] The NVGs might have triggered similar kinds of effects in other companies, at least in those that were already engaged in CSR and therefore sensitive to normative evolutions in this field. But no information suggests that the NVGs had much effect beyond this receptive circle.

The sole structural impact of the guidelines we could observe comes from the circular on Business Responsibility Reports issued by SEBI in 2012, which defined the principles and the reporting framework outlined in the NVGs as the template for mandatory CSR reporting for the 100 largest companies listed on the Bombay Stock Exchange and the National Stock Exchange. According

---

[52] Interview conducted by the author, 15 September 2014.

to a study conducted by KPMG,[53] 96 per cent of the targeted companies complied with this circular, and 65 per cent of them reported having internal policies and practices on all of the principles outlined in the guidelines. These policies and practices include, for instance, having a code of conduct, registering complaints of stakeholders related to human rights, having products or services whose design took social and/or environmental concerns into account, or having sustainable sourcing procedures. However, it is likely that at least part of these CSR policies and practices predate the NVGs, and without further empirical material, it is not possible to assess the extent to which the NVGs contributed to the adoption of new CSR elements. Moreover, the information provided by companies in their CSR reports says little about the substance and concrete outcomes of these policies and practices. For instance, according to the study of KPMG, while 95 per cent of the companies provided information on complaints received by stakeholders in relation to human rights, most of them indicated 'nil complaint', and only 3 per cent of them provided additional information on the process of collection of the complaints. Whether the 'nil complaint' indicates no actual human rights issues, or rather the absence of a transparent mechanism to register complaints, and whether the received complaints were properly addressed and human rights abuses redressed, remain open questions.

According to a CSR executive of Vedanta, which is a multinational metals and mining company, the impact of the NVGs was further limited by the overriding effects of the Companies Act:

> Now with the Companies Act of 2013, all this NVGs thing is old history. NVGs are there for the 100 largest companies per market capitalization. But not for the rest of companies, which all focus on the 2 per cent now.[54]

In fact, while the CSR clause of the Companies Act offers significant leeway in terms of implementation, it was perceived by most companies operating in India as the defining form within which they had to conceive their CSR policies and practices. As the case of Vedanta suggests, this also applies at least partly to companies that must report to SEBI along the lines of the NVGs:

> Vedanta is a multinational company. It is listed on the London Stock Exchange and has lots of lenders from Western countries, institutional investors ... so we are looking at the international criteria. The international frameworks on

---

[53] KPMG (2017a).
[54] Interview conducted by the author, 12 September 2014.

CSR are already there, they apply to companies like us. Now with the new Act, as a CSR manager at Vedanta in India, I don't have to look at these CSR standards. Now I just have to focus on community relations, because this is what the government asks. It is very frustrating. Now I only have to implement and to report. The only discussion which we have now internally is: 'Does it fit the Schedule VII?'

... I will give you an example. In his speech for Independence Day on August 15, the new Prime Minister said that India should have proper toilets for sanitation. The next morning, Airtel and Tata Consultancy Services made an announcement in the newspapers saying that they will allocate that much CSR funds to build toilets. And the next morning, I was questioned internally about how many toilets Vedanta has been constructing, and what our plans for toilet construction are.[55]

The case of Cairn India, which is a major Indian oil and gas exploration and production company, provides similar insights. As one of its CSR executives explained:

There is no creativity going with this policy. We now have to work as per the rules. If we have some project ideas which are outside the scope defined by the law, there is no chance that we can do it. Also, CSR has a business linkage. For instance Unilever, they have this big 'Bottom of the Pyramid' project where they train poor women to sell their products. Such project is both for women empowerment and for market development, to get products to new markets. But such project will not be considered as being CSR by the law. For us it is the same thing. We have a programme in Barmer, where we train villagers to become welders, and they work for the maintenance of our pipelines. This is also some kind of CSR, but it is not recognized as such by the law. For the law, CSR should not be a business case.

According to official data from the Ministry of Corporate Affairs,[56] for the financial year 2014–2015, 10,475 public and private companies were falling within the scope of section 135, representing a potential spending amount of about ₹140 billion (about $2.2 billion). For the same year, the ministry notes

---

[55] Interview conducted by the author, 12 September 2014.

[56] The MCA published a PowerPoint presentation on its website that synthesizes key data on the implementation of section 135 of the Companies Act for the financial year 2014–2015. See www.mca.gov.in/Ministry/pdf/CSRPRESENTATION15092016. pptx (accessed on 17 January 2018).

that 7,334 companies reported on their CSR activities as per the law, and 3,139 declared having spent some amount of money for CSR. In total, the latter spent about ₹88 billion (about $1.3 billion), which is 74 per cent of what they should have spent as per the 2 per cent rule, and 62 per cent of what section 135 required companies to spend. The top 10 and the top 100 spenders account for about 31.5 per cent and 69 per cent of actual CSR spending reported under the Companies Act respectively.[57] Regarding the main areas in which companies spent for CSR, education comes first (32 per cent), followed by health, water, sanitation and hygiene (26 per cent), the environment (14 per cent), and rural development (12 per cent). While less information is available for the financial year 2015–2016, data provided by the MCA indicates that the number of companies that spent on CSR decreased, while the total amount they spent increased: 5,097 companies reported on their CSR spending, among which 2,691 had positive spending amounting to ₹98 billion (about $1.5 billion).[58] Among the spending companies, the top 10 and the top 100 spenders accounted for about 32 per cent and 76 per cent of total CSR spending respectively.

Overall, these empirical observations provide a mixed picture with regard to the impacts of the Companies Act on companies' CSR behaviour. Section 135 seems to have had a structuring effect on companies' definition of CSR. As it formally institutionalized the 'philanthropic' acceptation of CSR, the Companies Act hampered the emergence of alternative meanings and practices such as those promoted by the NVGs. However, so far, the Companies Act has had limited impact with regard to the prevalence of CSR policies and practices among large companies operating in the subcontinent. In 2014–2015, only 29 per cent of the targeted companies complied at least partly with the spending requirement of section 135, and the total funds generated by this CSR policy were only about two-thirds of what the law requires. Moreover, CSR spending was highly concentrated among a limited number of companies.

This latter point is confirmed by a survey based on a sample of 223 companies, which differentiates two kinds of companies falling under the CSR clause of the Companies Act.[59] The first category comprises companies that

---

[57] The top ten spenders, which include both private and state-owned companies, were Reliance Industries Ltd., ONGC Ltd., Infosys Ltd., Tata Consultancy Services Ltd., ITC Ltd., NTPC Ltd., NMDC Ltd., Tata Steel Ltd., ICICI Bank Ltd., and Oil India Ltd.

[58] See www.mca.gov.in/Ministry/pdf/CSRExpenditureDetails_2015_16_29042017.xlsx (accessed on 17 January 2018).

[59] Mukherjee and Bird (2016).

were already conducting CSR activities before the law was adopted. These companies are also the largest companies of the sample in financial terms (net profit and net worth). Their main reaction to section 135 has been to increase the level of their CSR spending. The second category comprises companies that fell under the scope of section 135 but had no prior CSR activity. In average, their financial size is a third of the size of companies with prior CSR activities. Unlike companies from the first category, a majority of these smaller companies with no prior CSR activities stated that they did not plan to increase their level of CSR spending in the next five years. In short, the Companies Act might have intensified CSR practices among the country's largest firms, but it seems to have fallen short of widening the prevalence of CSR outside this corporate elite.

Finally, examining the impacts of India's two CSR public policies requires to look at their effects on economic responsiveness at the level of interplays between business organizations and their social surrounding. This third aspect of the analysis is not only more complex than the two previous ones, but also the less covered by available empirical studies. In terms of perspectives for future empirical research, it would be particularly interesting to explore the effects of the Companies Act on local political dynamics involving companies. As suggested earlier, one reason why most MPs and their political parties supported section 135 is that they expected to benefit from enhanced CSR spending for their local clientelistic strategies. If more detailed empirical research was to confirm that local and regional political actors exert pressures on companies to finance CSR projects that serve their political interests, it would be interesting to investigate the concrete effects of this practice in interplays between profit-driven economic processes and power-driven politics. For instance, as suggested by the case of Lafarge India and other empirical studies,[60] higher CSR spending might reinforce occasions for companies and political actors to develop mutually beneficial ties and arrangements, at the expense of the ability of weaker actors (for example, poor lower-caste villagers, unskilled workers) to get their elected representatives defend their values and interests against profitable but harmful business practices.

Another area that calls for empirical research concerns relationships between companies and civil society organizations. Many NGOs welcomed the adoption of section 135, as they expected increased CSR spending to provide new funding sources to develop their activities. Partnerships with

---

[60] See, for instance, Varman and Al-Amoudi (2016).

which companies subcontract CSR activities to NGOs were also encouraged by the government. In 2012, the MCA created a National Foundation for Corporate Social Responsibility (NFCSR) within the Indian Institute for Corporate Affairs, which is a think tank affiliated to the MCA and directed by one of the key architects of section 135. As part of its activities that support the implementation of section 135, the NFCSR has provided information and training on CSR to both companies and NGOs. In addition, it set up a CSR Implementation Agency Hub, which is a platform designed to facilitate contact between companies looking for NGO partners and NGOs looking for corporate partners. This propitious institutional context is likely to have strengthened collaborations between companies and NGOs in the design and implementation of CSR-related development projects, for instance, in areas such as education, health and sanitation, and rural development.

Besides the outcomes of such collaborations for the projects' beneficiaries, it would be interesting to study their effects on relationships between companies and civil society organizations. Studies conducted in other contexts find that business–NGO partnerships can de-radicalize civil society organizations, as incentives for collaboration can encourage critical organizations to soften their stance and become more business-friendly.[61] In a report on Indian CSR commissioned by the Corporate Responsibility Watch, which was written by NGOs and consultants specialized in this field, Pradeep Patra from the National Foundation for India suggests that the Companies Act has favoured such de-radicalization:

> A lot of organizations that were working with a rights based approach are now turning into service delivery entities. Thus the alternative views on development (the dissenting voices), which are equally significant to a democratic and pluralistic society are not only occupying a shrinking space but are also feeling a severe threat to their continuity.[62]

While Patra's claim is not substantiated with empirical evidence, it is a hypothesis worth exploring, particularly in the light of recent changes in India's political context. Since the 1990s, social movements and organizations operating therein have gained increasing power as 'watch-dogs' who oppose public policies and business practices that, according to them, generate financial profit at the expense of values such as social justice, environmental protection,

---

[61] See, for instance, Shamir (2004).

[62] Patra (2016, 37).

and democracy (see Chapters 4 and 5). In 2014, a leaked note of the Indian Intelligence Bureau was found to accuse critic-minded NGOs, in particular those with foreign funding such as Greenpeace, of using 'people-centric issues' such as 'protection of human rights, "just deal" for project-affected displaced persons, protection of livelihood of indigenous people' to stall economic development projects. Subsequently, Narendra Modi's government revoked the licences of several NGOs that were deemed to be 'anti-national' and 'anti-development'. In recent years, the central government has also made it more difficult for citizens to use the Right to Information Act, introduced in 2005, which had become an important tool used by activists to access sensitive information. Besides, the government has multiplied decisions intended to facilitate economic growth by weakening the National Green Tribunal as well as by softening labour laws and environmental restrictions. Against this backdrop, it would be useful to examine how CSR and related business–NGO partnerships affect the ability of civil society organizations to question the dominant pro-business narrative and the related policy choices, as well as to politicize social problems related to corporate profit-making in India's democracy.

Chapter 7

✠

Conclusion

CSR as an intermediary institution for economic responsiveness

Companies are core institutions of modern society, and their role as both problem-making and problem-solving entities has become a major cause for concerns. While such concerns are not new, it has become hard to find any societal problem that does not involve companies in one way or another. Unemployment, child labour, occupational hazards and suffering at the workplace, growing financial instability, socio-economic inequalities, poverty and related hardships, public health issues such as cancer and obesity, militarized conflicts, energy (in)security, and the multiple manifestations of a global ecological crisis exemplify this vast entanglement in society between corporate conduct, problem genesis, and problem solution.

The phenomenon of CSR has grown out of this entanglement. At first, CSR emerged as an idea developed by American business ethicists and corporate executives who argued that companies can and should not focus single-mindedly on profit maximization. Companies were rather supposed to follow business practices that combine profit-making with moral standards and what was referred to as 'service to the nation'. Building on this synergistic view, CSR has expanded globally and concretized into specialized knowledge, discursive frames, organizational structures and management practices, inter-organizational partnerships, collaborative governance structures, and a vast corpus of public and private regulatory norms. These multiple facets of the global CSR phenomenon are held together and stabilized by the same core idea that was at the origin of the CSR *doxa*: companies can and should go beyond legal compliance and business as usual, and invest resources in finding ways to minimize societal problem-making while maximizing their contributions to societal problem-solving.

Notwithstanding this stable core, CSR has been caught in ongoing academic and popular contention regarding its scope and meaning. For some, CSR is a managerial fancy that should not be taken too seriously. Others conceive of CSR as a phenomenon of major significance, as it could potentially redeem capitalism by channelling ethical, social, and environmental concerns into the functioning of firms. Yet another standpoint also views CSR as a significant phenomenon, but in a negative way. For critical commentators, CSR is primarily a vehicle of corporate hegemony which ends up subordinating non-economic spheres of society to the capitalist logic of monetary accumulation. In view of these debates, *whether and how CSR actually changes the way social systems observe and address social problems* remains an open question.

The present study approached this research question from a perspective that relies primarily on SST. Among other advantages, this theoretical perspective allows us to go beyond the basic dichotomy between 'companies' and 'society' which pervades CSR scholarship. By distinguishing organizations and the function systems of modern society, SST provides a suitable conceptual framework to apprehend how CSR changes business organizations *in relation to* function systems such as the economy, politics, law, and morality. In fact, monetary transactions, the use of political power in the formulation and enforcement of collectively binding decisions, adjudication in courts of law, the production of scientific knowledge, information by mass media, the education of people, their medical treatment, moral expressions of praise and contempt, and so on, constitute as many meaning contexts in which social problems are being described and addressed. This functional differentiation conditions the way corporate conduct is observed as a source of social problems and/ or of solutions. Moreover, as poly-contextual organizations, companies can articulate multiple functional logics. Depending on how their decision-making processes take monetary transactions, political alternatives, legal criteria, moral judgements, and other functional distinctions into account, companies end up coordinating function systems in different ways. As a consequence, CSR is not only likely to affect the role of companies in the genesis and processing of social problems, but is also likely to impact the respective roles of function systems in this regard.

To grasp the complex relations between CSR, companies, and function systems more accurately, the present study made use of Poul Kjaer's concept of intermediary institutions. This concept points at general characteristics of the CSR phenomenon. First, CSR has been co-produced by multiple social systems, and it encompasses multiple – economic, political, legal, moral, and so on – dimensions. As an intermediary institution, CSR operates in between social systems as a 'hinge' of modern society. Second, CSR provides social systems with new possibilities to observe one another as well as to coordinate their operations, for instance, by institutionalizing normative expectations or by exercising self-restraint. This makes CSR both a complement and an alternative to the state, which usually aims to regulate inter-systemic relations through collectively binding decisions. Finally, CSR is particularly concerned with interrelations between the economy and other spheres of society. More specifically, CSR focuses on the role of companies in economic responsiveness – the observation and processing of social problems by a functionally differentiated economic system.

Through their business activities, companies take part in a basic mechanism of responsiveness that characterizes market economies. Companies observe social problems in the form of actual or potential needs located on the demand side of markets. And profit-making motivates them to address these needs by producing commodities that can be sold on these markets for a profit. But the role of companies with regard to economic responsiveness extends beyond markets. It also covers the way companies articulate the economy with concerns located in other meaning contexts. More precisely, companies can enhance or reduce economic responsiveness depending on how they deal with instances of contradiction between profit-making, which is based on monetary cost–benefit calculations, and competing collective values and interests, such as labour welfare, public health, democracy, or environmental protection. In this case, profit-making is not an incentive for but a constraint on economic responsiveness. The more companies' economic decisions focus on profit-making, which is a purely self-referential economic operation, the less they can take competing values and interests into account. Conversely, the less profit-making dominates corporate conduct, the more the economic operations of companies can tolerate the costs of taking non-profit concerns into account.

To examine how the CSR phenomenon changes economic responsiveness, in particular vis-à-vis problems arising from tensions between profit-making and competing collective values and interests, adequate empirical investigation is required. But such investigation runs into the difficulty of circumscribing the CSR phenomenon, as the meaning of 'CSR' is essentially contested. Where does the concrete CSR phenomenon start, and where does it stop? What does 'corporate social responsibility' actually entail? To overcome this obstacle, the present study adopted a constructivist approach that envisages CSR as a contested concept, which is part of the semantic (cultural) dimension of social systems. As an essentially contested concept, CSR has no stabilized and consensual meaning. However, whenever it is selected in social communication, CSR and the underlying distinction 'socially responsible/irresponsible company' introduce a specific horizon of potential meaning construction. Social systems construct the actual meaning of CSR out of this horizon of potentials, as their communicative operations relate CSR in certain ways with certain distinctions – and not others. These communicative processes of meaning construction, which can also involve contention and power, are not carried out in an unstructured social context. They are conditioned by more or less formalized institutions, and they contribute to reproducing and to changing these institutions, either through gradual norm displacement by way of deviant behaviour or through formal procedures. The concrete CSR phenomenon results from and is delineated by these interrelated processes of semantic selection, meaning construction, and institutionalization.

This conceptualization of the CSR phenomenon allows us to break down the research question formulated here in a series of analytical steps. To investigate how CSR changes economic responsiveness, a first step examines the concrete contexts (for example, institutional settings, social movements, conflicts) in which social systems identify the meaning horizon provided by CSR as a useful opportunity, and subsequently select CSR in their operations. This step allows us to find out who uses CSR, within which meaning context, and in relation to which problems. A second step refines the analysis by investigating the meanings given to CSR by social systems, and how these meanings contribute to institutional reproduction and change. At this point, the focus is set on the processes underlying the social construction of the CSR phenomenon. Finally, a third step analyses empirically how the resulting CSR phenomenon changes the way social systems – including in particular companies and the economy – observe and address social problems. This third step is the occasion to examine how CSR changes business organizations, for instance, by increasing their ability to intervene in their non-market environment. It also allows us to examine how CSR contributes to restructuring relationships between function systems such as the economy and the political system in the processing of social problems.

Functional differentiation and the rise of CSR: Insights from the Indian case

Guided by this conceptual framework, the present study analysed CSR and economic responsiveness in the Indian context. The study reconstructed empirically how, from the late eighteenth century onwards, India's modern economy differentiated itself from other spheres of society by way of an increasing monetization, a growing marketization of economic transactions, and an increasing incorporation of economic production in modern companies. This macro-sociological empirical analysis shows the gradual and incomplete character of economic differentiation in the subcontinent. Besides the survival of informal institutions and modes of production in parts of India's economic life, in particular in agriculture and in the so-called unorganized sector, large companies from the 'organized' corporate sector have remained embedded to various degrees in family affairs, in ethnic community ties, and in the socio-political project of building India as a free and prosperous nation. The incompleteness of economic differentiation with regard to companies has not been static. It has varied over the course of time as a result of complex dynamics of institutional change, which the study examined in four selected domains: corporate governance, labour relations, state–business relations, as well as corporate philanthropy and CSR.

Besides incremental institutional evolution, independence in 1947 and the constitution of India as a sovereign nation-state initiated major political-economic changes. Industrial families continued to control most of India's large private companies, and the role of caste-based community ties did not disappear overnight. But the state took over the so-called commanding heights of the economy through five-year planning, state-based industrialization, and a growing political-administrative regulation of the private sector. The state's extensive efforts to steer economic processes towards political goals were not always successful. Nonetheless, they contributed directly and indirectly to limiting the role of profit-making in the economy.

By contrast, India's shift from state interventionism to a 'pro-business' development model since the 1980s has significantly strengthened the role of profit-making as a guiding value of economic operations. As part of this pro-business reorientation, most governments at the central level and at the regional state level have gradually eased regulatory constraints on corporate conduct and strengthened political support to business profitability, in an effort to stimulate private investment and economic growth. Simultaneously, economic reforms strengthened competitive pressures on companies by opening up the economy to foreign capital and imported commodities. Overall, the resulting institutional setting has increased companies' operational autonomy vis-à-vis non-profit considerations. Conversely, higher market competition and growing pressures to deliver financial returns on investment have pushed large companies to focus increasingly on profit-driven cost–benefit calculations. As the case of Lafarge India illustrates, the growing integration of India's economy within global markets, financial flows, and production networks means that these national and sub-national political-economic changes have been deeply intertwined with transnational processes of economic marketization and financialization.

The growing significance of profit-making as a guiding value of economic processes, which increases the functional differentiation of the economy, has had ambivalent consequences in terms of economic responsiveness. On the one hand, India's corporate economy has become more cost-efficient, more dynamic, more agile, and more innovative.[1] While the 1990s were characterized by considerable efforts of adjustment by companies that had developed under the influence of the interventionist regime, the 2000s were the years of economic boom, growing investment, and a 'bully' optimism of entrepreneurs regarding the country's economic prospects. An economic slowdown during the second term of the United Progressive Alliance coalition (2009–2014) cast shadow over the dreams of India's aspiring middle and upper-middle classes. And since the election of Narendra Modi in 2014, economic indicators have been rather unstable. But all in all, when compared with previous periods, companies' appetite for profit-making in the new pro-business context has galvanized the responsiveness of India's market economy towards customers' needs and preferences.

Notwithstanding this positive effect, the growing significance of profit-making in the Indian economy has also constrained the ability of firms to observe and process social problems that cannot be addressed through the supply of commodities in markets. Not only has the mushrooming of private industrial and infrastructure projects throughout the country multiplied the occurrence of tensions between profit-making and competing collective values and interests, but companies' focus on financial profit has also reduced their organizational ability to take these values and interests into account.

This combination has favoured the multiplication of conflicts which feed social and political protest against business practices that are deemed harmful to society. According to these protest movements, India's pro-business development strategy might have improved economic responsiveness towards problems experienced by India's upper-middle and upper classes: since this

---

[1] For vivid depictions of this new dynamism of the Indian corporate economy, see, for instance, *Time* (2006), Cappelli, Singh, Singh, and Useem (2010), and *The Economist* (2013).

privileged fraction of the population has captured most of the wealth generated by the economic boom, it has also improved its ability to solve its problems through the market, for instance, by paying for private education and healthcare services.[2] But for the 'ghosts' of India's capitalism, as Arundhati Roy[3] describes them, the corporate economy would have become rather less responsive. This assessment might divide experts, political commentators, and scholars. What matters is the growing significance of this critical argument in India's public sphere. According to prominent intellectuals and the many voices of protest movements, companies' bully expansion and cost-cutting strategies often mean, inter alia, economic growth through the dispossession of rights and natural resources, limited income opportunities for the poor, large-scale environmental destruction, and resourceful corporate 'citizens' finding ways to secure the support of politicians and bureaucrats including at the cost of human citizens and democracy.

This growing polarization between the pro-business discourse, which supports profit-making as a source of economic responsiveness, and the counter-narrative, which indicts profit-making as a source of social problems, has been propitious for the rise of CSR in India over the past two decades. Departing from a tradition of corporate philanthropy, large domestic companies such as the Tata and the Birla conglomerates became increasingly interested in the semantic resources provided by the CSR concept to legitimize their organizations. Unlike philanthropy, whose meaning-horizon is restricted to problem-solving redistributive practices, CSR allows the attribution of problem-solving qualities to core business activities, and even to companies themselves through claims of essential moral qualities ('being' a responsible company). Indian subsidiaries of foreign MNCs became interested in CSR for similar reasons. Both were encouraged by India's apex business associations, which identified CSR as a timely resource to minimize anti-corporate protest movements and limit the development of costly regulatory policies. Some NGOs also invested the CSR field as a way of promoting what they perceive

---

[2] This perception of inequalities, which is widespread among participants of India's protest movements, has been substantiated recently by Lucas Chancel and Thomas Piketty' study of inequalities in India, conducted for the *World Inequality Report 2018* (Alvaredo, Chancel, Piketty, Saez, and Zucman 2018). The trend among India's upper-middle and upper classes that consists in compensating deficient public goods with market-based solutions is described, for instance, by Kohli (2012) and Drèze and Sen (2013).

[3] Roy (2014).

as socially more responsible business practices. And from 2007 onwards, the central government in New Delhi joined the CSR movement with public policies based on formal regulatory institutions.

The construction of the intermediary institution of CSR in India: Companies and politics

To gain a more detailed and subtle understanding of these processes underlying the expansion of CSR in the subcontinent, the present investigation complemented the macro-sociological analysis with in-depth qualitative research on the development of CSR within Lafarge India's organization and within India's political system. Among the various social systems involved in the social construction of CSR, companies and political systems are particularly interesting to look at. With regard to companies, they are obviously operating at the core of CSR, since the issue at hand is the 'social responsibility' of their practices. As for political systems, which concentrate political power, their involvement in CSR stands out because of its structural effects: by defining formal norms that 'socially responsible' companies are expected to implement, CSR public policies contribute to shaping the institutional arrangements on the basis of which interplays between the economy and other spheres of society are politically and legally regulated.

Findings resulting from the case study of Lafarge India substantiate the relations between increasing functional differentiation, contentious changes in patterns of economic responsiveness, and the rise of CSR.

Lafarge's acquisition of cements plants operated by Tata Steel in 1999 and of Raymond Cement's plant in Arasmeta in 2001 participated directly in the political-economic changes initiated by India's economic reforms, in a broader context of economic globalization. Lured by the prospects of fast economic growth characterizing the BRICS in the late 1990s and early 2000s, which contrasted with saturated markets in OECD countries, Lafarge put India and other emerging countries at the centre of its investment strategy. Conversely, India's central government and most of its regional state governments were keen on supporting investors such as Lafarge to boost economic growth and reap related electoral benefits. The resulting increase in FDIs strengthened competitive pressures in India's cement sector. While domestic cement manufacturers needed to match the efficiency of their foreign rivals if they wanted to stay in the market, multinational cement manufacturers were competing against each other and with domestic companies to grab a share of

India's expanding cement market. As exemplified by the case of Lafarge India, these market pressures came together with the growing weight of financial objectives in corporate governance and favoured an increasing organizational focus of companies on financial profit-making.

The detailed study of the cement plants of Sonadih and Arasmeta acquired by Lafarge shows how such organizational focus on profit-making impacts patterns of economic responsiveness. On the one hand, after being taken over by Lafarge India, the two cement plants gained in productivity. Investments in new machinery, human resources management geared towards productivity and flexibility, selective mining for high quality of limestone, and the implementation of an all-round cost-cutting programme improved the ability of the plants to turn financial investments into profit *and* into cement that was badly needed by India's booming construction industry. On the other hand, however, Lafarge India's focus on profit-making reduced its organizational sensitivity towards competing collective values and interests. These include values and interests related directly to business processes, such as the social welfare of low-skilled workers and their families, or the life chances of neighbouring villagers who are exposed to local industrial pollution, depleting water resources, and the loss of land due to mining expansion. Lafarge India also lost sensitivity towards more peripheral values and interests, such as institutionalized 'philanthropic' practices directed towards both the socio-economic development of surrounding villages and the requirements of local political patronage.

The relative closure of Lafarge India vis-à-vis these collective values and interests contrasts with the former relative openness of Tata Steel and Raymond Cement in this area. It induced frustration and resentment among a part of the company's workforce, leftist trade unions, neighbouring villagers, activists, and local as well as regional politicians and bureaucrats. While low-skilled workers and common villagers were mostly helpless, trade union leaders, activists, and some political actors built on this frustration and resentment to put Lafarge India under pressure. They publicly described tensions between the company's profit-making and competing collective values and interests as pressing problems. In addition, they confronted Lafarge India economically, politically, and legally through strikes, road blocks, electoral campaigning, letters of complaint addressed to public administration, as well as litigations filed in Chhattisgarh's Labour Court, Industrial Relations Court, and High Court.

These instances of public indictment of Lafarge India's behaviour were not isolated events. Lafarge India was experiencing similar pressures and conflicts in other locations, such as in its major investment projects in Meghalaya. Moreover, Lafarge India could observe through mass media and informal channels that other large companies, including cement manufacturers, were facing similar opposition. Taken together, this flow of information pointed at an emerging dynamic of contention that seemed to threaten the company's business prospects in the subcontinent. Simultaneously, CSR was gaining momentum in India and internationally, and it promised to help companies manage contention and strengthen their social legitimacy. The presence of CSR in Lafarge India's environment and its perceived relevance to manage threatening contention led the company to explore CSR's potential.

The decision to look into the resources CSR could provide to Lafarge India set subsequent decision-making processes in motion, through which CSR was increasingly integrated in the organization's structures and operations. Meetings with experts were organized, CSR managers were hired, benchmarking was conducted to assess the CSR policies and practices of other cement manufacturers, and general objectives and guidelines were formulated. The cement plant project of Alsindi was subsequently selected as a pilot project to design and test a full-fledged CSR strategy. Besides, a corporate foundation project that had been abandoned was revived, budget lines were set in place, managerial frameworks and tools were introduced to support plant-level CSR management, partnerships with NGOs were encouraged, and so on.

These decision-making processes, which include the formulation of 'decision premises' meant to guide Lafarge India's operations in the field of CSR, were also processes of meaning construction. By selecting the CSR concept and relating it selectively with other distinctions, Lafarge India contributed directly to the social construction of the CSR phenomenon in the subcontinent. Three characteristics of this contribution can be isolated. First, the meaning given to CSR by Lafarge India is typical of the country's post-philanthropic transition. The company still connected CSR with redistributive expectations and practices directed towards the socio-economic development of village communities located near its plants and plant projects. But Lafarge India also made use of the broader meaning horizon provided by the CSR concept to emphasize synergies between the company and India's developmental aspirations. For instance, it related CSR to issues more directly connected with its business processes, such as pollution abatement, mason training for unemployed youth, or the promotion of cheap housing constructed with Lafarge's cement. And internally, CSR was not only about social work sponsored by the company but also about other functions such as strategic stakeholder analysis and management.

A second characteristic is that Lafarge India envisaged CSR mostly in relation to profit-oriented business processes. While the company emphasized concerns for social development and environmental sustainability when communicating on CSR with external audiences, the meaning given to CSR internally was dominated by an instrumental economic logic geared towards profitable business expansion. In other words, CSR was designed to support profit-driven economic processes, rather than to look for more compromise between profit-making and competing collective values and interests.

Third, CSR was subjected to the same programme of cost-cutting and efficiency that prevailed in other areas of management. While the budget allocated to CSR was increased, CSR managers were required to use these means to maximize contributions of CSR activities to the fulfilment of the objectives attributed to CSR by the company.

The growing institutionalization of CSR in the organizational structures and practices of companies such as Lafarge India has been accompanied by an increasing involvement of India's political system in this field. As showcased by the Indo-German CSR initiative, which also involved a benchmarking of CSR public policies from around the world, the CSR public policies adopted by the central government over the past decade were not insulated from a transnational trend of 'government of self-regulation'. Nonetheless, the government's political interest for CSR, and the policy-making processes underlying the CSR policies it adopted, were primarily reactions to domestic concerns. More specifically, they were political attempts to attenuate the dynamic of contention, as this dynamic not only threatened companies' business prospects but also the electoral prospects of pro-business politicians.

This political threat arising from rising tensions and conflicts between profit-making and competing collective values and interests was multifaceted. First, protest movements acting for the defence of these collective values and interests, be it on the ground of abstract principles (for example, 'social justice', 'environmental justice', 'democracy') and/or in the name of perceived victims of unbridled profit-making (for example, land-losing peasants, indigenous groups, contract workers), were not only indicting companies, but were also overtly criticizing policy-makers for pursuing 'development' policies that, in their view, put the capitalist interests of powerful business groups first. In a context where the material benefits of India's private sector–led economic boom seemed to concentrate in the hands of the country's elite, instead of 'trickling down' to the poor as promised during the electoral campaign of 2004, the United Progressive Alliance was worried about the resonance of such critiques in public opinion. A second cause for concerns was that protest movements publicly advocated for stronger regulation and fiscal redistribution. Moreover, by filing PILs in the High Courts and in the Supreme Court, protest movements enhanced regulatory pressures by way of jurisprudence, as well as through court orders that required the government to ensure the proper implementation of regulatory norms and of the Directive Principles of the Constitution. Finally, highly mediatized conflicts in which protest movements blocked major industrial projects, such as Tata Motor's car factory project in West Bengal, Vedanta and POSCO's mining projects in Odisha, or a number of flagship SEZ projects, were tarnishing India's reputation as a competitive destination for investments.

Around the mid-2000s, policy-makers started identifying CSR as a promising policy option to try to reduce this politically damaging dynamic of contention. Thanks to its broad and open-ended thematic relevance, CSR seemed appropriate to tackle the multiple tensions and conflicts opposing profit-making and pro-business policies to competing collective values and interests. Hence, by adopting policies that promote CSR, the government could display concrete measures that address at once the multitude of tensions between 'business' and 'development'. CSR was also interesting as it could relieve political pressure on the state by attributing the responsibility for harmonizing profit-making and development-related concerns to companies. Moreover, the forward-looking outlook of CSR, which is presented as a movement that will transform problem-making companies into socially responsible problem-solvers, could be expected to appease concerns raised by protest movements in public opinion.

As in the case of companies such as Lafarge India, the identification of CSR as a potential resource in Indian politics motivated decisions to explore this potential. This resulted in a series of CSR public policies being adopted by the Indian state. The CSR Charter outlined by Prime Minister Manmohan Singh at the CII General Assembly in 2007 was followed by the formulation of the National Voluntary Guidelines (NVGs) as part of the Indo-German CSR initiative, and the NVGs were subsequently integrated in the Business Responsibility Reporting circular of SEBI. Around the same period, CSR spending obligations were introduced for large enterprises of the public sector, and the crafting of a new Companies Act (2013) provided the opportunity to impose a similar CSR spending obligation on large companies of the private sector. In short, India's political system intervened with increasing might in the field of CSR. In doing so, the government strengthened the institutionalization of CSR both as an integral part of India's regulatory norms and as an established management domain for large companies operating in the subcontinent.

The impacts of CSR on economic responsiveness

As CSR has become an integral part of the organizational structures and activities of most large companies operating in India, and as it has expanded in other social systems as well, such as in Indian politics and law, or in moral communication, one can wonder about the changes induced by this phenomenon. While management studies often focus on the impacts of CSR with regard to companies' objectives and performance, and while public policy analysis generally focuses on policy outputs in relation to policy objectives and inputs, the present study examined the changes induced by CSR from another angle. As the intermediary institution of CSR arises from societal problems involving tensions between profit-driven economic processes and competing collective values and interests, the study analysed how CSR changes the ways social systems – here companies, politics, and the economy – observe and process these problems.

With regard to companies, the case of Lafarge India suggests that the main change introduced by CSR is the enhancement of their organizational ability to perform second-order observation (observing how they are observed by other social systems) in support of their business activities. In fact, CSR became operationally relevant for Lafarge India after a period when the company's growing organizational focus on profit-making had restricted its ability to take non-economic meaning contexts into account. As the organization's self-observation *and* its observation of its environment had been predominated by economic cost–benefit calculations, it had disregarded how its operations were observed by others from different perspectives. For instance, downsizing the permanent workforce, increasing the use of flexible contract workers, and pushing up pressures on productivity seemed obvious decisions for Lafarge to meet its financial objectives. While doing so, the company paid little attention to the economic, political, and moral concerns for labour welfare that preoccupied low-skilled workers, trade unions, activists, and some politicians. Similarly, disengaging from traditional peripheral development activities seemed a logical decision for a company that focused on producing and commercializing cement for a profit. But in doing so, the company overlooked the moral condemnations and the local political contention such a decision could trigger.

By contrast, the CSR-related organizational structures introduced by Lafarge India from 2008 onwards enhanced its capacity to observe how other social systems observe its operations within and in particular outside market transactions. Such second-order observation was performed by a dedicated team of CSR professionals. Based on sources such as interactions with so-called stakeholders (bureaucrats, politicians, villagers, and so on), these CSR managers generated and processed information within the company on how it was perceived by the outside world, and whether external perceptions could endanger its business prospects. While the company previously envisaged the dynamics of contention surrounding its business operations as dangers, which by definition consist in possibilities of losses attached to external circumstances, second-order observation transformed these perceived dangers into risks, which combine possibilities of gains and losses attached to decisions.

This transformation of dangers into risks has far-reaching consequences. While companies can only prepare for dangers by fortifying their defence systems (for example, crisis management), risks can be managed proactively. To put it differently, while one is exposed to external dangers, to which one can react, one *takes* risks by anticipating calculated risk parameters and by deciding accordingly. This calculation of risk parameters also allows organizations to translate information from one meaning context to another. More precisely, risk management can relate *potential political dynamics, litigations, or moral sanctions* with *prospects of economic gains and losses* attached to a given decision option. In the case of Lafarge India, for instance, the presence of a CSR manager in the Alsindi plant project helped the company consider information on local politics and the mindset of villagers when comparing the economic advantages of alternative decision options, such as decisions about land acquisition and the modalities of displacement of villagers living within the limestone mining concession.

Such translation of non-economic values and interests into parameters of economic risks is constitutive of the ability of the intermediary institution of CSR to enhance the coordination of profit-driven economic processes with non-economic spheres of society. It is through such translation and coordination that CSR changes patterns of economic responsiveness. While advanced functional differentiation – the organizational focusing of companies on profit-making – reduces economic responsiveness vis-à-vis competing collective values and interests, CSR helps profit-driven economic processes take these collective values and interests into account, not as such, but inasmuch as they seem relevant as parameters of profit-driven economic risk management.

Besides enhancing companies' capacity to observe non-economic collective values and interests as parameters of economic risks, CSR also provides companies with resources to handle these risks. These resources are of different kinds. For instance, they include trained CSR professionals, practice-oriented knowledge elaborated in particular by management studies, and institutionalized CSR practices (for example, CSR reporting, business–NGO partnerships) that companies can integrate into their own CSR portfolio. Underlying these managerial resources, CSR provides companies with useful opportunities of meaning construction to process risk parameters. These opportunities of meaning construction are configured by the properties of the CSR concept.

In the *factual dimension of meaning*, thanks to the thematic breadth of 'social responsibility', companies can use CSR to address a wide and open-ended range of problems. In fact, the scope of relevance of CSR covers any collective value or interest that, in any given circumstance, seems to stand in the way of profit-oriented business operations. Moreover, the thematic scope of CSR encompasses any scale at which issues are being raised, from localized tensions and conflicts, such as issues pertaining to a specific investment project, to global challenges such as rising inequalities or climate change. This semantic openness and flexibility provides companies with the opportunity to adapt to uncertain dynamics of contention, as organizational structures and activities dedicated to CSR can easily absorb and process unexpected points of tension and conflict. While doing so, companies' CSR operations can move easily between local, regional, national, and supra-national scales, for instance, by addressing a local conflict within a national or global CSR programme, or by using a local CSR activity to showcase the company's commitment to addressing issues of global significance.

In the *social dimension of meaning*, the indication of 'corporate' social responsibility can be used by companies to generalize claims of moral and civic qualities out of selected CSR activities. A partnership with an NGO to fight child labour in international supply chains, a corporate programme to reduce CO_2 emissions, or any other CSR-related activity that contributes to realizing collective values and interests can be put forward as evidence for the company's claim of being a 'socially responsible' company and a 'good corporate citizen'. This semantic resource provided by CSR does not mean that the CSR programmes and activities displayed by companies are necessarily inconsistent 'window dressing', as critical commentators often contend. Companies' CSR programmes and activities can also provide substantial and long-lasting contributions to societal problem-solving. In any case, the semantic possibility to turn '*doing* CSR' into '*being* socially responsible' allows companies to use CSR activities as input in the construction of cultural narratives that represent these companies as 'socially responsible' problem-solvers. In doing so, companies can amplify reputational assets gained through specific CSR activities. Moreover, by turning specific CSR activities into claims of general moral and civic qualities, companies can outshine instances where their business operations hurt competing collective values and interests.

Finally, in the *temporal dimension of meaning*, CSR activities can be used by companies to manifest their participation in the worldwide CSR 'movement', which sets out to gradually turn socially irresponsible problem-making companies into socially responsible problem-solving companies. This allows companies to address actual tensions and conflicts between their business operations and competing collective values and interests by pointing at promising outlooks for the progressive harmonization of business–society interplays. Such forward-looking optimism is particularly well suited to counter the business-unfriendly pessimistic views advanced by protest movements, which describe contentious business operations as destructive capitalist forces that jeopardize chances for the advancement of social justice, peace, democracy, the conservation of nature, and other such values and interests.

The development of CSR impacts not only companies but also the other social systems involved. Regarding the Indian political system, the present study showed how CSR public policies induced a number of changes in the institutional arrangements underlying the political regulation of corporate conduct. CSR being an essentially contested concept, CSR public policies can institutionalize various definitions of CSR, which are not necessarily compatible with one another. And CSR public policies can institutionalize various behavioural expectations that companies have to implement to be considered 'socially responsible'. These regulatory structures can differ not only in terms of which behaviour is expected but also in terms of the resources and constraints these structures rely on to change corporate conduct. These regulatory mechanisms include, inter alia, motivational narratives that rely on persuasion (for example, the 'business case' argument), practical toolkits designed to help companies integrate CSR within their organizational structures and processes, guidelines that companies are invited to follow, as well as more constraining legal norms such as the CSR clause of India's Companies Act.

The Indian case provides a striking illustration of this variety of institutional changes that CSR policy-making can produce. Crafted in a deliberative setting dominated by experts, the NVGs are mostly rooted in the global CSR *doxa*. The guidelines define CSR as a movement entailing opportunities of convergence between profit-making, social welfare, and environmental sustainability. They associate CSR with issue-areas that are directly connected with companies' core business processes, and emphasize the voluntary character of CSR. Produced in a parliamentary setting dominated by the central government and MPs, section 135 of the Companies Act is rather rooted in India's philanthropic tradition. It defines CSR as the redistribution of profit in non-profit development projects and programmes which are only indirectly connected with companies' core business processes. Unlike the NVGs, the Companies Act formulates legally binding normative expectations – though enforcement relies on a flexible 'comply or explain' mechanism instead of bureaucratic monitoring and coercive sanctions.

Notwithstanding their variety, Indian CSR public policies and the institutional changes they induced also share common characteristics. These commonalities can be traced back to the properties of the contested CSR concept. More precisely, the CSR concept provides attractive semantic resources to public policy-makers, but using these resources requires policy-makers to stay within certain common parameters.

With regard to the factual dimension of meaning, the wide and flexible scope of CSR enables the government to address in one stroke a large number of wicked and multifaceted societal problems. Using this resource leads policy-makers to design CSR policies whose regulatory expectations towards corporate conduct remain general and flexible, if not vague. Both the NVGs and section 135 cover broad and blurry issue-areas, in which companies can choose strategically which social problems they want to address and which they want to leave untouched.

With regard to the social dimension of meaning, CSR offers opportunities for the government to relieve some political pressure by transferring or sharing responsibilities for societal problem-solving with companies. Using this resource leads policy-makers to design CSR policies that avoid hard constraints, as such constraints would require enforcement mechanisms that increase rather than lower the burden of the state. Both the NVGs and section 135 emphasize the responsibility of *companies* in areas where the state describes itself as insufficient and/or deficient, and both policies avoid bureaucratic enforcement mechanisms based on monitoring and sanctions.

Finally, with regard to the temporal dimension of meaning, politicians are interested in the ability of CSR to promise a convergence between profit-making and the common good, as such promise might attenuate social tensions and conflicts that are costly not only economically but also politically. Using this resource leads policy-makers to design CSR policies that legitimize profit-making by defining it as an engine of societal problem-solving. In India, while the NVGs point to a movement that can harmonize profit-making, social welfare, and environmental sustainability, section 135 defines profit-making as a source of corporate contributions to the country's development.

Taken together, these institutional variations and commonalities characterizing CSR public policies tend to weaken the role of the political system while reinforcing the role of the economic system in the processing of tensions and conflicts between profit-making and competing collective values and interests. CSR public policies use more or less constraining means to involve companies in the performance of various regulatory and redistributive problem-solving functions, which are more or less connected with the core business processes of firms. But at the operational level, CSR public policies remain highly flexible with regard to *how* companies are to perform these functions. Moreover, CSR public policies avoid imposing constraints that would hurt profit-making, as profit-making is defined in these policies as a positive source of societal problem-solving. Regulatory arrangements institutionalized by CSR policy-making originate from the state, and their design reflects primarily political processes guided by concerns for the control of political power. However, unlike conventional state-based regulation of the economy through legal norms, taxation, and redistributive social policies, CSR public policies institutionalize regulatory and redistributive arrangements that rely primarily on companies' profit-driven economic risk calculations. In other words, CSR public policies might contribute to making profit-driven economic processes more responsive to social problems, as they promote and institutionalize structures of second-order observation among targeted companies. But CSR public policies are unlikely to ease the constraints on economic responsiveness arising from increased functional differentiation, as self-referential profit-making remains the primary logic through which companies selectively observe and address social problems involving non-profit collective values and interests.

This analysis raises questions regarding how the growing institutionalization of CSR in the subcontinent plays out in the broader context of interactions between India's capitalist economy and its democratic politics. Political-economic changes characterizing the country's pro-business development regime have significantly increased economic responsiveness based on the market mechanism. But the economy has also contributed to generating social problems of significant proportion. Socio-economic inequalities have increased rapidly, as most of the wealth generated by India's economic emergence has been concentrated in the hands of the country's elite: the share of economic growth captured by the top 0.1 per cent earners since 1980 is higher than the share of the bottom 50 per cent, and while the top 10 per cent earners captured about 55 per cent of economic growth in 2014, the middle 40 per cent captured about 30 per cent, leaving about 15 per cent of economic growth for the lower 50 per cent earners.[4] Capitalist economic processes have also harmed the life chances of millions among weak social groups, for instance, by imposing particularly harsh working conditions on labourers, by depriving rural households of their livelihood and uprooting village communities to acquire land, by diverting natural resources such as water for industrial use, or by creating health problems through industrial pollution and the commercialization of toxic products. Companies' business expansion is often also contributing directly and indirectly to the deterioration of India's natural environment. And arrangements between business actors and politicians at various levels of India's political system have sometimes impeded the democratic implementation of the preferences of (non-corporate) citizens.

Considering the high degree of complexity and uncertainty that characterizes these wicked problems, no solution seems to be on hand. But society tackles – that is, observes and processes – these intractable problems nonetheless. There are many ways society can do so, and the way society tackles these problems can have concrete consequences for the life chances of hundreds of millions of people. In the functionally differentiated social order that currently prevails, the political system is only one of the many social systems that contribute to tackling these problems. Law, science, mass media, education, health, morality, and religion can and do also play a role. The economy itself can provide relevant contributions as well, both through market-based responsiveness (for example, green innovation, fair trade, social business models) and through CSR-based risk management. However, in a democratic political context, the political system might have a peculiar role to play. Public policy-makers who formally represent and act in the interest of the Indian polity can devise legitimate collectively binding decisions to arbitrate trade-offs between profit-driven economic processes, which generate monetary wealth and supply markets with useful goods and services, and competing collective values and interests, whose realization requires an effective political regulation of the economy.

---

[4] See Alvaredo, Chancel, Piketty, Saez, and Zucman (2018).

In India, democratic politics has provided limited contributions in this regard. In electoral periods, political parties in the opposition have often vehemently criticized incumbents for pursuing economic reforms that would hurt the poor and disadvantaged masses. But if elected, the same parties have usually continued the work of their predecessors, while the new opposition has voiced similar critiques in the next electoral round.[5] Moreover, while socio-economic inequalities and promises of 'inclusive growth' have featured prominently in political rhetoric, other issue-areas such as environmental concerns have remained at the margins of Indian elections. Overall, debates on the country's pro-business development policies have not been decisive for electoral outcomes. Other variables have been more decisive, such as caste-based identity politics, local systems of patronage, material promises such as subsidies and loan-waver programmes for over-indebted farmers, and with particular intensity since the general elections of 2014, a populist brand of Hindu nationalism.[6] However, while elections have not prevented most central and state governments from pursuing pro-business development policies, India's dynamic protest movements and its powerful judiciary have exerted growing political pressure. In multiple instances, the combined action of protest movements and judicial institutions has forced governments to deviate from their pro-business political line to safeguard collective values and interests that are protected by law – including the Fundamental Rights and the Directive Principles of State Policy entailed in India's Constitution.

As the present study showed, the growing institutionalization of CSR in India is not set to reinforce the role of democratic politics in the regulation of economic processes that hurt competing collective values and interests. As indicated in Chapters 4 and 6, the adoption of CSR public policies by the central government is not unrelated to other political interventions that have weakened labour laws and eased environmental regulations to boost industrialization and economic growth. More generally, companies and pro-business political actors have institutionalized CSR precisely to minimize economic, legal, and political challenges coming from protest movements and the judiciary. Besides, companies and pro-business politicians have purposefully used CSR as a means to limit discontent within the general public. In the words of the former central minister of corporate affairs, Sachin Pilot, who oversaw the introduction of section 135 in India's Companies Act, CSR was about initiating a 'perception

---

[5] See Suri (2004).
[6] See, for instance, Palshikar (2015) and Jaffrelot (2017).

correction' in a context where 'the divide between the rich and the poor is getting bigger and bigger'.[7]

More detailed empirical research would be required to gain a more subtle understanding of the interplays between CSR and democratic politics in the processing of tensions between profit-driven economic processes and competing collective values and interests. The conceptual and analytical framework elaborated for the purpose of the present study might prove useful to guide such empirical research. In particular, the analysis of CSR and economic responsiveness outlined here could be complemented by an analysis of CSR and the responsiveness of other social systems.

Furthermore, using sociological systems theory to conceptualize CSR as an intermediary institution allows us to expand research perspectives beyond the political-economic spectrum. While political economy is a broad category that encompasses multiple research traditions and theoretical approaches, it envisages and explains social phenomena by referring primarily to interactions between the economy and politics. Conversely, Luhmann's sociological theory of functional differentiation considers the economy and politics as two function systems among many others. While these two function systems play a key role in most areas of social life, they do not dominate other spheres of society.[8] For instance, law is as important for politics and economic life as politics and the economy are for law. Similarly, mass media communication is highly significant for politics, the economy, and law, but political decisions, economic payments, and courts of law cannot easily control the autopoietic processes of mass media communication. In this perspective, the analytical framework devised in the present study could also be applied to study the properties and outcomes of CSR in other spheres of society: as an intermediary institution, CSR is also set to change to various degrees legal proceedings involving contentious corporate conduct; the reporting on companies' behaviour in mass media; moral praises and condemnations of companies; scientific research on companies, CSR being already an established academic field of research; the way companies are described and involved in the education system, including in business schools;

---

[7] Minister of Corporate Affairs, minutes of the plenary session of the Lok Sabha on 18 December 2012.

[8] See, for instance, Strulik (2012). But this point is debated, as other theorists argue that asymmetrical relations between function systems and a propensity of capitalism to 'ecological dominance' provide the economy with a dominant position in modern society (Jessop 2008; Schimank 2015).

the role of the pharmaceutical industry, private healthcare providers, and other companies in the health system, and so on.

Finally, the three-dimensional constructivist definition of CSR as a combination of an essentially contested concept (*semantic dimension*) with meaning-generating communicative processes (*operative dimension*) and institutionalized expectations (*structural dimension*) could prove useful for cross-national comparative CSR research. The gradual expansion of the CSR phenomenon within world society, which has gained pace over the past two decades, is a historical process of interactions between global meaning-patterns (culture) and social structures (institutions) on the one hand, and regional/ local meaning-patterns and social structures, on the other. As the present study of the Indian context showed, these historical interactions result in a complex mix of commonalities and variations. The semantic properties of the CSR concept and the related horizons of potential meaning-construction are stable. But the way social systems exploit these potentials is conditioned by varied cultural patterns and social structures such as, in India, the philanthropic tradition of family-managed business conglomerates or the institution of the 'village community' in rural areas. Building on existing CSR scholarship and further empirical research, cross-national comparative analysis could not only foster the understanding of commonalities and variations characterizing the global CSR phenomenon, but could also shed light on the ability of this intermediary institution to articulate multiple perspectives and deal with the variety of regional and local contexts in the stabilization of disrupted relations between the global capitalist market economy and collective values and interests anchored in other social spheres.

References

Abend, Gabriel. 2014. *The Moral Background: An Inquiry into the History of Business Ethics*. Princeton: Princeton University Press.

Ackerman, Robert W. and Raymond A. Bauer. 1976. *Corporate Social Responsiveness: The Modern Dilemma*. Reston, VA: Reston Publishing & Co.

Acquier, Aurélien, Thibault Daudigeos, and Bertrand Valiorgue. 2011. 'Corporate Social Responsibility as an Organizational and Managerial Challenge: The Forgotten Legacy of the Corporate Social Responsiveness Movement'. *M@n@gement* 14 (4): 250.

Albareda, Laura, Josep M. Lozano, Antonio Tencati, Atle Midttun, and Francesco Perrini. 2008. 'The Changing Role of Governments in Corporate Social Responsibility: Drivers and Responses'. *Business Ethics: A European Review* 17 (4): 347–63.

Alvaredo, Facundo, Lucas Chancel, Thomas Piketty, Emmanuel Saez, and Gabriel Zucman. 2018. *World Inequality Report 2018*. Cambridge, MA: Harvard University Press.

Andersen, Niels Åkerstrøm. 2011. 'Conceptual History and the Diagnostics of the Present'. *Management & Organizational History* 6 (3): 248–67.

Andonova, Liliana B. and Ronald B. Mitchell. 2010. 'The Rescaling of Global Environmental Politics'. *Annual Review of Environment and Resources* 35 (1): 255–82.

Archel, Pablo, Javier Husillos, and Crawford Spence. 2011. 'The Institutionalisation of Unaccountability: Loading the Dice of Corporate Social Responsibility Discourse'. *Accounting, Organizations and Society* 36 (6): 327–43.

Arora, Saurabh and Henny Romijn. 2012. 'The Empty Rhetoric of Poverty Reduction at the Base of the Pyramid'. *Organization* 19 (4): 481–505.

Bagchi, Amaresh. 2007. 'Role of Planning and the Planning Commission in the New Indian Economy: Case for a Review'. *Economic and Political Weekly* 42 (44): 92–100.

Bagchi, Amiya Kumar. 1972. *Private Investment in India: 1900–1939*. Cambridge South Asian Studies. Cambridge: Cambridge University Press.

———. 1985. 'Transition from Indian to British Indian Systems of Money and Banking 1800–1850'. *Modern Asian Studies* 19 (3): 501–19.

Bakken, Tore and Tor Hernes. 2003. *Autopoietic Organization Theory: Drawing on Niklas Luhmann's Social Systems Perspective*. Oslo, Norway: Abstrakt forlag.

Banerjee-Guha, Swapna. 2013. 'Accumulation and Dispossession: Contradictions of Growth and Development in Contemporary India'. *South Asia: Journal of South Asian Studies* 36 (2): 165–79.

Banerjee, Subhabrata Bobby. 2008. 'Corporate Social Responsibility: The Good, the Bad and the Ugly'. *Critical Sociology* 34 (1): 51–79.

Bansal, Pratima, Jijun Gao, and Israr Qureshi. 2014. 'The Extensiveness of Corporate Social and Environmental Commitment across Firms over Time'. *Organization Studies* 35 (7): 949–66.

Baraldi, Claudio, Giancarlo Corsi, and Elena Esposito. 1997. *Glossar zu Niklas Luhmanns Theorie sozialer Systeme*. Frankfurt am Main, Germany: Suhrkamp.

Bardhan, Pranab. 2012. 'Distributive Conflicts and Indian Economic Policy'. In *The Oxford Handbook of the Indian Economy*, edited by Chetan Ghate, 581–90. Oxford: Oxford University Press.

Barkan, Joanne. 2013. 'Plutocrats at Work: How Big Philanthropy Undermines Democracy'. *Social Research: An International Quarterly* 82 (2): 635–52.

Bartley, Tim. 2018. *Rules without Rights: Land, Labor, and Private Authority in the Global Economy*. Oxford: Oxford University Press.

Baviskar, Amita. 2005. 'Red in Tooth and Claw? Looking for Class in Struggles Over Nature'. In *Social Movements in India: Poverty, Power, and Politics*, edited by Raka Ray and Mary Fainsod, 161–78. Katzenstein. Lanham: Rowman & Littlefield.

Baviskar, Amita and Raka Ray, eds. 2011. *Elite and Everyman: The Cultural Politics of the Indian Middle Classes*. New Delhi: Routledge.

Becker, Howard S. 1966. *Social Problems: A Modern Approach*. New York: John Wiley.

Beckert, Jens. 2002. *Beyond the Market: The Social Foundations of Economic Efficiency*. Princeton, NJ: Princeton University Press.

———. 2010. ‚Sind Unternehmen sozial verantwortlich?‘ In *Unternehmensethik: Forschungsperspektiven zur Verhältnisbestimmung von Unternehmen und Gesellschaft*, edited by Olaf Schumann, Alexander Brink, and Thomas Beschorner, 109–24. Marburg, Germany: Metropolis-Verlag.

Bedajna, Sutirtha. 2012. 'Between Ecology and Economy: Environmental Governance in India'. In *New Subjects and New Governance in India*, edited by ýRanabir Samaddar and Suhit K. Sen, 154–210. New Delhi: Routledge.

Bernhard, Ungericht and Hirt Christian. 2010. 'CSR as a Political Arena: The Struggle for a European Framework'. *Business and Politics* 12 (4): 1–24.

Besio, Cristina and Andrea Pronzini. 2008. 'Niklas Luhmann as an Empirical Sociologist: Methodological Implications of the System Theory of Society'. *Cybernetics & Human Knowing* 15 (2): 9–31.

Bhagwati, Jagdish N. and Arvind Panagariya. 2012. *India's Reforms: How They Produced Inclusive Growth*. Oxford: Oxford University Press.

Bhattacharya, C. B., Sankar Sen, and Daniel Korschun. 2011. *Leveraging Corporate Responsibility : The Stakeholder Route to Maximizing Business and Social Value*. Cambridge: Cambridge University Press.

Bhattacherjee, Debashish. 1999. 'Organized Labor and Economic Liberalization in India: Past, Present, and Future'. ILO Discussion Paper DP/105/1999.

————. 2001. 'The Evolution of Indian Industrial Relations: A Comparative Perspective'. *Industrial Relations Journal* 32 (3): 244–63.

Blowfield, Michael. 2010. 'Business, Corporate Responsibility and Poverty Reduction'. In *Corporate Social Responsibility and Regulatory Governance: Towards Inclusive Development?* edited by Peter Utting and José Carlos Marques, 124–50. Basingstoke, UK: Palgrave Macmillan.

Bose, Pablo S. 2004. 'Critics and Experts, Activists and Academics: Intellectuals in the Fight for Social and Ecological Justice in the Narmada Valley, India'. *International Review of Social History* 49 (SupplementS12): 133–57.

Brammer, S., G. Jackson, and D. Matten. 2012. 'Corporate Social Responsibility and Institutional Theory: New Perspectives on Private Governance'. *Socio-Economic Review* 10 (1): 3–28.

Breman, J. 1999. 'The Study of Industrial Labour in Post-colonial India – The Formal Sector: An Introductory Review'. *Contributions to Indian Sociology* 33 (1–2): 1–41.

Brenkert, George G. 2012. *The Oxford Handbook of Business Ethics*. Oxford: Oxford University Press.

Business Standard. 2014. 'Government Planning to Clip National Green Tribunal's Wings'. 6 August 2014.

Candland, Christopher. 2007. *Labor, Democratization and Development in India and Pakistan*. Abingdon, UK: Routledge.

Cappelli, Peter, Harbir Singh, Jitendra Singh, and Michael Useem. 2010. *The India Way: How India's Top Business Leaders are Revolutionizing Management*. Boston, MA: Harvard Business Press.

Carroll, Archie B. 1979. 'A Three-Dimensional Conceptual Model of Corporate Performance'. *The Academy of Management Review* 4 (4): 497–505.

Carroll, Archie B., Kenneth J. Lipartito, James E. Post, Patricia H. Werhane, and Kenneth E. Goodpaster. 2012. *Corporate Responsibility: The American Experience*. New York: Cambridge University Press.

Cazal, Didier. 2009. 'RSE et théorie des parties prenantes: l'impasse du contrat'. *Revue de la Régulation* 9: online.

Chakrabarty, Bidyut. 2011. *Corporate Social Responsibility in India*. Abingdon, UK: Routledge.

Chakravarti, S. 2008. *Red Sun: Travels in Naxalite Country*. New Delhi: Penguin Books.

Chakravarty, Seshadri M. 1989. *Indian Cement Industry: From Control to Decontrol*. Bombay: Wadhera Publications.

Chandavarkar, A. G. 1983. 'Money and Credit, 1858–1947'. In *The Cambridge Economic History of India*, edited by Dharma Kumar and Tapan Raychaudhuri, 762–803. Cambridge: Cambridge University Press.

Chandrachud, Abhinav. 2011. 'The Emerging Market for Corporate Control in India: Assessing (and Devising) Shark Repellents for India's Regulatory Environment'. *Washington University Global Studies Law Review* 10 (2): 187–238.

Chassagnon, Virgile. 2014. 'Toward a Social Ontology of the Firm: Reconstitution, Organizing Entity, Institution, Social Emergence and Power'. *Journal of Business Ethics* 124 (2): 197–208.

Chen, Stephen and Petra Bouvain. 2009. 'Is Corporate Responsibility Converging? A Comparison of Corporate Responsibility Reporting in the USA, UK, Australia, and Germany'. *Journal of Business Ethics* 87 (1): 299–317.

Chopra, Rohit. 2003. 'Neoliberalism as Doxa: Bourdieu's Theory of the State and the Contemporary Indian Discourse on Globalization and Liberalization'. *Cultural Studies* 17 (3–4): 419–44.

Christensen, Lars Thøger, Mette Morsing, and Ole Thyssen. 2013. 'CSR as Aspirational Talk'. *Organization* 20 (3): 372–93.

Ciepley, David. 2013. 'Beyond Public and Private: Toward a Political Theory of the Corporation'. *The American Political Science Review* 107 (1): 139–58.

CII and WWF. 2008. *Indian Companies with Solutions that the World Needs: Sustainability as a Driver for Innovation and Profit*. New Delhi: Confederation of Indian Industries and World Wildlife Fund. Available at https://www.wwfindia.org/?6363/Indian-Companies-with-solutions-that-the-World-Needs-Report.

Clark, John M. 1916. 'The Changing Basis of Economic Responsibility'. *Journal of Political Economy* 24 (3): 209–29.

Coen, David, Wyn Grant, and Graham K. Wilson, eds. 2010. *The Oxford Handbook of Business and Government*. Oxford: Oxford University Press.

Collomb, Bertrand, and Emmanuel Soupre. 2003. 'Le PDG rencontre l'actionnaire: une heure pour convaincre'. *Les Amis de l'Ecole de Paris* 43: 7–15.

Cooper, Stuart M. and David Owen. 2007. 'Corporate Social Reporting and Stakeholder Accountability: The Missing Link'. *Accounting, Organizations and Society: An International Journal Devoted to the Behavioural, Organizational and Social Aspects of Accounting* 32 (7/8, 10/11): 649–67.

Corbridge, Stuart, John Harriss, and Craig Jeffrey. 2013. *India Today: Economy, Politics and Society*. Cambridge: Polity Press.

Corporate Europe Observatory, The Austrian Federal Chamber of Labour, and The Austrian Trade Union Federation. 2014. *The Fire Power of the Financial Lobby: A Survey of the Size of the Financial Lobby at the EU level*. Available at https://corporateeurope.org/sites/default/files/attachments/financial_lobby_report.pdf.

Crane, Andrew and Dirk Matten. 2016. *Business Ethics: Managing Corporate Citizenship and Sustainability in the Age of Globalization*. Oxford: Oxford University Press.

Crane, Andrew, Abagail McWilliams, Dirk Matten, Jeremy Moon, and Donald S. Siegel, eds. 2008. *The Oxford Handbook of Corporate Social Responsibility*. Oxford: Oxford University Press.

Crouch, C. 2011. *The Strange Non-death of Neo-liberalism*. Cambridge: Polity Press.

CSE. 2005. *Concrete Facts: The Lifecycle of the Indian Cement Industry*. New Delhi: Centre for Science and Environment.

———. 2008. *Rich Lands, Poor People: Is 'Sustainable Mining' Possible?* Vol. 6, *State of India's Environment Report*. New Delhi: Centre for Science and Environment.

Damodaran, Harish. 2008. *India's New Capitalists*. New Delhi: Permanent Black.

Dashwood, Hevina S. 2012. *The Rise of Global Corporate Social Responsibility: Mining and the Spread of Global Norms*. Cambridge: Cambridge University Press.

Daugareilh, Isabelle, ed. 2010. *Responsabilité sociale de l'entreprise transnationale et globalisation de l'économie*. Bruxelles: Bruylant.

Dentchev, Nikolay A., Mitchell van Balen, and Elvira Haezendonck. 2015. 'On Voluntarism and the Role of Governments in CSR: Towards a Contingency Approach'. *Business Ethics: A European Review* 24 (4): 378–97.

Derry, Robbin. 2012. 'Reclaiming Marginalized Stakeholders'. *Journal of Business Ethics* 111 (2): 253–64.

Dhanesh, Ganga S. 2015. 'Why Corporate Social Responsibility? An Analysis of Drivers of CSR in India'. *Management Communication Quarterly* 29 (1): 114–29.

Djelic, Marie-Laure, and Philippe Zarlowski. 2005. 'Entreprises et gouvernance en France : perspectives historiques et évolutions récentes'. *Sociologie du Travail* 47 (4): 451–69.

Drèze, Jean and Amartya Sen. 2013. *An Uncertain Glory: India and Its Contradictions*. London: Penguin Books.

Dubois, Léon. 1988. *Lafarge-Coppée: 150 ans d'industrie une mémoire pour demain, Histoire et vie des entreprises*. Paris: P. Belfond.

Dwivedi, Ranjit. 1998. 'Resisting Dams and "Development": Contemporary Significance of the Campaign against the Narmada Projects in India'. *The European Journal of Development Research* 10 (2): 135–83.

Eckerman, Ingrid. 2005. *The Bhopal Saga: Causes and Consequences of the World's Largest Industrial Disaster*. Hyderabad: University Press.

Eckstein, Lars and Christoph Reinfandt. 2016. 'Luhmann in da Contact Zone: Towards a Postcolonial Critique of Sociological Systems Theory'. In *Theory Matters: The Place of Theory in Literary and Cultural Studies Today*, edited by Martin Middeke and Christoph Reinfandt, 151–66. London: Palgrave Macmillan UK.

Elkington, John. 1998. *Cannibals With Forks: The Triple Bottom Line of 21st Century Business, Conscientious Commerce*. Gabriola Island, Canada: New Society Publishers.

European Commission. 2007. *Corporate Social Responsibility National Public Policies in the European Union*. Luxembourg: Office for Official Publications of the European Communities.

Fernandes, Leela and Patrick Heller. 2006. 'Hegemonic Aspirations: New Middle Class Politics and India's Democracy in Comparative Perspective'. *Critical Asian Studies* 38 (4): 495–522.

FICCI. 2014. *Shaping India's Development Story: CSR Ideology and Investment*. New Delhi: Federation of Indian Chambers of Commerce and Industry .

Fleming, Peter and Marc T. Jones. 2013. *The End of Corporate Social Responsibility: Crisis and Critique*. London: SAGE Publications.

Fourcade, Marion. 2013. 'The Material and Symbolic Construction of the BRICs: Reflections Inspired by the RIPE Special Issue'. *Review of International Political Economy* 20 (2): 256–67.

Fox, Tom, Halina Ward, and Bruce Howard. 2002. *Public Sector Roles in Strengthening Corporate Social Responsibility: A Baseline Study*. Washington D.C.: World Bank.

Frederick, William C. 1994 [1978]. 'From CSR1 to CSR2: The Maturing of Business-and-Society Thought'. *Business & Society* 33 (2): 150–64.

Freeman, Edward R., Kirsten E. Martin, and Bidhan L. Parmar. 2007. 'Stakeholder Capitalism'. *Journal of Business Ethics* 74 (4): 303–14.

Freeman, R. Edward. 1984. *Strategic Management: A Stakeholder Approach*. Pitman Series in Business and Public Policy. Boston: Pitman.

Fuchs, Doris. 2007. *Business Power in Global Governance*. Boulder, CO.: Lynne Rienner Publishers.

Fuchs, Stephan. 2010. 'Kinds of Observers and Types of Distinctions'. In *Die Methodologien des Systems*, edited by René John, Anna Henkel, and Jana Rückert-John, 81–96. Wiesbaden, Germany: VS Verlag für Sozialwissenschaften.

―――. 2013. 'Ontological and Constructivist Observing'. In *Ontologien der Moderne*, edited by René John, Jana Rückert-John, and Elena Esposito, 15–33. Wiesbaden, Germany: Springer.

Fuller, C. J. and Haripriya Narasimhan. 2007. 'Information Technology Professionals and the New-Rich Middle Class in Chennai (Madras)'. *Modern Asian Studies* 41 (1): 121–50.

Gilberthorpe, Emma and Glenn Banks. 2012. 'Development on Whose Terms? CSR Discourse and Social Realities in Papua New Guinea's Extractive Industries Sector'. *Resources Policy* 37 (2): 185–93.

Gill, Gitanjali Nain. 2012. 'Human Rights and the Environment in India: Access through Public Interest Litigation'. *Environmental Law Review* 14 (3): 200–18.

Gjølberg, Maria. 2010. 'Varieties of Corporate Social Responsibility (CSR): CSR Meets the "Nordic Model"'. *Regulation & Governance* 4 (2): 203–29.

Goldar, B. N. 2014. 'Globalisation, Growth and Employment in the Organised Sector of the Indian Economy'. Institute for Human Development WP 06/2014.

Gollakota, Kamala and Vipin Gupta. 2006. 'History, Ownership Forms and Corporate Governance in India'. *Journal of Management History* 12 (2): 185–98.

Gond, Jean-Pascal, Nahee Kang, and Jeremy Moon. 2011. 'The Government of Self-Regulation: On the Comparative Dynamics of Corporate Social Responsibility'. *Economy and Society* 40 (4): 640–71.

Gond, Jean-Pascal and Jeremy Moon, eds. 2011. *Corporate Social Responsibility: A Reader*. New York: Routledge.

Goody, Jack. 1996. *The East in the West*. New York: Cambridge University Press.

Government of Himachal Pradesh. 2004. *Industrial Policy 2004 and Package of Incentives*. Shimla: Department of Industries.

Government of India. 1956. *Industrial Policy Resolution (30th April,1956)*. New-Delhi: Ministry of Industry.

―――. 2009. 'Corporate Social Responsibility Voluntary Guidelines'. Ministry of Corporate Affairs, Government of India, New Delhi.

———. 2011. 'National Voluntary Guidelines for the Social, Environmental and Economic Responsibilities of Business'. Ministry of Corporate Affairs, Government of India, New Delhi.

———. 2014. Ministry of Corporate Affairs Notification (27 February 2014). *The Gazette of India* No. 95, Extraordinary, Part II, section 3, sub-section (i). Art.2 (http://www.mca.gov.in/Ministry/pdf/CompaniesActNotification2_2014.pdf, accessed on 8 February 2019).

Goyder, George. 1961. *The Responsible Company*. Oxford: Blackwell.

Graz, Jean-Christophe, and Andreas Nölke, eds. 2007. *Transnational Private Governance and Its Limits*. Abingdon, UK: Routledge.

GTZ. 2011. *Corporate Social Responsibility und Entwicklungszusammenarbeit: Der Beitrag der GTZ*. Eshborn, Germany: Gesellschaft für Technische Zusammenarbeit.

Guha, Atulan. 2009. 'Labour Market Flexibility: An Empirical Inquiry into Neoliberal Propositions'. *Economic and Political Weekly* 44 (19): 45–52.

de Haan, Arjan. 1999. 'The Badli System in Industrial Labour Recruitment: Managers' and Workers' Strategies in Calcutta's Jute Industry'. *Contributions to Indian Sociology* 33 (1–2): 271–301.

Haas, Peter M. 1992. 'Introduction: Epistemic Communities and International Policy Coordination'. *International Organization* 46 (1): 1–35.

Hasan, Zoya. 2012. *Congress after Indira: Policy, Power, Political Change (1984–2009)*. New Delhi: Oxford University Press.

Haynes, D. E. 1987. 'From Tribute to Philanthropy: The Politics of Gift Giving in a Western Indian City'. *Journal of Asian Studies* 46 (2): 339–60.

Hazra, Sugato. 2011. *Influencing India: Lobbying in the World's Largest Democracy*. Kolkata: Bridging Borders.

Helin, Sven, Tommy Jensen, and Johan Sandström. 2013. '"Like a Battalion of Tanks": A Critical Analysis of Stakeholder Management'. *Scandinavian Journal of Management* 29 (3): 209–18.

Hertz, Noreena. 2001. *The Silent Takeover: Global Capitalism and the Death of Democracy*. London: Heinemann.

Hill, Elizabeth. 2009. 'The Indian Industrial Relations System: Struggling to Address the Dynamics of a Globalizing Economy'. *Journal of Industrial Relations* 51 (3): 395–410.

Hilliard, Darnell. 2005. 'On Defining the Multinational Corporation: A Systems-theoretical Perspective'. In *Niklas Luhmann and Organization Studies*, edited by David Seidl and Kai Helge Becker, 324–47. Malmö, Sweden: Liber.

Hindustan Times. 2015. 'Under New Norms, 36 Industries May Not Need Environmental Clearance'. 18 September 2015.

———. 2017. 'Govt Tweaks Rules, Reduces Judiciary Control on India's Environmental Watchdog'. 4 July 2017.

Hofferberth, Matthias. 2011. 'The Binding Dynamics of Non-Binding Governance Arrangements: The Voluntary Principles on Security and Human Rights and the Cases of BP and Chevron'. *Business and Politics* 13 (4): Online.

Holmström, Susanne. 2010. 'Society's Constitution and Corporate Legitimacy, or Why It Might Be Unethical for Business Leaders to Think with Their Heart'. In *Power and Principle in the Market Place: On Ethics and Economics*, edited by J. D. Rendtorff, 133–60. Farnham, UK: Ashgate Publishing.

Holzer, Boris, Fatima Kastner, and Tobias Werron, eds. 2014. *From Globalization to World Society: Neo-Institutional and Systems-Theoretical Perspectives*. Abingdon, UK: Routledge.

India Today. 2012. 'Green Terror'. 05 October 2012.

———. 2015. 'Centre Liberalises Environment Laws for Ease of Business'. 11 May 2015.

Ishwaran, K. 1966. *Tradition and Economy in Village India*. London: Routledge & Kegan Paul.

Jackson, Gregory and Androniki Apostolakou. 2010. 'Corporate Social Responsibility in Western Europe: An Institutional Mirror or Substitute?' *Journal of Business Ethics* 94 (3): 371–94.

Jacobsson, Kerstin and Christina Garsten. 2012. 'Post-Political Regulation: Soft Power and Post-Political Visions in Global Governance'. *Critical Sociology* 39 (3): 421–37.

Jaffrelot, Christophe. 2008. '"Why Should We Vote?" The Indian Middle Class and the Functioning of the World's Largest Democracy'. In *Patterns of Middle Class Consumption in India and China*, edited by Christophe Jaffrelot and Peter Van Der Veer, 35–54. New Delhi: Sage Publications.

———. 2011. *Religion, Caste and Politics in India*. London: C. Hurst & Co.

———. 2015. 'What "Gujarat Model"? – Growth without Development – and with Socio-Political Polarisation'. *South Asia: Journal of South Asian Studies* 38 (4): 820–38.

———. 2017. 'India's Democracy at 70: Toward a Hindu State?' *Journal of Democracy* 28 (3): 52–63.

Jaffrelot, Christophe and Cynthia Schoch. 2008. *Emerging States: The Wellspring of a New World Order*. Series in Comparative Politics and International Studies. London: Hurst & Co.

Jaffrelot, Christophe and Peter Van Der Veer, eds. 2008. *Patterns of Middle Class Consumption in India and China*. New Delhi: Sage Publications.

Jamali, Dima, Peter Lund-Thomsen, and Navjote Khara. 2017. 'CSR Institutionalized Myths in Developing Countries'. *Business & Society* 56 (3): 454–86.

Jenkins, Rob. 1999. *Democratic Politics and Economic Reform in India, Contemporary South Asia*. Cambridge: Cambridge University Press.

———. 2004. 'Labor Policy and the Second Generation of Economic Reform in India'. *India Review* 3 (4): 333–63.

Jenkins, Rob, Loraine Kennedy, and Partha Mukhopadhyay, eds. 2014. *Power, Policy, and Protest: The Politics of India's Special Economic Zones*. New Delhi: Oxford University Press.

Jeppesen, Søren and Peter Lund-Thomsen. 2010. 'Special Issue on "New Perspectives on Business, Development, and Society Research"'. *Journal of Business Ethics* 93 (2): 139–42.

Jessop, Bob. 1997. 'The Governance of Complexity and the Complexity of Governance: Preliminary Remarks on Some Problems and Limits of Economic Guidance'. In *Beyond Market and Hierarchy: Interactive Governance and Social Complexity*, edited by A. Amin and J. Hausner, 95–128. Cheltenham: Elgar.

————. 2008. ‚Zur Relevanz von Luhmanns Systemtheorie und von Laclau und Mouffes Diskursanalyse für die Weiterentwicklung der marxistischen Staatstheorie'. In *Der Staat der Bürgerlichen Gesellschaft: Zum Staatsverständnis von Karl Marx*, edited by Joachim Hirsch, John Kannankulam, and Jens Wissel, 155–80. Baden-Baden, Germany: Nomos.

Jodhka, Surinder S. 2012. *Caste, Oxford India Short Introductions*. New Delhi: Oxford University Press.

Kakar, Sudhir. 1971. 'Authority Patterns and Subordinate Behavior in Indian Organizations'. *Administrative Science Quarterly* 16 (3): 298–307.

Kaplan, Rami. 2015. 'Who Has Been Regulating Whom, Business or Society? The Mid-20th-Century Institutionalization of "Corporate Responsibility" in the USA'. *Socio-Economic Review* 13 (1): 125–55.

Kaplan, Rami and Daniel Kinderman. 2017. 'The Business-Led Globalization of CSR: Channels of Diffusion From the United States Into Venezuela and Britain, 1962–1981'. *Business & Society* preprint.

Karnani, Aneel G. 2011. '"Doing Well by Doing Good': The Grand Illusion'. *California Management Review* 53 (2): 69–86.

Kennedy, Loraine. 2014. *The Politics of Economic Restructuring in India: Economic Governance and State Spatial Rescaling*. Abingdon, UK: Routledge.

Khanna, Tarun and Krishna Palepu. 2005. 'The Evolution of Concentrated Ownership in India: Broad Patterns and a History of the Indian Software Industry'. In *A History of Corporate Governance around the World: Family Business Groups to Professional Managers*, edited by Randall K. Morck, 283–324. Chicago, IL: University of Chicago Press.

Khilnani, Sunil. 1997. *The Idea of India*. London: Penguin Books.

————. 2012 [1997]. *The Idea of India*. New Delhi: Penguin Books.

Kinderman, Daniel. 2013. 'Corporate Social Responsibility in the EU, 1993–2013: Institutional Ambiguity, Economic Crises, Business Legitimacy and Bureaucratic Politics'. *Journal of Common Market Studies* 51 (4): 701–20.

————. 2016. 'Time for a Reality Check: Is Business Willing to Support a Smart Mix of Complementary Regulation in Private Governance?' *Policy and Society* 35 (1): 29–42.

Kjaer, Poul F. 2014. 'Towards a Sociology of Intermediary Institutions: The Role of Law in Corporatism, Neo-Corporatism and Governance'. In *Law and the Formation of Modern Europe: Perspectives from the Historical Sociology of Law*, edited by Mikael Rask Madsen and Chris Thornhill, 117–41. Cambridge: Cambridge University Press.

————. 2015a. 'From Corporatism to Governance: Dimensions of a Theory of Intermediary Institutions'. In *The Evolution of Intermediary Institutions in Europe: From Corporatism to Governance*, edited by Eva Hartmann and Poul F. Kjaer, 11–28. Basingstoke, UK: Palgrave Macmillan.

————. 2015b. 'The Function of Justification in Transnational Governance'. WZB Discussion Paper SP IV (2015–808).

Knudsen, Jette S. and Jeremy Moon. 2017. *Visible Hands: Government Regulation and International Business Responsibility*. Cambridge: Cambridge University Press.

Knudsen, Jette S., Jeremy Moon, and Rieneke Slager. 2015. 'Government Policies for Corporate Social Responsibility in Europe: A Comparative Analysis of Institutionalisation'. *Policy & Politics* 43 (1): 81–99.

Kochanek, Stanley A. 1974. *Business and Politics in India*. Berkeley, CA: University of California Press.

————. 1987. 'Briefcase Politics in India: The Congress Party and the Business Elite'. *Asian Survey* 27 (12): 1278–301.

Kohli, Atul. 2012. *Poverty Amid Plenty in the New India*. New York: Cambridge University Press.

Kohli, Kanchi, and Manju Menon, eds. 2016. *Business Interests and the Environmental Crisis*. New Delhi: Sage Publications.

KPMG. 2011. *Corporate Responsibility Survey 2011: Marching towards Embracing Sustainable Development*. Mumbai: KPMG.

————. 2013. *India Corporate Responsibility Reporting Survey 2013*. Mumbai: KPMG.

————. 2017a. *Business Responsibility Reporting*. Mumbai: KPMG. Available at https://assets.kpmg/content/dam/kpmg/in/pdf/2017/07/Business-Responsibility-Reporting.pdf.

————. 2017b. *India's CSR reporting survey 2016*. Mumbai: KPMG. Available at https://assets.kpmg/content/dam/kpmg/in/pdf/2017/02/CSR-Survey-2016.pdf.

Krichewsky, Damien. 2011. 'Crise et modalités d'élaboration d'un compromis social dans le nouveau capitalisme indien'. *Revue de la régulation* (9): https://journals.openedition.org/regulation/9197.

————. 2017. 'CSR Public Policies in India's Democracy: Ambiguities in the Political Regulation of Corporate Conduct'. *Business & Politics* 19 (3): 510–47.

Krishnamurty, J. 1983. 'The Occupational Structure'. In *The Cambridge Economic History of India*, edited by Dharma Kumar and Tapan Raychaudhuri, 533–52. Cambridge: Cambridge University Press.

Krishnan, Sandhya and Neeraj Hatekar. 2017. 'Rise of the New Middle Class in India and Its Changing Structure'. *Economic and Political Weekly* 52 (22): 40–48.

Kühl, Stefan. 2018. *Arbeit - Marxistische und systemtheoretische Zugänge*. Wiesbaden, Germany: Springer VS.

Kurien, C. T. 1994. *Global Capitalism and the Indian Economy*. London: Sangam Books.

Lachaier, Pierre. 1999. *Firmes et entreprises en Inde: la firme lignagière dans ses réseaux*. Paris: Karthala.

————. 2003. 'The Socio-Cultural World: Family, Community, Value-Concepts'. In *The Indian Entrepreneur*, edited by Bruno Dorin, 19–64. New Delhi: Manohar.

Lafarge India. 2010. *2010 NIDHEE Annual Report: Corporate Social Responsibility*. Mumbai: Lafarge India Pvt. Ltd.

Lampert, Matthew. 2016. 'Corporate Social Responsibility and the Supposed Moral Agency of Corporations'. *Ephemera* 16 (1): 79–105.

Lee, Daniel B. and Achim Brosziewski. 2009. *Observing Society: Meaning, Communication, and Social System*. Amherst: Cambria Press.

Lievens, Matthias. 2015. 'From Government to Governance: A Symbolic Mutation and Its Repercussions for Democracy'. *Political Studies* 63 (S1): 2–17.

Locke, Richard M. and Hiram Samel. 2018. 'Beyond the Workplace: "Upstream" Business Practices and Labor Standards in the Global Electronics Industry'. *Studies in Comparative International Development* 53 (1): 1–24.

Lokanathan, P. S. 1945. 'The Bombay Plan'. *Foreign Affairs* 23 (4): 680–86.

Luhmann, Niklas. 1982. *The Differentiation of Society*. New York: Columbia University Press.

———. 1988. *Die Wirtschaft der Gesellschaft*. Frankfurt am Main, Germany: Suhrkamp.

———. 1989. *Ecological Communication*. Chicago: University of Chicago Press.

———. 1993. *Risk : A Sociological Theory*. New York: de Gruyter.

———. 1995. *Social Systems*. Stanford: Stanford University Press.

———. 1997. 'Globalization or World Society: How to Conceive of Modern Society?' *International Review of Sociology* 7 (1): 67–79.

———. 2000. *Organisation und Entscheidung*. Wiesbaden, Germany: VS Verlag für Sozialwissenschaften.

———. 2008. *Die Moral der Gesellschaft*. Frankfurt am Main, Germany: Suhrkamp.

———. 2012. *Theory of Society*. 2 vols. Vol. 1: *Cultural Memory in the Present*. Stanford: Stanford University Press.

———. 2013. *Theory of Society*. 2 vols. Vol. 2: *Cultural Memory in the Present*. Stanford: Stanford University Press.

Mansell, Samuel F. 2013. *Capitalism, Corporations and the Social Contract: A Critique of Stakeholder Theory*. Cambridge: Cambridge University Press.

March, J. G. 1962. 'The Business Firm as a Political Coalition'. *Journal of Politics* 24 (4): 662–78.

Marchildon, Allison. 2016. 'Corporate Responsibility or Corporate Power? CSR and the Shaping of the Definitions and Solutions to Our Public Problems'. *Journal of Political Power* 9 (1): 45–64.

Markovits, Claude. 2008. *Merchants, Traders, Entrepreneurs: Indian Business in the Colonial Era*. Basingstoke, UK: Palgrave Macmillan.

———, ed. 2002. *A History of Modern India, 1480–1950*. London: Anthem Press.

Mascareño, Aldo. 2012. *Die Moderne Lateinamerikas: Weltgesellschaft, Region und funktionale Differenzierung*. Bielefeld, Germany: Transcript.

Mathur, Nita. 2010. 'Shopping Malls, Credit Cards and Global Brands: Consumer Culture and Lifestyle of India's New Middle Class'. *South Asia Research* 30 (3): 211–31.

Matten, Dirk and Jeremy Moon. 2008. '"Implicit" and "Explicit" CSR: A Conceptual Framework for a Comparative Understanding of Corporate Social Responsibility'. *Academy of Management Review* 33 (2): 404–24.

McWilliams, Abagail and Donald Siegel. 2001. 'Corporate Social Responsibility: A Theory of the Firm Perspective'. *Academy of Management Review* 26 (1): 117–27.

Meadowcroft, James. 2007. 'Who Is in Charge Here? Governance for Sustainable Development in a Complex World'. *Journal of Environmental Policy & Planning* 9 (3–4): 299–314.

Mehrotra, Santosh, Jajati Parida, Sharmistha Sinha, and Ankita Gandhi. 2014. 'Explaining Employment Trends in the Indian Economy: 1993–94 to 2011–12'. *Economic and Political Weekly* XLIX (32): 49–57.

Mehta, Balwant Singh and Sandip Sarkar. 2010. 'Income Inequality in India: Pre- and Post-Reform Periods'. *Economic and Political Weekly* XLV (37): 45–55.

Mejia, Robin. 2009. 'The Challenge of Environmental Regulation in India'. *Environmental Science & Technology* 43 (23): 8714–15.

Menon, Manju and Kanchi Kohli. 2014. 'Executive's Environmental Dilemmas'. *Economic and Political Weekly* XLIX (50): 10–13.

Merton, Robert K. and Rober A. Nisbet, eds. 1971. *Contemporary Social Problems*. New York: Harcourt Brace Janovich.

Miklian, Jason. 2009. 'The Purification Hunt: The Salwa Judum Counterinsurgency in Chhattisgarh, India'. *Dialectical Anthropology* 33 (3): 441.

———. 2012. 'The Political Ecology of War in Maoist India'. *Politics, Religion & Ideology* 13 (4): 561–76.

Mishra, Girish. 1994. *An Economic History of Modern India*. New-Delhi: Pragati Publications.

Mitchell, Ronald K. Bradley R. Agle, and Donna J. Wood. 1997. 'Toward a Theory of Stakeholder Identification and Salience: Defining the Principle of Who and What Really Counts'. *The Academy of Management Review* 22 (4): 853–86.

Moon, Jeremy Andrew Crane, and Dirk Matten. 2011. 'Corporations and Citizenship in New Institutions of Global Governance'. In *The Responsible Corporation in a Global Economy*, edited by Colin Crouch and Camilla Maclean, 203–24. Oxford: Oxford University Press.

Moriarty, Jeffrey. 2008. 'Business Ethics: An Overview'. *Philosophy Compass* 3 (5): 956–72.

———. 2014. 'The Connection Between Stakeholder Theory and Stakeholder Democracy: An Excavation and Defense'. *Business & Society* 53 (6): 820–52.

Mukherjee-Reed, A. and D. Reed. 2004. 'Corporate Governance in India: Three Historical Models and Their Development Impact'. In *Corporate Governance, Economic Reforms and Development*, edited by D. Reed and S. Mukherjee, 25–63. New Delhi: Oxford India Paperbacks.

Mukherjee, Abhishek and Ron Bird. 2016. 'Analysis of Mandatory CSR Expenditure in India: A Survey'. *International Journal of Corporate Governance* 7 (1): 32–59.

Mukherjee, Aditya. 2002. *Imperialism, Nationalism, and the Making of the Indian Capitalis Class*. New Delhi: Sage Publications.

Mukherjee Reed, Ananya. 2001. *Perspectives on the Indian Corporate Economy: Exploring the Paradox of Profits*. International Political Economy Series. Basingstoke, UK: Palgrave.

Mukherji, Rahul. 2009. 'The State, Economic Growth, and Development in India'. *India Review* 8 (1): 81–106.

———. 2013. 'Ideas, Interests, and the Tipping Point: Economic Change in India'. *Review of International Political Economy* 20 (2): 363–89.

Mushtaq, Sehrish and Fawad Baig. 2016. 'Indian Media System: An Application of Comparative Media Approach'. *South Asian Studies (1026-678X)* 31 (2): 45–63.

Naudet, Jules and Claire-Lise Dubost. 2017. 'The Indian Exception: The Densification of the Network of Corporate Interlocks and the Specificities of the Indian Business System (2000–2012)'. *Socio-Economic Review* 15 (2): 405–34.

Nayar, Baldev Raj. 2012. 'Economic Planning as an Integrative Mechanism in India: Changes and Challenges After Economic Liberalization'. *India Review* 11 (4): 226–58.

Newell, Peter, Philipp Pattberg, and Heike Schroeder. 2012. 'Multiactor Governance and the Environment'. *Annual Review of Environment and Resources* 37 (1): 365–87.

Norman, Wayne and Chris MacDonald. 2004. 'Getting to the Bottom of "Triple Bottom Line"'. *Business Ethics Quarterly* 14 (2): 243–62.

OECD. 2006. *Environmental Compliance and Enforcement in India: Rapid Assessment*. Paris: Organisation for Economic Co-operation and Development. Available at http://www.oecd.org/environment/outreach/37838061.pdf.

Okoye, Adaeze. 2009. 'Theorising Corporate Social Responsibility as an Essentially Contested Concept: Is a Definition Necessary?' *Journal of Business Ethics* 89 (4): 613–27.

Outlook Business. 2008. 'India: Making of a Superpower'. 23 August 2008.

Outlook India. 2011. 'Putting Growth in Its Place'. 14 November 2011.

Oza, A. N. 1988. 'Integrated Entrepreneurship Development Programmes: The Indian Experience'. *Economic and Political Weekly* 23 (22): 73–79.

Palshikar, Suhas. 2015. 'The BJP and Hindu Nationalism: Centrist Politics and Majoritarian Impulses'. *South Asia: Journal of South Asian Studies* 38 (4): 719–35.

Panagariya, Arvind. 2008. *India: The Emerging Giant*. New Delhi: Oxford University Press.

Panth, Prabha and Rahul A. Shastri. 2008. 'Patterns of Pollution Compliance: A Cross-State Analysis of Industrial Pollution Compliance in India'. In *Corporate Accountability and Sustainable Development*, edited by Peter Utting and Jennifer Clapp, 199–234. New Delhi: Oxford University Press.

Parekh, Bhikhu. 1991. 'Nehru and the National Philosophy of India'. *Economic and Political Weekly* 26 (1/2): 35–48.

Patra, Pradeep. 2016. 'The Companies Act and CSR: the landscape in India'. In *CSR in India, 2016*, edited by Corporate Responsibility Watch, 34–37. New Delhi: CRW.

Polanyi, Karl. 1957. "Aristotles Discovers the Economy." In *Trade and Market in the Early Empires: Economies in History and Theory*, edited by Karl Polanyi, Conrad Maynadier Arensberg, and Harry W. Pearson, 64–94. New York: The Free Press.

———. 1957 [1944]. *The Great Transformation: The Political and Economic Origins of Our Time*. Boston: Beacon Press.

Porter, M. E. and M. R. Kramer. 2006. 'Strategy and Society: The Link Between Competitive Advantage and Corporate Social Responsibility'. *Harvard Business Review* 84 (12): 78–92.

Prahalad, Coimbatore Krishna. 2005. *The Fortune at the Bottom of the Pyramid: Eradicating Poverty Through Profits*. Upper Saddle River, NJ: Wharton School Publishing.

Rahoof, Abdul T. K. and P. G. Arul. 2016. 'An Evaluation of Special Economic Zones (SEZs): Performance Post SEZs Act 2005'. *Universal Journal of Industrial and Business Management* 4 (2): 44–52.

Rajak, Dinah. 2011. *In Good Company : An Anatomy of Corporate Social Responsibility*. Stanford: Stanford University Press.

Rajakumar, Dennis. 2011. 'Size and Growth of Private Corporate Sector in Indian Manufacturing'. *Economic and Political Weekly* 46 (18): 95–101.

———. 2014. 'Corporate Financing Pattern in India: Changing Composition and Its Implications'. *The IUP Journal of Applied Finance* 20 (4): 5–21.

Rajalakshmi, T. K. 2014. 'Labour under Attack'. *Frontline*, 14 November 2014.

Rao, C. K. S. and A. Guha. 2006. 'Ownership Pattern of the Indian Corporate Sector: Implications for Corporate Governance'. ISID Working Paper (2006/09).

Ray, Raka and Mary Fainsod Katzenstein. 2005. *Social Movements in India: Poverty, Power, and Politics*. Lanham, UK: Rowman & Littlefield.

Raychaudhuri, Tapan. 1983. 'The Mid-Eighteenth-Century Background'. In *The Cambridge Economic History of India*, edited by Dharma Kumar and Tapan Raychaudhuri, 3–35. Cambridge: Cambridge University Press.

Reed, Darryl and Sanjoy Mukherjee. 2004. *Corporate Governance, Economic Reforms, and Development: The Indian Experience*. New Delhi and Oxford: Oxford University Press.

Reich, Robert B. 2007. *Supercapitalism: The Transformation of Business, Democracy, and Everyday Life*. New York: Alfred A. Knopf.

Robé, Jean-Philippe. 2011. 'The Legal Structure of the Firm'. *Accounting, Economics, and Law* 1 (1): Article 5.

Rodrik, Dani and Arvind Subramanian. 2005. 'From "Hindu Growth" to Productivity Surge: The Mystery of the Indian Growth Transition'. IMF Staff Papers 52 (2): 193–228.

Rosa, Hartmut, Klaus Dörre, and Stephan Lessenich. 2017. 'Appropriation, Activation and Acceleration: The Escalatory Logics of Capitalist Modernity and the Crises of Dynamic Stabilization'. *Theory, Culture & Society* 34 (1): 53–73.

Rothermund, Dietmar. 1970. 'The Monetary Policy of British Imperialism'. *The Indian Economic & Social History Review* 7 (1): 91–107.

Roy, Arundhati. 2014. *Capitalism: A Ghost Story*. Chicago: Haymarket Books.

Roy, Srirupa. 2007. *Beyond Belief: India and the Politics of Postcolonial Nationalism*. Durham: Duke University Press.

Roy, Tirthankar. 2000. *The Economic History of India, 1857–1947*. New Delhi: Oxford University Press.

Roy, Tirthankar and Anand V. Swamy. 2016. *Law and the Economy in Colonial India*. Chicago: Chicago University Press.

Ruggie, John G. 2007. 'Global Markets and Global Governance: The Prospects for Convergence'. In *Global Liberalism and Political Order: Toward a New Great Compromise?* edited by S. Bernstein and L. W. Pauly, 23–50. Albany: State University of New York Press.

Ruparelia, Sanjay. 2015. '"Minimum Government, Maximum Governance": The Restructuring of Power in Modi's India'. *South Asia: Journal of South Asian Studies* 38 (4): 755–75.

Ruparelia, Sanjay, Sanjay Reddy, John Hariss, and Stuart Corbridge, eds. 2011. *Understanding India's New Political Economy: A Great Transformation?* Abingdon, UK: Routledge.

Sacher Committee. 1978. *Report of the High-Powered Expert Committee on Companies and MRTP Acts.* New Delhi: Government of India.

Salmon, Anne. 2009. *Moraliser le capitalisme ?* Paris: CNRS Edition.

Sarangi, Prakash. 2016. 'Politics as Business: An Analysis of the Political Parties in Contemporary India'. *Studies in Indian Politics* 4 (1): 37–48.

Sarathy, Partha R. and Seshadri M. Chakravarty. 1998. *Indian Cement Industry: Emerging Trends.* New Delhi: Contact Avertising & Communication.

Scherer, Andreas Georg and Guido Palazzo. 2011. 'The New Political Role of Business in a Globalized World: A Review of a New Perspective on CSR and Its Implications for the Firm, Governance, and Democracy'. *Journal of Management Studies* 48 (4): 899–931.

Scheyvens, Regina, Glenn Banks, and Emma Hughes. 2016. 'The Private Sector and the SDGs: The Need to Move Beyond "Business as Usual"'. *Sustainable Development* 24 (6): 371–82.

Schimank, Uwe. 2015. '"Modernity as a Functionally Differentiated Capitalist Society: A General Theoretical Model'. *European Journal of Social Theory* 18 (4): 413–30.

Seidl, David and Kai Helge Becker, eds. 2005. *Niklas Luhmann and Organization Studies.* Malmö, Sweden: Liber.

Seitz, Karolin and Jens Martens. 2017. 'Philanthrolateralism: Private Funding and Corporate Influence in the United Nations'. *Global Policy* 8 (S5): 46–50.

Sen, Ronojoy. 2009. 'Walking a Tightrope: Judicial Activism and Indian Democracy'. *India Review* 8 (1): 63–80.

Sen, Sunanda and Byasdeb Dasgupta. 2009. *Unfreedom and Waged Work: Labour in India's Manufacturing Industry.* New Delhi: SAGE Publications.

Sethi, S. Prakash. 1975. 'Dimensions of Corporate Social Performance: An Analytical Framework'. *California Management Review* 17 (3): 58–64.

Shamir, Ronen. 2004. 'The De-Radicalization of Corporate Social Responsibility'. *Critical Sociology* 30 (3): 669–89.

———. 2010. 'Capitalism, Governance, and Authority: The Case of Corporate Social Responsibility'. *Annual Review of Law and Social Science* 6 (1): 531–53.

Sharma, Seema. 2011. 'Corporate Social Responsibility in India'. *The Indian Journal of Industrial Relations* 46 (4): 637–49.

Sikka, Prem. 2010. 'Smoke and Mirrors: Corporate Social Responsibility and Tax Avoidance'. *Accounting Forum* 34 (3–4): 153–68.

Simon, Herbert A. 1991. 'Organizations and Markets'. *Journal of Economic Perspectives* 5 (2): 25–44.

Singh, J. 2008a. 'Tight Rope Walk at Tata Steel: Balancing Profits and CSR'. *South Asian Journal of Management* 15 (1): 118–36.

Singh, Jaivir. 2008b. 'Labour Law and Special Economic Zones in India'. Working Paper Series – Centre for the Study of Law and Governance CSLG/WP/08.

Sinha, Aseema. 2005. 'Understanding the Rise and Transformation of Business Collective Action in India'. *Business and Politics* 7 (2): 1–35.

———. 2007. 'Economic Growth and Political Accomodation'. *Journal of Democracy* 18 (2): 41–54.

Sivramkrishna, Sashi. 2017. *In Search of Stability: Economics of Money, History of the Rupee.* Abingdon, UK: Routledge.

Standing Committee on Finance. 2010. 'The Companies Bill, 2009: Twenty-First Report'. New Delhi: Lok Sabha Secretariat.

Steurer, Reinhard. 2011. 'Soft Instruments, Few Networks: How "New Governance" Materializes in Public Policies on Corporate Social Responsibility Across Europe'. *Environmental Policy and Governance* 21 (4): 270–90.

Stichweh, Rudolf. 2006., Semantik und Sozialstruktur: Zur Logik einer systemtheoretischen Unterscheidung'. In *Neue Perspektiven der Wissenssoziologie*, edited by Dirk Tänzler, Hubert Knoblauch and Hans-Georg Soeffner, 157–71. Konstanz, Germany: UVK.

———. 2007a. 'The Eigenstructures of World Society and the Regional Cultures of the World'. In *Frontiers of Globalization Research: Theoretical and Methodological Approaches*, edited by Ino Rossi, 133–49. Boston: Springer US.

———. 2007b. 'Evolutionary Theory and the Theory of World Society'. *Soziale Systeme* 13 (1–2): 528–42.

———. 2009. ,Das Konzept der Weltgesellschaft: Genese und Strukturbildung eines globalen Gesellschaftssystems'. *Workingpaper des Soziologischen Seminars* (01/09).

———. 2015. 'Luhmann, Niklas (1927–1998)'. In *International Encyclopedia of the Social & Behavioral Sciences*, edited by James D. Wright, 382–89. Oxford: Elsevier.

Strulik, Torsten. 2012. ,Die Gesellschaft der „neuen Wirtschaftssoziologie". Eine Replik auf Jens Beckerts Artikel „Wirtschaftssoziologie als Gesellschaftstheorie".' *Zeitschrift für Soziologie* 41 (1): 58–74.

Sum, Ngai-Ling. 2010. 'Wal-Martization and CSR-ization in Developing Countries'. In *Corporate Social Responsibility and Regulatory Governance: Towards Inclusive Development?* edited by Peter Utting and José Carlos Marques, 50–76. Basingstoke, UK: Palgrave MacMillan.

Sundar, Pushpa. 2000. *Beyond Business: From Merchant Charity to Corporate Citizenship.* New Delhi: Tata McGraw Hill.

———. 2013. *Business and Community: The Story of Corporate Social Responsibility in India.* New Delhi: SAGE Publications.

Suri, K. C. 2004. 'Democracy, Economic Reforms and Election Results in India'. *Economic and Political Weekly* 39 (51): 5404–11.

Suryanarayana, M. H. and Mousumi Das. 2014. 'How Inclusive Is India's Reform(ed) Growth?' *Economic and Political Weekly* 49 (6): 44–52.

Tandon, Rajesh and Ranjita Mohanty. 2002. *Civil Society and Governance.* New Delhi: Samskriti.

Thakur, C. P. 2008. *Labour Policy and Legal Framework in India: A Review.* Edited by T. S. Papola. Vol. 1, *Labour Regulation in Indian Industry.* New Delhi: Bookwell.

The Economist. 2006. 'Can India Fly?' 01 June 2006.

———. 2013. 'India's Surprising Economic Miracle'. 30 September 2013.

The Guardian. 2015. 'India's War on Greenpeace'. 11 August 2015.

The Hindu. 2004. 'UPA Government to Adhere to Six Basic Principles of Governance'. 28 May 2004.

———. 2015. 'Greenpeace India's Registration Cancelled'. 04 September 2015.

The New York Review of Books. 2011. 'Quality of Life: India vs. China'. 12 May 2011.

Timberg, Thomas A. 1978. *The Marwaris: From Traders to Industrialists.* New Delhi: Vikas.

Time. 2006. 'India Inc.: Why the World's Biggest Democracy Is the Next Great Economic Superpower – And What It Means for America'. *Time*, 26 June 2006.

Tripathi, D. and J. Jumani. 2007. *The Concise Oxford History of Indian Business.* New Delhi: Oxford University Press.

Tsutsui, Kiyoteru and Alwyn Lim, eds. 2015. *Corporate Social Responsibility in a Globalizing World.* Cambridge: Cambridge University Press.

Utting, Peter. 2015. 'Corporate Social Responsibility and the Evolving Standards Regime: Regulatory and Political Dynamics'. In *Corporate Social Responsibility in a Globalizing World*, edited by Kiyoteru Tsutsui And Alwyn Lim, 73–106. Cambridge: Cambridge University Press.

Utting, Peter and José Carlos Marques. 2010a. *Corporate Social Responsibility and Regulatory Governance: Towards Inclusive Development?* Basingstoke, UK: Palgrave Macmillan.

———. 2010b. 'Introduction: The Intellectual Crisis of CSR'. In *Corporate Social Responsibility and Regulatory Governance: Towards Inclusive Development?* edited by Peter Utting and José Carlos Marques, 1–25. Basingstoke, UK: Palgrave Macmillan.

Vaid, D. 2014. 'Caste in Contemporary India: Flexibility and Persistence'. *Annual Review of Sociology* 40: 391–410.

Vaishnav, Milan. 2017. *When Crime Pays: Money and Muscle in Indian Politics.* Yale: Yale University Press.

Valente, Mike and Andrew Crane. 2010. 'Public Responsibility and Private Enterprise in Developing Countries'. *California Management Review* 52 (3): 52–78.

Valentinov, Vladislav, Steffen Roth, and Matthias Georg Will. 2018. 'Stakeholder Theory: A Luhmannian Perspective'. *Administration & Society* First view online (18 July 2018): journals.sagepub.com/doi/abs/10.1177/0095399718789076.

Vallentin, Steen. 2015. 'Governmentalities of CSR: Danish Government Policy as a Reflection of Political Difference'. *Journal of Business Ethics* 127 (1): 33–47.

Vandenbergh, Michael P. 2007. 'The New Wal-Mart Effect: The Role of Private Contracting in Global Governance'. *UCLA Law Review* 54 (4): 913–70.

Varman, Rohit and Ismael Al-Amoudi. 2016. 'Accumulation through Derealization: How Corporate Violence Remains Unchecked'. *Human Relations* 69 (10): 1909–35.

Varshney, Ashutosh. 1998. 'Mass Politics or Elite Politics? India's Economic Reforms in Comparative Perspective'. *The Journal of Policy Reform* 2 (4): 301–35.

Veldman, Jeroen and Martin Parker. 2012. 'Specters, Inc.: The Elusive Basis of the Corporation'. *Business and Society Review* 117 (4): 413–41.

Verma, Arvind. 2004. 'Taking Justice Outside the Courts: Judicial Activism in India'. *The Howard Journal of Criminal Justice* 40 (2): 148–65.

Vogel, D. 2008. 'Private Global Business Regulation'. *Annual Review of Political Science* 11: 261–82.

Voß, Jan-Peter and Basil Bornemann. 2011. 'The Politics of Reflexive Governance: Challenges for Designing Adaptive Management and Transition Management'. *Ecology and Society* 16 (2): Art. 9 (https://journals.openedition.org/regulation/9197).

Whitcombe, Elisabeth. 1983. 'Irrigation and Railways'. In *The Cambridge Economic History of India*, edited by Dharma Kumar and Tapan Raychaudhuri, 677–761. Cambridge: Cambridge University Press.

Wilks, Stephen. 2013. *The Political Power of the Business Corporation*. Cheltenham: Edward Elgar Publishing.

Williams, Cynthia A. and Peer Zumbansen. 2011. *The Embedded Firm: Corporate Governance, Labor, and Finance Capitalism*. Cambridge: Cambridge University Press.

Williams, E. Freya. 2015. *Green Giants: How Smart Companies Turn Sustainability into Billion-Dollar Businesses*. New York: AMACOM.

Williams, Glyn and Emma Mawdsley. 2006. 'Postcolonial Environmental Justice: Government and Governance in India'. *Geoforum* 37 (5): 660–70.

Willke, Helmut. 2009. *Governance in a Disenchanted World: The End of Moral Society*. Cheltenham; Northampton, MA: Edward Elgar.

Wimmer, Andreas and Yuval Feinstein. 2010. 'The Rise of the Nation-State across the World, 1816 to 2001'. *American Sociological Review* 75 (5): 764–90.

Wolcott, Susan. 2010. 'An Examination of the Supply of Financial Credit to Entrepreneurs in Colonial India'. In *The Invention of Enterprise: Entrepreneurship from Ancient Mesopotamia to Modern Times*, edited by David S. Landir, Joel Mokyr, and William J. Baumol, 443–68. Princeton: Princeton University Press.

Yadav, Yogendra. 1999. 'Electoral Politics in the Time of Change: India's Third Electoral System, 1989–99'. *Economic and Political Weekly* 34 (34/35): 2393–99.

Index